THE ALCHEMY OF ACTING

THE ALCHEMY OF ACTING

The Evolution of Craft in Film

JIM BLUMETTI

ISBN (Hardcover): 979-8-9914204-3-3
ISBN (Paperback): 979-8-9914204-9-5

First Edition

Published by Arcane Pen Press
Dallas, Texas
www.jimblumettibooks.com

Printed in the United States of America

U.S. Copyright Registration Number: TXu 2-504-612

Library of Congress Control Number: [to be assigned]

DEDICATION

To the teachers who bore my rough edges with patience,
and to the students whose presence kept me awake to the work.

To the words offered in youth that returned again and again,
changing with time, as if time itself were the alchemist—
turning fragments into something greater, enduring, deeper.

What I once resisted now rings clear;
what I once dismissed has shaped me.

May this book, in its own way, act the same for you—
a vessel that echoes,
a reminder that the smallest guidance can transmute,
given years enough, into gold.

*—In the end, nothing is wasted. The lessons we resist wait in silence until we
are ready to know them for the first time—*

CONTENTS

"Ars longa, vita brevis."
— Hippocrates

WHO IS THIS BOOK FOR?

All art is a theft from death. A soft rebellion against the dark. Every gesture, every glance, every breath-caught word is a refusal — the deep, human need to leave something behind. We all fear it: to vanish without a trace, to pass through life and be forgotten.

Long before science, before history, there was alchemy — not a quest for wealth, but for permanence. For the philosopher's stone that would not merely turn lead to gold, but flesh to memory. A way to whisper across time: *We were here.*

Actors are heirs to that ancient defiance. We slip inside other lives — strangers, sinners, kings, lovers — and lend them breath again. Through the lens's indifferent eye, we are captured. Preserved. Not in stone or ink — but in light. A flicker. A heartbeat. Stitched into the fabric of forever.

"Pain is brief," Martin Scorsese once said. *"Celluloid is forever."*

This isn't merely craft. It's a kind of sacred theft. A private alchemy. The work of turning what is mortal into what will not die. A quiet mark, left in the hidden places of those who watch... and remember.

And this book?

It's not for dreamers chasing neon-lit illusions of instant fame or effortless acclaim. Not for those hoping acting will hand them stardom, success, or the admiration of strangers.

No — this book is for the restless. The ones with a hunger they can't explain. Who won't leave well enough alone. Who hear their own whisper: *I cannot... not do it.*

You know who you are. You find yourself reciting lines alone, watching films that haunt your gestures. You study strangers — not what they say, but how they move. If this is you, acting didn't invite you. It claimed you.

That first private whisper — *I want to be an actor* — seemed harmless enough. But behind it? A path paved with rejection, resilience, and revelation. If you're chasing fantasy, you'll crumble. But if the calling runs deeper — if the work itself feels like the reward — then welcome.

Acting is for you.

You'll build the external tools: headshots, resumes, demo reels. Learn the dance — auditions, agents, protocols. But those are just the surface. The real journey lies within: patience, presence, empathy, adaptability, courage. You'll need that — and your temperament will matter too. More than your training.

I've seen brilliant actors falter under pressure. And others — less polished, more grounded — thrive within the chaos. Why? Because readiness isn't purely technical. It's internal. It's the discipline to stay grounded in the storm.

This book is for those willing to be cracked open. Who understand failure is not the end, but the forge. For those who choose generosity over ego. Endless practice over perfection. For actors who know: the real alchemy doesn't live in the fame — it lives in the work. In quiet triumphs. In honest moments. In the courage to be seen — completely, uncovered. If that sounds like you, then turn the page.

PART I

THE CALLING
& THE CONTEXT

"Presence isn't something you 'do' —
it's what remains when you stop trying."

C raft isn't just talent or instinct; it's the cultivated language of storytelling through body, voice, and spirit.

It's the quiet pause before a word that changes everything. The subtle tilt in posture that gives away what a character won't say. The kind of silence that lands louder than speech.

This *Craft* means knowing when to press forward, when to retreat, and when to disappear behind another life completely.

To Act begins with a spark. A pull you can't explain. A need to inhabit other lives, other realities. It's not a choice. It's a compulsion.

But this calling doesn't happen in isolation. It rises inside of culture, history, and the art that shaped the stage before you ever stepped onto it.

Here, we explore twin forces shaping the actor's path — the private, restless drive that pulls you toward the craft whether you like it or not, and the public evolution of cinema that keeps changing what the work demands. One is instinct. The other, machinery. One is ancient. Instinctual. The hunger to embody, to transform. The other is newer. But a moving target.

From the exaggerated physical language of the silent film era — where gesture spoke louder than words — to today's microscopic thought-visibility captured by high-definition lenses that see what you dare not fake. Each shift in the medium carved new demands into the actor's flesh.

We trace that history not for nostalgia, but because it changed the rules. With every movement in film came a shift in what was possible — and what was required. You're not just learning tradition. You're learning survival.

You inherit not just the brilliance of those before you, but their baggage. Their habits. Their risks. And all of it, like it or not, lives in you now.

Context isn't just some academic exercise. It's a survival skill. A foundation. Without it, your choices drift. They answer questions no one's asking.

Every era wrote new rules — out of necessity, or out of rebellion. Technological shifts, cultural fractures, and audience appetites changing without warning. Yesterday's camera caught gesture. Today's catches thought. Yesterday's actor could hide behind the words. Today's has nowhere to hide.

Different era. Different truth. Different instinct.

Film movements weren't trends, they were evolutionary survival strategies. Each one rewired the actor's instrument, reshaped the frame, shifted the weight of a single glance. And those shifts — didn't vanish. They're sediment. They're what you're standing on.

Most of the time, you carry that history without even knowing it. A tilt of the head, an unnecessary huff? That glance too sharp? That's inheritance.

But the serious actor doesn't leave that to accident. They reach back, study the lineage. Not out of reverence but out of need. Because to survive what's coming, you have to understand what came before.

The Alchemy of Acting – Chaos to Craft

This book speaks to your inheritance. Complex, contradictory, essential. The starting point for everything that follows. This is not about the past for past's sake, but rather it's about the layers of influence that actors all carry. Consciously or not.

Acting has changed, yes. Yet again. And if you're paying attention — really paying attention — you've seen it, felt it in your bones, and recognized its shifting sands beneath your feet.

This is the alchemy at the heart of our craft — the mysterious transformation process where the base elements of technique, history, and personal truth combine to create the new gold of authentic performance. Like the ancient alchemists who sought to transmute common metals into precious ones, actors undergo a similar metamorphosis, converting mundane reality into transcendent art.

Understanding this lineage isn't optional. It's the foundation upon which all modern performance builds.

What once passed as honest now feels adorned, theatrical, false. What once lit up a stage now falls flat on the screen — energy dissipating before it reaches the lens. Why? Because the lens itself has changed. The stories have changed. And the audience? They've changed most of all. More perceptive. Less forgiving. They don't want to be overtly shown anything. They want to believe — quietly, immediately, viscerally — that they're witnessing real life unfolding before them.

This is our dilemma: most actors are training for a world in flux, slipping, shifting away as we go. And yet, perhaps that's always been the actor's paradox — to chase mastery in an art form forever reshaping itself beneath our very feet.

The books remain unchanged. The syllabi. The vocabulary. The workshops. They're all echoing lessons forged in a different age — in the glow of proscenium arches or the measured pace of mid-century cinema. They teach performance as something to deliver, to present, to execute with precision.

But the work now? It's more of something to... inhabit. To sometimes barely whisper. But to *think loud* — and let the thought ripple through your being before you speak it. That is, if you speak it at all.

This isn't to dismiss the classics. Far from it. I've studied them. Still do. Their wisdom lives deeply within these pages. Stanislavski, Hagen, Meisner, Adler, Chekhov — they laid the bones, constructed the skeleton upon which all modern acting hangs. But the flesh has changed. The nervous system, too. If you're reading these as scripture, unadapted, you're preparing for a craft that's already left the station, a train disappearing over the horizon while you stand on the platform, ticket in hand for a journey that's already gone.

I relished diving deep into them all — repeatedly, sometimes as a near-religious zealot. Then did the only thing left to do: I went into the fire and tested what actually worked — for me. What worked for others. What held up on set, under pressure, with nerves high and time short. And over time, what emerged wasn't a purist's lineage — it was a hybrid. A system shaped not by theory, but by results.

As passionate and committed as I was then about the classics, I think of what I teach now, as more of a *Mixed Martial Arts of Acting*. Not my *method*, but a *fast-track* system. Not one of lineage, but an integration. A quick, flexible, practical way forward. Built on what delivers, not just inspires.

> *"Create your own method. Don't depend slavishly on mine. Make up something that will work for you. But keep breaking traditions, I beg you."*
> — Stanislavski

From Italian Neorealism to the French New Wave, from New Hollywood to Dogme 95 and Mumblecore, and now the fractured stylistics of streaming — each wave has rewritten the rules. Not just for how stories are told, but how actors must respond to them. The grammar of performance remains fluid, adaptive, evolving. And today's dialect is something else entirely, a language some actors speak fluently while others struggle to form basic sentences.

Let's look at today's bleeding edge: The Bear. Succession. Beef. Atlanta. Normal People. Euphoria. Better Call Saul... and so many more. These aren't just popular shows — they are blueprints for the new language of performance. Watch closely. The acting isn't loud. It isn't grand. It's granular. Internal. Often micro-expressed. A flick of thought crosses the actor's eyes, we feel it in our chest. The actor doesn't perform the emotion — they think it, and because they do, so do we. The camera catches the internal life long before the dialogue lands. The space between the beats has become the scene itself. A sacred place I want to help you find.

As I write his book, we're deep into a new wave — but it's subtler, more personal than previous movements. Less of a revolution and more of a murmur spreading through an evolving list of mediums. You see it in the directors who prioritize instinct over instruction, stillness over spectacle. Spike Jonze. Charlie Kaufman. David Lynch. Yorgos Lanthimos. Lars von Trier. Each one, in their way, has bent reality around performance — pushing actors to live inside the surreal, the awkward, the fragmented, the raw.

And it's not just in film. The rise of prestige television and streaming has created space for a new breed of storyteller — voices like Noah Baumbach, Greta Gerwig, the Duplass brothers, Kelly Reichardt. Directors who cast for presence, not strictly for performance. Who build stories around rhythm, texture, feeling. Who trust their actors to think it, not show it. And the actors who can't? They'll get left behind, relics of an approach that no longer serves the medium.

This is the work now. This is where the audience lives — in that subtle transmission. That breath before the line. The space where the actor's thought becomes the viewer's intuition. If you're not tuned to that frequency, you're missing the current. You're playing the craft like it's still 1982. The lens can see it, capture the falseness, the striving, the performance rather than the being.

But most actors' training hasn't caught up. It still rewards that overly expressive show of emotion, which reads as *false intending*. And when it reads this loudly, it breaks, and the illusion shatters. The truth thins out, becomes transparent, and reveals all the mechanisms practiced so painfully beneath.

This book is my response and hopefully your answer to that gap.

The Alchemy of Acting is both a reckoning and a translation. It doesn't ask you to throw out the past — it teaches you how to transmute it. To carry those old tools into this moment's movement, but with new hands. It's about boiling down the chaos of influence and instruction down to something usable. Something alive. Something tailored to the demands of now.

It's personal. It's practical. And yes — it, too, will one day be out of date.

And that's the point.

Because if you're doing it right — if you're really alive in this craft — you already know: Acting doesn't stand still. It can't. Not if the medium keeps moving. Not if the world keeps shifting.

This is where I've arrived. And the map I've drawn. Let's walk it together and see where it leads.

In Part I, we'll examine major film movements, their distinct performance demands, and how they've collectively shaped the actor's craft we know it today.

In Part II, we'll shift from art to industry — unpacking the realities of the business, the power of champions, and the strategies every working actor must master to endure.

In Part III, we'll return to the artist, exploring the internal toolkit, the actor's instrument, and the lifelong practice required to transform chaos into craft.

—Jim Blumetti

EMBRACING
THE CHAOS

Chaos isn't something actors should avoid —
it's the very stuff to mine for gold.

The new actor will rush straight to emotion — usually anger, if it's remotely available to play in the scene. It's the easiest emotion to access for most people, and the beginning actor assumes it's impressive. But more often than not, it's a worn trope and a *tell* of the actor's limitation. A desperate reach toward something — anything that might register as truthful and impressive. What they're chasing isn't truth. It's sensation. They dive into scenes without maps, without compasses, without the faintest idea of the territory they're meant to inhabit. Then, wonder why their performances feel generic, untethered, floating in theatrical limbo.

The truly extraordinary actors understand a paradox that defies conventional wisdom: the most authentic performances happen at the edge of surrender. Think of it as leaping from an airplane without your parachute pre-attached — you'll have to organize on the way down, fingers working against the rushing wind, mind calculating trajectory, altitude, body adjusting to forces you can't control. This isn't recklessness. You wouldn't have done it if you didn't know you absolutely could. It's post-ultimate preparation — knowing your tools so intimately, you can construct what you need in the midst of chaos. The adrenaline, the focus, and the absolute necessity of the moment create a state of heightened awareness, where your finest work emerges — as it must. Anything becomes possible precisely because nothing is certain.

This metaphor is more than interesting imagery. It's fundamental to what happens when the camera rolls and when you're suddenly face-to-face with another actor whose choices rewrite everything you've meticulously planned. The actor who can't adapt in free fall thinks only about hitting their mark, waiting for their cue, and nothing else. The one who trusts the chaos, senses opportunity, and knows the magic is near — That actor is ready to soar.

Acting, at its core, is alchemy. The mysterious art of transforming raw human emotions into pure cinematic gold. Yet this journey is rarely linear; it's tumultuous, uncertain, chaotic. In that chaos lies both challenge and possibility. Actors wrestle daily with doubt, vulnerability, and unpredictability. Harnessing these raw forces can produce something genuine, something resonant. Something organic and beautifully real.

The first time I watched Gena Rowlands in "A Woman Under the Influence," something shifted a bit for me. Her performance wasn't just good — it was dangerous. Unpredictable. You couldn't look away because you genuinely didn't know what she might do next. That's not technique. That's surrender at the scale of her DNA.

Most books on acting will offer formulas, the mechanics. Step-by-step guides for accessing emotion on cue. Guaranteed methods for building character. Reliable procedures to repeat a performance under pressure. This isn't that book. Not because those methods have no value — they do, and we'll explore them, keep what works, and question what doesn't for our work *today*. But you don't need another rigid system. What you need is permission — permission to embrace uncertainty.

Because the only thing you can count on is this: in every moment, there's something brilliant and beautiful to be played — if you're awake enough to catch it.

"No one wants to watch your homework."
— Cate Blanchett

That's how Cate Blanchett describes her process. Ruthless preparation followed by radical release. She marks every beat of the scene. Charts tactics. Builds arcs. She does the work — privately, obsessively. And then... she lets it all go. *Throws it away*, as the saying goes.

Because the audience isn't there to admire structure. They don't want to see the cogs turning. They want to be *transported*.

Blanchett glances at her notes before shooting — once — then buries them. Not to forget them, but now given over to trust. To let technique live beneath the surface and let her instinct *breathe*.

Control is useful in rehearsal. But on set? It becomes interference. So, she trades it for presence. The work remains — invisible, intact — a quiet framework beneath her skin. That's the paradox: you prepare to the edge of mastery so you can step off the clip... or out of the plane.

That kind of surrender built atop layers of unseen discipline is exactly why we draw from every corner of the craft: Meisner, Strasberg, Adler, Hagen, and the practical instincts shared by today's A-list actors. We'll combine them like a kind of mixed martial art. A personal, evolving technique forged from what each of us can bring to this moment — with the tools we've got right now. And we'll keep refining those tools, knowing that with time, they'll sharpen. So will our instincts. So will our capacity to comprehend new ones.

What feels like revelation today will feel entirely different in a few years. That's not failure — it's growth. Every instruction — from any method, any teacher, any director, even mine — will shift its meaning as you age inside the craft. That's how you know you're on the right path.

It's a practice — like medicine. Never mastered. Always evolving. You don't conquer it; you engage with it. You return to it again and again, adjusting, refining, learning. You don't arrive. You get better if you stay open and willing to change.

This book charts the evolution of acting through the lens of major film movements, each era leaving its distinct mark on how we understand the craft of today. From the initial exaggerated gestures of silent films to the unpolished realism of Dogme 95, each movement has shifted the paradigm, forcing actors to reinvent themselves and their methods.

This reflection may reveal something mystical — Alchemical. The silent era actors — they knew something we've forgotten. Without words, they developed a fine-tuned physicality, a language of the body so precise it can break your heart still, from across the decades.

Watch Renée Jeanne Falconetti in "The Passion of Joan of Arc." Those eyes. That trembling. No dialogue necessary. The close-up revealed everything words would have obscured. Or Chaplin in "City Lights" — that final scene when the flower girl realizes who he is. His hesitation, the hope that flickers across his face. Buster Keaton's deadpan in "The General" communicates more with stillness than most actors manage with monologues.

German Expressionism pushed further — distorting the body to reveal the twisted landscapes of the mind. Conrad Veidt in "The Cabinet of Dr. Caligari," his body twisted into impossible angles, his eyes bulging with madness. Max Schreck in "Nosferatu," inhuman yet somehow vulnerable. The actor as a psychological cartographer. Then, Italian Neorealism stripped everything away. De Sica cast Lamberto Maggiorani, an actual factory worker, in "Bicycle Thieves." The exhaustion in his eyes wasn't performed — it was lived. Anna Magnani in "Rome, Open City" her raw grief when her husband is shot. Non-professionals carrying entire films through sheer presence. The French New Wave followed, capturing moments so intimate they felt like trespassing. Jean-Pierre Léaud growing up before our eyes across Truffaut's Antoine Doinel films. Anna Karina's face in Godard's "Vivre Sa Vie," the camera lingering as she watches "The Passion of Joan of Arc" — Cinema watching itself, watching it weep.

American Cinema in the 70s, a beautiful, messy decade that brought us actors willing to shatter themselves on screen. Pacino in "Dog Day Afternoon," when he chants "Attica! Attica!" and you can't tell where the character ends and the actor begins. Nicholson, in "Five Easy Pieces," the diner monologue revealing the broken man beneath the swagger. De Niro's physical transformation in "Raging Bull" — not just his body, but the way his eyes changed. Jane Fonda, in "Klute," balances vulnerability and defiance as she listens to recordings of herself with clients. Ellen Burstyn in "The Exorcist," her terror not for demons but for her child. Sissy Spacek in "Badlands," her affectless voiceover creating a dissonance that haunts you.

They weren't performing emotion... they were experiencing it. Being in it — and allowing us in to watch.

Such a beautiful, raw, generous lineage — not owed to us, but offered. A legacy stepped into by commitment. If you dare to enter this arena, enter with reverence. Because to stand on the same ground, to breathe in the same craft, is to carve your mark into the long, weathered grain of the art itself. Honor it with your own fearless truth — whatever shape that might take. This is the debt you must pay to those who came before: not by matching their brilliance, but by having the courage to add your own.

Myths about acting persist. That you need to be damaged to access depth. That suffering equals artistry. That you must lose yourself to find the character. All bullshit.

The path is much simpler... and yet much harder.

After briefly exploring these historical currents, we'll dive deeper into the actor's journey — the myths that mislead, the commitments it demands, and the daily realities actors face. It's a path strewn with disappointment, joy, and relentless growth — one that requires more than talent. It demands discipline, resilience, and a bulldog-like refusal to let go of the dream.

I've watched actors clutching their techniques like impenetrable shields. Strasberg. Meisner. Adler. Desperate for structure. For safety. For the illusion of control. Hoping for guarantees that out the other end, applause and praise wait for them from cast and crew the moment the director yells, "Cut."

But there are no guarantees. No certainty. The path disappears as you walk it.

The work happens in the gap. That's a terrifying space between preparation and performance. Between knowing and not knowing. Between control and surrender. And that's where the magic lives. That's where the alchemy happens.

Let's Be Honest About the Method

Before I get into what I teach — and what I've found works for today's craft — let's clear something up.

The Method has become a loaded term. A mythology. You hear "Method actor" and think of someone refusing to break character between takes, or dragging themselves through trauma just to access a scene. Somewhere along the line, this technique became theater-kid folklore, press bait, or worse — an excuse for self-indulgence.

We might blame Daniel Day-Lewis, as the closest thing to the fully modern method myth — equal parts artist and apparition. Of course, there are also these guys as well:

Marlon Brando — the icon who first brought Method to film's mainstream.

Robert De Niro — gained 60 pounds for *Raging Bull*, drove a cab for *Taxi Driver*.

Christian Bale — famously fluctuates his body weight dangerously for roles (*The Machinist*, *Batman*, *Vice*).

Heath Ledger — locked himself in a hotel room for weeks to "find" the Joker.

Joaquin Phoenix — stayed in character for over a year while filming *I'm Still Here*.

But the truth is quieter. And far more useful.

Method Acting — real Method work — was never about self-destruction. It wasn't about staying in character for months or turning your life into a never-ending rehearsal. It was about locating truth within yourself, then letting that truth behave as if it were someone else.

The goal wasn't supposed to be torment. It was honesty.

I've coached actors who believed they had to suffer to be good. That their pain equaled depth. That torment was the path to authentic truth. My heart broke for them. This indulgent self-punishment, in the belief that agony off-screen would somehow show up on it. I worried all that sacrifice would go unseen, unrewarded but not unpunished. Because, more often than not, it doesn't translate. Not for everyone... and not all the time for anyone.

You can feel it in the work — the forced intensity, the strain behind the eyes. But audiences don't respond to what you pre-endured in the dark. They respond to what's alive in front of them. They don't need your narcissistic torment. They need your focused truth. And no, you don't have to rip out your own teeth like Shia LaBeouf to prove you care.

Real doesn't mean painful.

You don't need to bleed to be believable. You just need to be honest. Fully. Without apology. That's harder than it sounds — and infinitely more powerful.

The Three Pillars — Where It All Started

If you've studied acting here in the U.S., chances are your training traces back to one of these three voices — Strasberg, Adler, or Meisner. They all started from the same source: Stanislavski. But each took a different path.

Strasberg went inward — mining personal memory. Adler went outward — exploring imagination and circumstance. Meisner lived in the moment — reacting truthfully, without premeditation.

Three philosophies. Three lenses. Same journey. You don't have to choose one religion. You just have to understand what tools you're reaching for, and why.

I know many actors who think "choosing a teaching technique" means pledging allegiance. It doesn't. You're not joining a church. You're building a toolbox.

So here's where I pivot — not into theory, nor abstraction — but into the lived part. The messy, peculiar, irrefutable truth of what's actually worked... for me and my students. What's grown up through the floorboards of the classroom. Through late-night phone calls with actors on the verge. Through awkward silences before a breakthrough — or a breakdown. This didn't come from some neat system. It emerged — in me, and in them. Slowly. Unevenly. From the actors I've coached. The students who challenged me. The failures I couldn't explain. And those small moments of *ah-ha* that — somehow — became epiphanies.

Now it's layered in. Years of watching — not just what's happening in front of the camera, but what's breaking behind it. Thousands of hours —

studying, acting, writing, adjusting. Sitting with the unspoken. Listening to it all. Looking for the tell.

This isn't a method, not really. It's an accumulation. A sediment — years thick. Still settling. Still hungry. Greedy. Avaricious for more.

What follows is the shape that dogged, deliberate, circuitous process took.

My *method,* if you will, doesn't reject these proto-primary foundations. It folds them in. But with edges sanded off and the practical demands of today's on-camera performance laid bare.

Stanislavski Didn't Want You Trapped in Theory

We toss the name around so often that it's easy to forget: Stanislavski didn't want actors stuck in their heads.

He spent the second half of his life trying to get actors out of their chairs and into the scene. Less theory. More action. Less feeling about feeling. More *doing.*

What he called the "Method of Physical Action" wasn't about emotional recall or symbolic gestures—it was about finding the truth through behavior. Getting the actor moving with purpose. Living honestly within the moment's structure.

And that's where I began to shape my own approach. Something that draws from what's useful, burns off what isn't, and asks: what actually works when the camera is rolling?

What still breathes when the nerves hit... and there's no second take?

That's where we go next.

Finally, we'll ease into my approach — my way of working, if that sounds less grand. Hesitation creeps in when I call it a method, though perhaps it qualifies. It's not something I invented so much as something that slowly revealed itself. A personal rhythm. A way of making sense of the work — shaped over years of doing, years of watching others do it better, braver, or just... differently than I ever could.

From the first day on my first set, I was taken. Not just by the acting — though that spark has never left — but by the whole ecosystem. The script. The blocking. The strange silence just before a scene erupts to life. I fell in love with the invisible design. How writing leads to performance. How editing reshapes meaning. How tone, timing, and trust ripple through the frame. Even the marketing — the hustle — the curious machinery of getting a story into the world. All of it lit something in me.

This is where the artist, the teacher, and yes, the curious tinkerer in me found common ground. But underneath it all, one question has followed me: *What is it about the actor — the real one, the brave one — that moves us so deeply?* What pauses in us when a performance lands just right? What opens?

What I offer here isn't a shortcut. It's a scaffold. A lived process. Built from years of trial, missteps, late nights, and surprise. It leans into emotional chaos. It listens for honesty. And it waits — patiently — for that rare moment when the actor disappears... and truth is all that remains.

I once had an actor in a class who couldn't tap into the rage her character needed in a crucial moment, playing opposite a seasoned, mature man. Take after take — nothing. Just stiff, polite anger. Performative. Safe. Not bad, not what I call *uncastable*. But after my gentle notes, I could feel her discomfort grow. Each take tightened her down more. She was ready to shut down completely.

Trying to help her find a connection, I had sensed something.

"Are you thinking about your father when you're speaking to your scene partner?"

She stiffened. "That's off-limits," she said.

I nodded. "I understand." Waited a beat. Walked to her, leaned in, whispered so only she could hear, "And that's exactly where you need to go." Then I stepped to the back of the class and waited, watching.

After an awkward length of time, where I actually thought she might leave the classroom... Timidly, her eyes on the floor, she nodded a small "yes."

The next take... Volcanic. Primal. Terrifying. When it ended, she shook, trembling.

"I didn't know that was in there," she said.

"I did," I replied.

My lifelong fascination with what people hide — their body language, their voice, micro-movements of the eyes, face — has always been a bit of a superpower. I've trusted it completely, long before I ever knew I did it consciously or had discovered acting.

This technique, this method — call it what you will — isn't about exploitation. It's about permission. Permission to access what you already have. Permission to be messy, contradictory, human. And most importantly, permission to not know what comes next.

I've seen actors transform when they finally grasp that perfection is the enemy of authenticity. The most memorable performances in cinema history share this quality of dangerous unpredictability — a sense that anything could happen because the actor has surrendered fully to the moment.

Take Brando in *Last Tango in Paris.* The monologue over his wife's body wasn't in the script. Bertolucci just turned the camera on and let Brando excavate his own grief. Raw. Unfiltered. Almost unbearable to watch. That's not acting — it's exorcism.

Or Liv Ullmann in Bergman's *Persona,* the camera locked in extreme close-up as thoughts flicker beneath her skin like passing storms.

Jack Nicholson in *The Shining,* descending into madness so completely, we forget we're watching fiction.

Meryl Streep in *Sophie's Choice,* making an impossible choice in a language that's not even her own.

Daniel Day-Lewis in *There Will Be Blood,* transforming into a man so hollow and intense that we forget he was ever just an actor.

And then there's Cate Blanchett, the ultimate chameleon. Whether she's unraveling in *Blue Jasmine* or commanding the scene in *Tár,* she just melts away without truly disappearing. Her performances come from diving deep, moment by moment, breath by breath, until something authentic emerges. She once said, "If you know what you're doing, it's not worth doing." That's the cord. That's the point.

These performances don't just reveal characters — they reflect ourselves. Our fears, our desires, our little breakdowns. They remind us that the best acting isn't about pretending to be someone else. It's about being so fully invested that you forget anyone else is even in there. It's not forcing another spirit in; it's letting go of the one who's typically in control.

Whether you're a pro or just starting out, the magic remains the same. Embrace the chaos. That's when the real craft begins to shine, and the artistry emerges.

The pages ahead won't offer simple answers — the craft demands and deserves more than that. Instead, think of them as a map for the journey, given by someone who's navigated too many rough patches and has come back with insights and suggestions. Some, if not most, of which just might support your desire to find your own alchemy along the way.

Welcome to the journey.

CHAPTER ONE

A BRIEF
HISTORY OF FILM

Past Is Prelude: The Actor's Inheritance

Cinema evolves like water — changing form to fit the container of its age.

Film grows in intertwining spirals, like strands of DNA, not in straight, clearly demarcated lines. Each movement a reaction — often a rebellion and a reinvention of what came before.

Before we dive deeper, to set your mind at ease: this isn't a comprehensive academic history of Cinema. Film scholars have identified dozens of movements, schools, and styles across the global landscape of filmmaking. Our focus is narrower — we're tracing how specific movements transformed actors' craft, creating new possibilities for performance that continue to resonate today.

Cinema's evolution isn't just technological progression. It's an ongoing dialogue — a quiet murmur between actors past and present, urging us to adapt, grow, evolve. Dialogue between artists across time, across continents, across traditions. French New Wave directors didn't just invent new approaches — they responded to Italian Neorealism, to a Hollywood studio system, to their own obsessions with American genre films. Dogme 95 didn't emerge from a vacuum — it positioned itself explicitly against increasing digitalization and artifice of 1990s mainstream cinema.

Film history isn't dates and facts — it's the ghostly echo of every actor who ever stood before a lens.

Understanding these connections illuminates why certain performance styles emerged when they did. Why they matter. How they continue to influence what happens in front of cameras today.

Film as a medium has continually transformed, pushing boundaries of what actors are asked to do, sometimes dramatically changing the nature of performance itself. Cinematic movements I'll explore here laid the foundations for techniques you'll use today — techniques born from fertile ground of experimentation, rebellion, and reinvention.

We begin with the silent era — that foundational period when actors communicated solely through their physicality. But Cinema didn't stop evolving when it found its voice. The journey was just beginning.

Silent film actors developed a vocabulary of movement, gesture, facial expressions that communicated complex meaning without a single spoken word. They weren't primitive harbingers of "real" acting that would come with sound — they were *masters* of purely visual language, artists whose medium was physical presence itself.

The silence wasn't absence — it was presence in its rawest form.

Consider Chaplin's Tramp. An entire universe of emotion conveyed through the tilt of the bowler hat, angle of the cane, precise timing of physical gags that revealed profound humanity beneath comedy. Or Buster Keaton's stoic face — "The Great Stone Face," they called him — somehow communicating volumes precisely through what he refused to express. These weren't compensating for technological limitations. They were exploring the richest possibilities of visual storytelling.

When sound arrived, something gained, yes. But something was lost as well. New dimensions of performance became possible. But certain qualities of silent expression — that pure physical poetry — faded. Most silent film actors couldn't make the transition. Not because they lacked talent, but because they practiced a fundamentally different art form. One requiring different skills, different instincts, and different relationships to the camera.

Early sound actors often came from the stage, many bringing a heightened, grand-declamatory, theatrical delivery that, by today's standards, feels distinctly stylized. Add to that the technical restrictions of the time: actors had to plant themselves near hidden microphones, unable to move freely without losing the take. There's a wonderful, painful illustration of this in *Babylon*—Damien Chazelle's brilliant (and criminally overlooked) 2022 black comedy-drama. There's a scene where Nellie LaRoy, played by Margot Robbie, is shooting her first talkie. She's forced to hit rigid marks dictated not by the director, but by the sound engineer. Everyone on set is locked into claustrophobic positions, their freedom throttled by the new audio equipment.

If you haven't seen the film — or at least that scene — you owe it to yourself as an actor. I've watched it dozens of times. Not just because it captures the raw disorientation of a "first day on set," but because it's a masterclass in tension, rhythm, ensemble work, and controlled chaos. It reminds us how performance must constantly adapt — not just to character, but to the invisible pressures of the frame, the space, the tech... the moment.

So do your homework. Watch early talking pictures — the stiff formality, the declarative line readings, the static framing. Then, see how quickly actors and filmmakers adapted. Found ways to make dialogue seem natural rather than performed. Developed more intimate relationship with the microphone and camera. Created a new grammar of screen acting that wasn't purely visual but wasn't strictly theatrical either. Something unique. Cinema finding its voice — literally and figuratively.

Cinema's evolution reflects tension between realism and artifice, authenticity and stylization — each era reshaping the actor's approach to truthfulness on screen. From exaggerated gestures required by silent films to convey emotional intensity without sound, to psychological subtleties introduced by Method Acting, film has continually redefined what it means to deliver a compelling performance.

This redefinition wasn't merely aesthetic preference. Each shift responded to a specific cultural moment, changing audience expectations, new production contexts. An acting style that feels "natural" to contemporary viewers would appear bizarrely understated to a 1940s audience. Performance lauded as the pinnacle of realism in the 1970s now sometimes reads as mannered self-conscious. These aren't judgments of quality but recognitions of context — each era's "truth" responded to its moment.

Consider that the Method's emergence in post-war America wasn't just an artistic movement, but a response to social conditions — veterans returning from the horror of World War II, the nation confronting darker truths about itself, audiences no longer satisfied with the sanitized emotions of studio-era star performances. Method's raw psychological intensity answered a cultural need for entertainment that acknowledged complexity, contradiction, and darker corners of the human experience that had been previously kept off-screen.

Actors learned quickly that each shift in cinematic storytelling wasn't just a technical adjustment but fundamental rethinking of how to inhabit characters. With Soviet Montage, performance became deeply entwined with editing, shaping meaning through juxtaposition and rhythm. German Expressionism stretched the physical and emotional spectrum, emphasizing internal turmoil through distorted, heightened physicality. Italian Neorealism stripped away layers of artifice, demanding actors portray genuine human struggle with raw simplicity, bringing cinema closer to everyday reality.

The Kuleshov Effect — named after Soviet filmmaker Lev Kuleshov, who argued that "the soul of cinema is in the edit." He demonstrated how performance does not exist in isolation but in relationship to what surrounds it. His famous experiment showed the same neutral facial expression from actor Ivan Mosjoukine, juxtaposed with a bowl of soup, a dead child, and a beautiful woman. It highlights the power of editing and how seemingly unrelated shots can be manipulated to create a new meaning where audiences "see" hunger, grief, or desire in identical footage based solely on context. Establishing performance isn't self-contained — it exists in conversation with everything around it. An actor's understanding of this principle is crucial to their craft.

Hitchcock was a master of using the Kuleshov Effect, creating suspense to manipulate audience emotions.

As cameras shrank and became more portable in the 1960s, the possibilities for performance opened up. French New Wave filmmakers took their cameras to the streets and into apartments, capturing moments with a documentary-like immediacy. Jean-Pierre Léaud in Truffaut's films — spontaneous, unpredictable, seemingly improvised yet meticulously crafted — showcased a fresh approach to screen acting. It wasn't about theatrical declarations or stylized studio performances; it felt more like something caught in the act of being rather than something put on display.

Movements like the French New Wave and New Hollywood revolutionized acting yet again, pushing for authenticity through spontaneity and a direct, intimate connection with audiences. Actors didn't just recite lines; they became their characters, delving into complex inner lives with newfound nuance and depth.

The New Hollywood of the 1970s mixed the psychological intensity of Method acting with the formal experimentation and countercultural ethos of European art cinema, challenging the norms of American storytelling. Performances from icons like Pacino, De Niro, Nicholson, Streep, Dunaway, and Rowlands exemplified this blend, merging psychological depth with improvisational freedom and technical precision. This golden age didn't emerge from a singular vision but from a vibrant interplay of diverse influences, paving the way for an unprecedented array of performance styles.

Contemporary movements like Dogme 95 and Mumblecore continued this quest for authenticity, inviting actors to blur the lines between fiction and reality, scripted dialogue, and genuine conversation. Embracing improvisation and spontaneity, these movements lead to the performances of today that resonate with striking immediacy.

Dogme 95's "Vow of Chastity" — a manifesto urging filmmakers to ditch artificial lighting, special effects, and post-production tweaks — created a radical environment for performance. Without technical enhancements, actors had to tap into raw truth.

Emily Watson's role in "Breaking the Waves" exemplifies this, showcasing such brutal emotional honesty it's hard to watch.

Likewise, Paprika Steen in "The Celebration" navigates family trauma with unsettling authenticity. These performances weren't "natural" in the conventional sense; they pushed emotional boundaries precisely because they lacked typical cinematic shields.

Mumblecore emerged from a different impulse but shared a similar desire for authenticity. With digital cameras, minimal budgets, and largely improvised dialogue, performers — often non-professionals — simply existed on screen.

Greta Gerwig's early roles in films like "Hannah Takes the Stairs" and "Nights and Weekends" illustrate this — not polished or technically flawless, but infused with a kind of quirky specificity that conventional performance techniques would have dulled.

Every cinematic wave has pushed actors into uncharted territory, demanding adaptability, courage, and innovation. While film historians often examine these movements through the lenses of directors, cinematographers, or cultural impacts, it's the actors who've consistently stood at the forefront, navigating new stylistic demands and reshaping the audience's understanding of the human experience through their performances.

This historical context matters for today's actors, serving not as mere academic trivia but as a practical foundation. Contemporary performance synthesizes elements from various traditions — the physical precision of silent film, the psychological depth of Method acting, the experimentation of European art cinema, the unfiltered immediacy of documentary, and the casual intimacy of the digital era. Understanding these threads allows you to draw from a rich tapestry of techniques rather than confining yourself to a single tradition.

Cinema's rich history encompasses many significant movements:

- Silent Film Era (1890s–1920s)
- Soviet Montage Theory (1920s)
- German Expressionism (1920s–1930s)
- French Impressionism (1920s)
- Surrealism (1920s–1930s)
- Poetic Realism (1930s)
- Italian Neorealism (1940s–1950s)
- Film Noir (1940s–1950s)
- Japanese Golden Age (1950s)
- French New Wave (1950s–1960s)
- Free Cinema (British New Wave) (1950s–1960s)
- Cinema Novo (Brazil) (1960s)
- Direct Cinema and Cinéma Vérité (1960s)
- New Hollywood (American New Wave) (1960s–1980s)
- Parallel Cinema (India) (1970s–1980s)
- New German Cinema (1970s)
- Fifth Generation (China) (1980s–1990s)
- Korean New Wave & Contemporary Korean Cinema (1990s–present)
- Dogme 95 (1995–2005)
- Mumblecore (2000s–present)
- New Argentine Cinema (2000s–present)
- Romanian New Wave (2000s–present)

Cinema isn't a straight line — it's a constellation. Every movement lights up another, across time and space.

Each movement developed its own visual language, narrative approach, and — most relevant to our exploration — distinct demands on its actors.

For our purposes, we'll focus on just a few movements that dramatically shifted the paradigm of screen performance.

Art changes the actor — because it keeps changing what truth looks like.

These movements don't exist in isolation. They converse across time, influence each other, and sometimes react against one another. American cinema influenced Italian Neorealism, which influenced French New Wave, which in turn influenced New Hollywood, creating a complex web of inspiration, evolution, and reaction.

The actor isn't just adapting styles — they're absorbing the very heartbeat of each era.

As an actor in the digital age, you don't just perform — you inherit. You carry the embers of every rebellion, every experiment. Styles that once shook Paris in the 1960s now slip unnoticed into television commercials. Approaches considered experimental in 1970s New York now pop up in ads. You have the freedom to draw from an unprecedented range of techniques, approaches, and traditions — but also the responsibility to understand the context from which they emerged.

Knowing that Cassavetes pioneered an approach allowing actors to improvise extended scenes while maintaining character has given us all permission to explore similar territory. Understanding how Bresson achieved a rare, unselfconscious presence through non-actors offers techniques we can adapt. Studying how silent film actors conveyed complex emotions without dialogue grants us new tools for scenes where the voice or *words on the page* should yield to the body.

> *"It is about as much as you say as what you don't say. If I can put off the meaning of a paragraph with a look... go with the look. Not the words."*
> – Matthew McConaughey

Consequently, we explore film movement here not to categorize or academically classify them, but to better understand how the actor's task has shifted over time. Knowing where we've been isn't nostalgia — it's survival. It's the map we draw, so we don't lose our way forward.

Ultimately, cinema isn't just dialogue between characters. It's a conversation across time. Between past and present, tradition and innovation, artists separated by decades yet united in one pursuit: making visible the invisibility of human experience.

CHAPTER 2

EVOLUTION OF MAJOR FILM MOVEMENTS

Limitations as Liberation

Multimedia artist Phil Hansen didn't just adapt to limitation — he made it his compass. When a tremor in his hand threatened to derail his creativity, he didn't resist. He leaned in. In his TED Talk *Embrace the Shake*, Hansen reframes constraint not as a boundary but as a birthplace — a site where creativity isn't suffocated but summoned.

"Seize the limitation," he says. Not the day. Not the moment. The limitation.

There's a larger truth here — one that transcends art. In a culture addicted to freedom, expansion, and endless choice, we often overlook a hidden paradox: boundary isn't the enemy of expression — it's its condition. The frame gives meaning to the image. The silence gives shape to the song.

Limitations, whether physical, emotional, societal, or circumstantial, don't stifle the human spirit — they chisel it. They force ingenuity, summon resourcefulness, and demand a confrontation with what's essential. What remains when the excess is stripped away? Sometimes, something more honest. More alive. More human.

If you haven't watched Hansen's talk, do. Not just for artistic inspiration, but as a meditation on our species' strange capacity to turn confinement into flight. It's not just a lesson in creativity — it's a philosophy of becoming.

Orson Welles put it more starkly: "The enemy of art is the absence of limitations."

Actors know this in their bones — whether they name it or not. We carry more than lines and blocking. We carry the weight of history — not just the movements we study, but the personal ones etched into our bodies. The tremors we've tried to hide. The heartbreaks we've swallowed. The inherited silences we learned not to speak. All of it. All of it becomes part of the work.

And the best of it — the most revelatory, the most transcendent — often emerges precisely because we couldn't do it the way we first imagined. Because the straight path disappeared. Because we were forced to adapt — to reconfigure. To let the work rise not from ease, but from friction.

I was reminded of this years ago in Los Angeles.

I'd met up with an old friend, Patrick Kilpatrick — an ever-working actor and recognizable face in a sea of deeply flawed character roles. We hadn't seen each other in years. As we walked to lunch, I noticed something — his gait. Subtle, but different than I remembered. A kind of softness in the rhythm of his step.

I asked, gently, "Did you get hurt?"

He laughed, waved it off. "Nah, that's the famous Kilpatrick limp," he said.

Now, I'm paraphrasing here — he said more, and said it much better — but the essence stuck with me. He told me how he'd nearly died in a motorcycle accident when he was younger. Doctors weren't sure he'd ever walk again. He fought his way back, rebuilt what he could. But the limp remained. He couldn't do what he used to, not at the elite athletic level he once had. But instead of masking it, he made it part of the work. A signature. He "embraced the shake" decades before there was a Phil Hansen.

"I don't hide it," he said. "I lean into it. Most of the roles I get — villains, heavies, guys with a rough history — the limp tells their story before I even have to say a word."

What the world might see as a flaw — a limitation, a liability in casting — he turned into an asset. A built-in backstory. You had to think the moment he entered the scene. On screen or in life. Not just acceptance — authorship. He didn't just let you see it. He made sure you did, then dared you to look away. And in doing so, he reshaped the terms of how you'd have to regard him.

That hit me. Quietly, completely. If I hadn't already admired his significant acting talents, I respected him now for much more.

Actors carry more than lines and blocking.

We carry the weight of history — personal history, film history, and something deeper. Not just the movements we study, but the ones imprinted into our muscles. The ones no training can iron out. And shouldn't.

Let's accept this, then — the silent era wasn't crippled by the absence of sound. It was liberated by it. Stripped of dialogue, actors uncovered something elemental: the body contains multitudes. Every move, a paragraph. Every look, a confession.

Before film, acting belonged to the stage — vast spaces that demanded volume, gesture, exaggeration. You had to hurl emotion to the back row, carry the meaning on your breath, make yourself large enough to be believed from sixty feet away.

Then came this new medium: intimate, visual, silent. Yet somehow more intimately personal than anything that came before. No balconies. No distance. Just the camera — a witness watching inches away. The close-up.

It has crowned stars. Exposed pretenders. A monster, a lover — it can devour you or deliver you and everything you've ever hoped for. Every actor craves it, then dreads it, caught in that strange, schizophrenic dance between not enough... and one take too many. The close-up doesn't care about your effort. It doesn't flinch. The camera watches — unblinking — searching your face for something that can't be faked. Something felt. Not performed. Known. Lived. Then you hear the director call, "This next one's your close-up."

No matter how many times you've run the scene — hit the marks, mapped the beats — that moment always stirs something low and electric in your gut. That little knot of fear. That quiet voice whispering: *This is the one you have to get right.*

No art form had ever demanded quite this *collision* — the vastness of scale paired down with the subtlety of precision. Painting has canvas. Sculpture has stone. Music has notation, agreed-upon grammar. But acting — on film — requires a human being to become both medium and message, both instrument and interpretation.

There was no handbook for the silent era pioneers. No lineage to lean on.

Theater had its tradition, yes. But the camera — that unblinking witness — changed everything. It saw too much and forgave too little. It demanded truth stripped of the artifice of theatrics, emotion without truth. And in this new landscape, actors had to invent a vocabulary as they went along — each close-up a new verb, each silence a diverse syntax.

It couldn't be codified. It had to be conjured.

Through failure. Through improvisation. Through those long, disorienting days on set where nothing landed — until suddenly, it did. Discovery became the method. And when the work was honest — good or bad — it left no residue. Unlike a painting or sculpture, there was nothing to hold. Nothing to hang. It wasn't baked or birthed. Just a breath — caught in light. A flicker of meaning before the final cut, before picture wrap.

And then... you wait.

Because what comes next — what survives the edit — is out of your hands. Some of it is yours: your instincts, your mistakes, your grace. Some of it not: a director's taste, an editor's rhythm, the mood of the room that day. All of it unknowable until much later, if ever.

That's the life. The craft. Then and now, it continues.

Those early limitations weren't theoretical — they were brutal. Cameras were hand-cranked. Tripods, locked in place. The lights? Blinding. Hot. Unforgiving. There were no second chances — no zoom lenses, no slick post edits, no effects to clean it up or bail you out. Everything had to happen in the frame — in real-time, in real space, in full view.

Buster Keaton understood this better than most. The stone face. The elastic body. Watch *Steamboat Bill, Jr.* and you'll see it — the shot where the house collapses around him. A two-ton wall falls and lands exactly where it's supposed to, sparing him by inches. Not because of the simple luck inferred by his character — but because he's standing in the one place, the *only* place, where the open window... just happens to line up perfectly.

One breath too far forward, and he's gone. Flattened.

But he doesn't move. Doesn't brace. Doesn't flinch. No fear. No anticipation. No wink to the audience. Just that blank, brilliant stare — daring gravity to do its thing.

It wasn't performance. It was presence. Embodiment. A real human, in real danger, captured in one take — no safety rig, no visual effects, no second unit. Just Buster, dead center, standing on a nail, he'd driven into the ground to mark the spot. Miss it by a half-inch, and the window frame would've split his skull and the wall crush him.

It is said the crew couldn't even watch. But Keaton? Still. Silent. Steady.

Because for him, the body, the physicality, *was* the performance. And the danger — that was the punchline.

He understood something profound: that the joke wasn't the collapsing house — it was his refusal to react. No comment. No flinch. Just unblinking defiance in the face of chaos. That was the magic.

Audiences paid their nickel to see it again and again — and they waited. Leaned forward with a shared anticipation no matter how many times they'd seen it: *"Just wait. Just wait."* They knew the moment. Had seen it before. But still, they watched like it might go differently. It was the silence that made everything sharper. More dangerous. With sound, it might've played as cued spectacle. Without it, it became myth.

And maybe, in the back of their minds, a part of them wondered what it would look like if it went wrong. They laughed again when it didn't, out of relief. But something in the silence stayed with them.

The house-fall remains one of cinema's most astonishing moments. Not just because it's technically perfect, but because it's so nakedly *precise*. Stoicism as comedy. Stillness as rebellion. Precision as poetry. The silence? That was the killer. The silence wasn't the *limitation*. It was the punchline. It *was* the whole argument for what silent film could do that sound never could.

Steamboat Bill, Jr. (1928) arrived as one last, brilliant, defiant gasp of the silent era. A swan song. An elegy for physical storytelling. For a kind of wordless, weight-bearing grace — carved in motion, delivered without a word.

And then the silence would end as just months later, Jolson's Jazz Singer would usher in the talkies, flooding the frame with sound — and changing the craft forever.

Arguably, the greatest genius of the Silent Era, Chaplin, took a different path. Where Keaton was steel, Chaplin was mercury: expressive and elastic. His face was a symphony of micro-movements. The twitch of a mustache, the arc of an eyebrow. His body was a smorgasbord of language all its own... and audiences worldwide reveled in it.

Watch the final scene of *City Lights*. The flower girl, once blind, now sees. She reaches out and touches the Little Tramp's hand — and in that one moment, Chaplin's face becomes a kaleidoscope of feeling. Hope. Fear.

Love. Shame. And something Indefinable but lives in every human who has ever felt unworthy of being seen.

No words. No explanation. Just presence. Truth.

These weren't just funny men. They were poets of the body. Philosophers of movement. Cartographers of emotion mapping out new territory — moment by moment, frame by frame. Their limitations weren't obstacles. They were invitations. Silence gave them space. Even in that unforgiving framework, they found something timeless. They weren't making up for what was missing. They were discovering what had always been — the physicality of the human body in all its expressive glory.

This is where craft begins. And in many ways, where it ends.

In Chaplin's *The Gold Rush*, the sequence where the starving prospector cooks, serves, and eats his own shoe. Chaplin transforms a grim survival situation into a ballet of manners — twirling the shoelaces like spaghetti, delicately picking a nail from the sole as if removing a bone from fish, savoring the boiled leather with the expression of culinary delight. His comedy didn't emerge from mugging or indicating — it arose from total commitment to the character's reality.

These weren't just comedians. They were artists' pioneers, cartographers mapping uncharted territories of the human face and body. Their canvas limited. Their tools few.

Early cameras didn't help. Static angles. Primitive lighting. Rudimentary editing. Every technical element worked against subtlety. Causing most actors to respond by going bigger — exaggerating expressions, amplifying gestures, telegraphing emotions so broadly they'd be visible from in back row of a theater. Grand declamatory in style and gesture.

This approach created a generation of forgotten performers — actors whose work now appears dated, mannered, and excessive to modern eyes. But others discovered something profound about this new medium. They recognized that film required a kind of restraint unknown to the theater, that the camera caught the smallest details, that screen performance demanded precision over projection.

Consider Lillian Gish, D.W. Griffith's greatest collaborator, who understood the emotional power of stillness — of contained feelings threatening to break the surface. In *Way Down East*, her character is abandoned in a snowstorm, unconscious on an ice floe drifting toward a waterfall. To convey that truth on screen, Gish placed her bare hand in freezing water between takes so her physical suffering would translate. Not Method acting before the Method existed, but something more elemental: a recognition that the body's truth communicates directly to the audience in a way no *indicating* ever can.

Then came the close-up... that changed everything.

Suddenly, the canvas wasn't limited — it was infinite. The human face, now projected larger than life on seventy-foot screens, revealed new landscapes. Micro-expressions became grand gestures. The flicker of an eyelid could carry a secret. A quiver of the lip could convey more than an entire monologue.

D.W. Griffith did not invent the close-up, but he certainly recognized and elevated its emotional potential. Earlier filmmakers like George Albert Smith and Edwin S. Porter had already used close-ups, but Griffith, especially in *Broken Blossoms* (1919), explored their expressive power with unprecedented intensity.

The scene where Lillian Gish's character, Lucy, is locked in a closet and tries to calm herself by forcing a smile with her fingers is one of the most haunting close-ups in silent cinema history. The camera lingers. She is terrified, trembling, eyes darting, and then... the smile — pulled at the corners of her mouth with shaking fingers — not to comfort herself, but to appease the monster waiting outside. That moment became emblematic of how a close-up could render the *interior* world visible. It's horrifying. Heartbreaking. And yes — unforgettable.

That isn't stage acting captured on film. It's something entirely new. Something only cinema could create.

That scene reveals the silent era's remarkably sophisticated understanding of performance psychology, the ability to communicate not just surface emotion but complicated inner conflict. A character forcing herself to display a feeling she doesn't have for the sake of survival. Human behavior, distilled to its visual essence. Modern performance, even with dialogue, music and editing, rarely achieves such clarity without help.

The melodrama of the stage may have provided a loose framework for the narrative. But silent film actors quickly realized that theatrical techniques didn't translate. The camera was too intimate. Too revealing. It exposed broad strokes as artifice. It demanded a new language.

The *intertitles* of silent film complicated the equation. Those flashes of text — sometimes dialogue, sometimes description added a new layer of rhythm. Actors had to master the beat between image and word: the pause before an intertitle, the reaction after. It became a visual dance that required mathematical precision.

Gloria Swanson in *Sadie Thompson* plays a fallen woman seeking redemption, navigating a complex moral terrain without the benefit of dialogue. Her performance holds a dual awareness — growing recognition of her own compromised position, layered with defiance aimed squarely at those judging her. She communicates this through shifts in posture, glances that reveal calculation beneath contrition, hands that alternate between guarded and exposed. No words, yet nothing withheld.

Directors weren't just directing actors. They were co-inventing an entirely new grammar. Every shot, every cut, every choice was a step into the unknown. There were no rules. No proven techniques. Just artists stumbling through the dark, sometimes striking lightning.

It wasn't about compensating for silence. It was about discovering what silence made possible.

The Russians understood this. Sergei Eisenstein's montage theory proposed that meaning is born not from a single image, but from juxtaposition—the cut between images. Kuleshov's experiment (fascinating, look it up) proved it: the same neutral expression from an actor could convey hunger, grief, or desire depending entirely on what image followed. The performance didn't change. The context did. And the meaning emerged from that interplay.

In the experiment, actor Ivan Mosjoukine maintained the same passive expression throughout. When paired with a bowl of soup, viewers saw hunger. When followed by a child's coffin, they saw grief. When shown beside a reclining woman, they saw desire. The actor remained neutral, but the audience imbued the performance with emotion based on the surrounding imagery.

That principle remains foundational to screen performance: the actor's truth doesn't exist in isolation; it thrives in relationship with the light, the edit, the music, the frame. Silent cinema wasn't just a primitive version of modern film. It was a complete, sophisticated art form capable of emotional complexity and psychological depth. Sometimes, even surpassing what came after.

Sure, we gained a lot when movies learned to talk. But we lost something too: a direct visual line to the emotional cortex, a purity of communication — raw, unfiltered, bypassing language altogether.

Many great silent actors couldn't make the leap to sound, not because they lacked skill or had awkward voices, but because they had mastered a different form entirely. One that used different muscles, different instincts, a different relationship to the audience, and the lens. Sound didn't enhance their artistry. It replaced it.

And yet, modern actors still study these pioneers — often without realizing it. The physical specificity of Tom Hardy. The facial precision of Tilda Swinton. The comedic timing of Jackie Chan — all echo techniques born of silence.

Limitation isn't the enemy of art. It's the catalyst.

When actors complain to me about restrictions, a difficult director, horrible locations, uncomfortable wardrobe (I've had them all... and certainly complained enough early in my career) — I encourage them to look at Keaton standing perfectly still as the house falls around him. Or Chaplin, eating his own shoe, turning starvation into a ballet. Or Gish, trapped in that closet in *Broken Blossoms*, forcing her face into a grotesque smile that still haunts.

They didn't just work around their limitations. They created masterpieces because of them. So, the question isn't what you lack. It's what you do with what you have.

What those silent pioneers had — what they discovered through necessity and invention was a simple, durable truth: acting begins and ends with the body. Words can mislead. Words can be clever. But the body... the body doesn't lie.

The silent era wasn't a warm-up act. It wasn't an incomplete version of the real thing. It was its own sophisticated art form — whole, expressive, capable of emotional depths we still struggle to reach today. When sound arrived, we gained a lot. But we also lost something vital in the process: a direct line to the visual cortex, an unfiltered connection between audience and emotion. The raw poetry of pure cinema. A moving image that didn't need to explain itself.

Every actor should spend time in silence. A full week, if possible — no dialogue, no sound, no words to lean on. Just intention. Breath. Physicality. Presence without performance.

What would you communicate if the text were stripped away? How would you move? What would your posture say? Would your breath quicken? Would your listening deepen?

Try this: use a slightly different version of the Meisner Repetition Exercise — but remove your voice from the exercise. Let your partner speak the repeated phrase. You remain still. Silent. Let your response arise only in your body — a shift of weight, a glance, a hesitation, a slow exhale.

They speak. You respond — physically, truthfully. Let it land. Let it ripple. Then let them repeat the phrase, again and again. Each time, allow yourself to feel something new. To discover the emotional currents beneath the surface. Keep going until every possible response — every flicker of resistance, tenderness, fear, rage — has had its moment in the light.

The goal is not to perform. It's to feel. To listen with the whole body. To let silence do the talking.

The silent revolution didn't just pave the way — it reawakened something long buried. If we want to understand the deeper magic of acting, the part that hums beneath craft, beneath method — we have to look further back. The silent era didn't invent physical storytelling. It remembered it.

Older than cinema. Older than theater. Older, perhaps, than language itself.

Acting didn't begin in service of story or spectacle. It began as survival. As ritual. As the body's attempt to shape the unspeakable — to make sense of a world too vast, too unknowable, to face unguarded.

The first actors weren't actors at all. They were shamans. Healers. Story-keepers. The embodied link between seen and unseen. They didn't perform roles — they yielded to presence. Letting the mask, the movement, the rhythm of breath become something other. Their bodies became thresholds. Their silence, a summoning.

Ancient cave walls show masked figures, limbs frozen mid-dance. They weren't pretending. The bear mask wasn't a costume; it was possession. When the shaman became the bear, it wasn't performance; it was transformation. Complete. Irreversible. For the duration of the rite, he *was* the bear.

Sound familiar? It should.

When Daniel Day-Lewis stays in character for months or when Joaquin Phoenix dissolves into a role to the point where the actor is hard to locate, they're not being difficult.

Any criticism of the Method aside, these actors aren't being indulgent. They're accessing something ancient. One of our oldest traditions.

Transformation. Possession. Becoming.

The Greeks understood it, too. Their word for actor — *hypokrites* — shares its roots with *hypnosis*. A surrender of the self. An altered state. Their theater wasn't performance in the modern sense; it was communion. Tragic masks weren't props. They were thresholds. The Dionysian rites that predated Greek drama involved more than metaphor; they invited gods into the body.

And traces of that tradition remain, flickering in the best screen work of today. Jean-Louis Trintignant in *Amour*, portraying a husband caring for his dying wife. It's not a simulation. It's not technique. It's a *surrender*. The viewer doesn't observe — they receive. Emotional truth passes through the actor like current through a wire.

Or Isabelle Adjani in *Possession*. That subway tunnel scene — it's not performance, it's possession. Grief, rage, collapse, birth — her body convulses with something unspeakable. It's not choreography. It's not a breakdown. It's an exorcism.

What makes it unbearable and unforgettable is that it doesn't live in her technique. It lives in her ganglia. In the limbic system. In the pre-verbal, pre-rational storm of the body remembering something older than language.

She doesn't perform; she *becomes* a conduit for it. Her instrument stops being expressive and becomes responsive. Receptive. Transmitting something primal through skin and breath and tremor. The audience doesn't sit back and analyze — they flinch. They feel it in their solar plexus, their throat, the back of their neck. Not comprehension, but recognition. Their own nervous systems echoing back: *yes, I know this.*

Every culture developed its own doorway. In India, the classical Kathakali performer spends hours in sacred preparation, painting the face, binding the costume, layering symbol upon symbol until identity dissolves. In Japan, the Noh actor moves with precision until stillness becomes sublime. Across the Americas, Indigenous storytellers shape their bodies into spirits and ancestors, living vessels of memory.

Years ago, I once met an actor who had trained in Kathakali. I found this endlessly compelling. No dialogue. No spoken lines. Only movement, breath, and the discipline of gesture. Every flick of the eye, every held muscle, carried meaning, sacred, deliberate, precise. It wasn't performance as we know it. It was invocation.

I asked him, "So... when does the character take over?"

"With the first breath of preparation. By the time I enter the dressing room, I've already left whoever I am behind."

I remember thinking about not only the tradition of that process, but also being given permission and the acceptance to do so, must have been quite a freeing and exhilarating experience. To be *allowed* to become. Not to mimic or pretend, but to surrender. In that world, transformation isn't eccentric — it's expected.

Not so in the West. At least, not anymore. Modern culture has severed actor from role, art from ritual. We call it pretending. We flatten the sacred into craft and forget the deeper magic.

But it still shows up in those rare moments that rupture the frame.

Like Isabelle Adjani in *Possession*.

That subway tunnel scene isn't staged. It's unleashed. Her body becomes a battleground of grief, rage, collapse, birth. It's not technique. It's not even madness. It's something older. Something cellular.

What we're witnessing lives beneath language, in the ganglia, the limbic system, below the neocortex. This is pre-thought, pretense stripped away. Her body fires on ancestral circuitry. She doesn't "play" the moment, she channels it. Transmits it. Transmutes it.

And the audience doesn't analyze it. They flinch. They *feel*. Their nervous system lights up in recognition... *"I know this. I've been there. I've been broken like that."*

Before thought catches up, the body already understands.

The greatest screen actors instinctively reject this separation. By letting the body lead. By allowing themselves to become the role rather than perform it. They understand, often without articulating it, that their craft isn't about pretending; rather, it's about becoming.

Not fakery, but *Alchemy*. Genuine transformation of self into the other.

Still, we often get confused about these words: "pretending" "becoming," just as we frequently blur the lines between "method" and "technique." The language of acting can trap us if we aren't careful. It's easy to mistake simplicity for shallowness, or intensity for authentic, genuine truth.

Some actors bristle at the term *Method Acting* — and with good reason. They picture the excesses, the caricatures, the endless suffering mistaken for depth. They hear "method" and think of losing control, permissive madness, and self-indulgent parading as art.

Some actors reject the idea of *preparation,* diving headfirst into willpower, instinct, and pure imagination. They wait for something raw to emerge — an organic impulse bubbling up from who knows where.

I've tried myself and trained both extremes. Lived in the structure. Then let go into chaos.

And what I've found — what holds true for most to discover — is that the real work lives somewhere in the tension between them. Preparation meets imagination. Imagination meets surrender. And when all three are held in balance, something very real happens.

Famously, when Dustin Hoffman pushed himself into physical and emotional exhaustion for *Marathon Man,* Sir Laurence Olivier, ever the classical craftsman, is said to have looked at him kindly and quipped:

"My dear boy — why don't you just act?"

Ouch. There's truth in Olivier's barb — and also, a kind of concealment. Even Olivier, with all his classical brilliance, knew that true acting isn't mere *imitation* (this differs from *impersonation*, which can be *embodiment*). It isn't even technique. It's becoming.

The danger lies in thinking it's one or the other. That you must suffer endlessly to achieve truth, or that you can simply plaster technique on top, and go.

The real work lives in the *in-between.* Where imagination, discipline, physicality, breath, and surrender meet. Where pretending dissolves, and becoming — slowly, quietly — takes over.

Magic can happen, yes. But this isn't mystical nonsense. This is the history of our craft. The DNA of what we do.

Acting is a dance between method(ology) and mystery, technique and surrender.

When the actor truly surrenders — when the boundary between self and character dissolves — something happens. Science can't explain it. The body changes. The voice transforms. Even the eyes, those windows to the "soul," reflect a different light.

I've seen it happen. I've felt it, too. Every serious actor has. It's why we keep coming back — addicted to this wild, punishing, euphoric thing. This craft that breaks us open and stitches us back together, sometimes in the same breath.

It's that moment when *you're* no longer steering. The choices aren't yours — they're the character's, moving through you. The words don't feel memorized. They arrive as thought. As needed. As truth born in the instant.

You're fully present... and somehow *absent* simultaneously.

Weird, yes, but gloriously so.

I'm reminded of an interview I saw with Johnny Depp, where he described this mystery in his own way. Speaking about his process, he said,

"I could never be Jack Sparrow. So, I look around for something to imitate that reminds me of who this character might be. Sometimes it's a dog, or a cartoon. When I played Edward Scissorhands, I used my sister's newborn baby — the way he moved, the way he looked at the world — and just imagined being and acting like that."

Depp wasn't pretending. He wasn't performing in the traditional *shamanic* sense. He was searching for a living, breathing thread — something real he could hold onto —and letting it transform him from the inside out. The dog's loyalty. The baby's wonder. The cartoon's elasticity of spirit. All woven together until Johnny Depp, as we know him, slipped quietly into the background — and something other, now alive anew, and entirely of that moment, stepped forward. Shamanic.

Recently, I saw Christopher Walken in an interview. He was asked, "Who is the best actor you've ever seen?" His response. "Bugs Bunny."

So, ask yourself, *why*? Doesn't this sound a bit like Depp? What do they see so evidently clear that we might not see on its surface?

When Walken names "Bugs Bunny" as the greatest actor he'd ever seen — and meant it — he wasn't joking, and he wasn't being cute. He was pointing at something essential. Something most of us miss because we've been trained to look for *technique*, not *transcendence*.

What Walken saw in Bugs — and what mirrors Depp — is the ability to shapeshift at will, yet remain deeply specific and alive in every moment. Bugs isn't bound by realism. He violates all logic — gender, form, tone, species, rhythm, tempo — and yet never once feels false. He's fully committed, grounded in his own cartoon logic, and utterly fearless.

Here's why it matters:

- **Elasticity of Spirit** — Bugs Bunny embodies total *freedom*. He responds in the moment with whatever is truest — sometimes clever, sometimes ruthless, sometimes tender. He *bends the laws of the world*, but never loses *his own internal consistency*. Like Depp channeling his sister's baby's wonder or a dog's loyalty, Bugs takes the emotion that best serves the moment and *lives inside it fully* — then moves on to the next.
- **Presence + Play** — Bugs *isn't performing for you*, he's *being with you*. This is the core of shamanic performance. The same kind you see hinted

at in sacred ritual, clowning, and yes — Depp at his best. There's no artifice. There's just *now*.

- **Surprise + Agency** — Like a trickster deity, Bugs *rewrites the script* every second. He improvises, mocks power, shifts roles, and dances on the boundary between observer and participant — you know that you don't know — what's liable to come next. So you lean in and wait for it as something other steps forward and the actor, recedes.

Walken saw in Bugs what ancient performers, jesters, and medicine men knew: **to act is to conjure**. And what better example of a conjurer than a rabbit who never loses?

So, why "Bugs Bunny"?

Because sometimes the cartoon *knows more about truth* than the method actor. Because elasticity is not the opposite of discipline — it's a reward for total surrender. Because Bugs, like Depp, **disappears into the magic of the moment**.

And because Christopher Walken, with his own elastic timing and beautiful metaphysical weirdness, *knows a fellow traveler when he sees one*.

You can teach technique. You can teach theory. You can teach the mechanics of breath, voice, and movement. But that final leap — complete surrender — can only be experienced. It can't be explained. I've tried using a thousand different words, phrases, and metaphors. But ultimately, it can only be invited in by the actor. It must be welcomed. Allowed.

This is why acting at its best remains a holy act. A conjuring. The summoning of spirits that don't exist until we give them flesh. An egregore birthed into the world.

Silent Cinema, in stripping away language, accidentally returned acting to its primal roots — the body as a vessel of transformation. The face as a landscape of the soul. Movement as expression of being.

Remember this lineage when you work. You're not just an entertainer. You're the latest in a long line of ancient shamans, priests, mystics, and mediums. Your work, when done with full commitment, isn't just performance — it's transformation. Not just for yourself but for those witnessing. Not just as observers, but co-pilots, navigators, fellow sojourners now and in the future.

This is the burden of our craft. And its gift.

Each movement we've explored didn't vanish — it left a mark, a residue. Fossils in the frame. Micro-habits in the craft. What silent film actors discovered through pure physicality now lives in the flick of an eyelid during a close-up. German Expressionism's distortion echoes in performances that stretch reality to reveal the unconscious. Neorealism's raw ordinariness bled into mumblecore and today's prestige TV. We think of these movements as eras, but really... they're more like sediments. Layers. And today's actor? They stand atop them all. Inherited. Informed. Sometimes overwhelmed by the very weight of what came before.

But history doesn't just echo — it evolves.

As we move forward, we'll shift into practical navigation — because the evolution didn't end. It didn't freeze after New Hollywood or crest with Dogme 95. No, it kept moving. Quietly. Relentlessly. Almost unnoticed.

The craft keeps mutating — shaped by what the camera now demands, and what the audience no longer forgives. It lives in the silence between lines, the flicker before intention, the breath before a choice is made.

Welcome to now.

German Expressionism: The Distortion of Reality

Imagine a world tilted on its axis. Buildings that lean to the impossible. Shadows crawling up walls like living things. Faces painted in stark contrasts of black and white.

This was German Expressionism — cinema as a nightmare, a fever dream, a manifestation of a collective unconscious.

After World War I, Germany was a nation in existential crisis. Defeated, humiliated and economically devastated. The films that emerged from this crucible weren't interested in capturing reality — they wanted to distort it, to reveal psychological truths beneath the surface.

Reality itself had become suspect. How could conventional realism depict a world where millions died in trenches, where social order collapsed, where nothing made sense anymore? Expressionist filmmakers understood that distortion, exaggeration, and stylization might communicate emotional truth more effectively than documentary-like literalism. They sought not how the world looked, but how it felt to live in it.

This approach wasn't limited to production design and cinematography. It demanded an entirely new performance style — one where actors' bodies became extensions of the distorted visual landscape around them. Not separate from their environment but integrated within it. Not moving through space but transforming along with it.

Fritz Lang's "M" gave us Peter Lorre hunting children through shadowy streets, his face a mask of tormented compulsion. In "The Cabinet of Dr. Caligari," Conrad Veidt's sleepwalker moved through distorted sets like a man underwater, his body elongated, his movements strangely precise.

Look at Veidt closely. His character, Cesare, exists in a perpetual trance state, controlled by the mysterious Dr. Caligari. To embody his character, Veidt doesn't simply act as if he is sleepy or drugged. He reinvents human movement itself. His body becomes an instrument of uncanny precision, each gesture perfect yet fundamentally wrong. Too deliberate. Too controlled. Watch how he extends his arms at unnatural angles, how he holds positions that living bodies deliberately avoid. This isn't random stylization but a precise physical manifestation of the character's psychological reality — a man trapped between consciousness and unconsciousness, between life and death, between will and its absence.

The movement didn't end there.

F.W. Murnau's "Nosferatu" presented Max Schreck as Count Orlok — a creature more rat than man, his elongated fingers casting spider-like shadows across walls, his movements alternating between predatory stillness and unnatural speed. His vampire wasn't simply portrayed; he was structurally embodied. Schreck didn't act as if he were the monster — he became its physical manifestation, and a visual shock to the nervous system.

It may sound comical now, but his transformation was so unnerving that rumors persisted for decades that Max Schreck wasn't acting at all — he was an actual vampire.

These whispers became the inspiration for the 2000 film *Shadow of the Vampire* — a fictional retelling of *Nosferatu*'s production that leans fully into the myth. In it, director F.W. Murnau (played by John Malkovich) secretly hires a real vampire to play Orlok. Willem Dafoe portrays Max Schreck in the film — not as a man, but as an inhuman creature hiding in plain sight. Dafoe's eerie, mesmerizing performance earned him an Oscar nomination and helped cement the legend in modern pop culture.

But the truth, as it often is, may be even more remarkable than the fiction.

Max Schreck was not a vampire — obviously. He was a classically trained stage and film actor, with roots in the Berliner Staatstheater, with a long résumé of theatrical work. What disturbed audiences then, and still does, wasn't some supernatural essence, but his masterful control of his physical instrument. His Count Orlok didn't move like a human. He moved like something else entirely, something governed by alien laws of gravity.

In the original film, watch how he rises from the coffin. Not with effort, but in a single, fluid arc, like a figure drawn upward by an unseen force. Note how he stands in impossible stillness, unblinking, unbreathing, as if suspended outside of time. Even the curling of his fingers defies anatomy, each gesture deliberate, unsettling, inhuman.

This wasn't just character work. It was a full-body reimagining. A performance so committed, so physically transformed, it gave birth to a myth.

And in a way, the myth endures — not because Schreck was a vampire, but because for the length of that film, he made us believe he just could be.

Lang's "Metropolis" brilliantly took expressionism to the next level, presenting a mechanized dystopian world where workers move in synchronized exhaustion beneath the city, their bodies components in a vast machine. The transformation of humans into automatons wasn't accomplished through special effects, but through the actors' commitment to mechanical movement, their humanity deliberately suppressed, their individuality sacrificed to the rhythm of the industrial beast.

Watch the worker "Shift Change" sequence in *Metropolis*. Columns of laborers move with an identical gait, rhythm, and posture, all of which convey a sense of defeat. Each actor subordinates their individual expression to the collective movement, creating a visual metaphor of dehumanization more powerful than any dialogue could express. This physically demanding sequence required performers to maintain mechanical precision while conveying exhaustion — a physical contradiction.

Years earlier, Paul Wegener's *The Golem* (1920) offered a different kind of physical transformation. Wegener himself played the clay creature from Jewish legend, brought to life through an arcane ritual. His movements suggest both immense strength and a kind of childlike bewilderment. Every gesture held a tension, a brute force paired with emerging awareness, violence laced with rudimentary emotion. Far from being hampered by the limitations, Wegener's performance elevated the film through sheer physical commitment. His body *became* the metaphor, not just monster, but myth in motion.

The acting wasn't subtle. It wasn't meant to be. These weren't characters, they were archetypes. Manifestations of primal fears and desires. The actors understood that their bodies needed to match the twisted environments surrounding them. They developed a heightened physical vocabulary, angular, stylized, almost balletic in its precision.

What set this approach apart? These performers weren't attempting psychological realism or emotional authenticity as we understand it today. They worked from the outside in. The external form — physical silhouette, exaggerated gesture, and grotesque posture — became a gateway to revealing internal states. The somnambulist's stiff-armed movements in "Caligari" conveyed more about his compromised will than any modern method-acting approach might achieve.

In *M*, Peter Lorre doesn't just play a killer. He exposes one. His bulging eyes, that tortured face — all twitch and tremble — externalize a compulsion he can barely contain, let alone understand. It's horrifying. But not because it's overdone. Because it's precise. Controlled chaos.

There's a moment — maybe *the* moment — where he looks into a mirror. Not to preen. To deform. He contorts his own face with his hands, rehearsing grotesque expressions, watching himself become the thing others already believe him to be. A monster, yes. But a self-aware one. Not just practicing deception, performing recognition. Trying to see what they see. Trying to believe it himself.

Layer upon layer. The character performing for himself, for the imagined audience, for the voices in his head. It's not vanity. It's a kind of confession. A stylized exaggeration that somehow lands more truthfully than any naturalistic gesture ever could.

And here's the brilliance: Lorre doesn't signal technique. He disappears inside it. What should feel like a showcase of skill lands as a psychological revelation. Real. Raw. All the more chilling because it feels, inexplicably, like it was never acted at all.

This physical approach demanded complete commitment. Conrad Veidt didn't "indicate" Cesare's trance state — he transformed his entire body into an instrument of uncanny precision. His few movements felt at once mechanical and balletic, each gesture weighted with an unnatural significance. His eyes, ringed in black, stared with hypnotic stillness — a stare that wasn't performed but constructed through complete control of his facial musculature. These weren't casual choices. They were feats of physical discipline, held in place with exacting intention, frame after frame.

Swedish actress Greta Garbo — before arriving in Hollywood — appeared in German Expressionist-influenced films like *The Joyless Street*. She understood the power of containment. Of restraint. Of letting the camera come to her, rather than projecting emotion toward it. Her stillness wasn't passive — it was gravitational. She learned early that a single breath withheld, a glance suspended too long, could carry entire subplots beneath the surface. Expressionism shaped her. And in Hollywood, she carried that stylized precision forward — refined, softened, but never forgotten.

And yet, even before Garbo. Even before Veidt. There was Lon Chaney.

"The Man of a Thousand Faces." A phrase often repeated — rarely understood. Chaney wasn't just a master of disguise. He was an architect of embodiment. His transformations in *The Hunchback of Notre Dame, The Phantom of the Opera*, and dozens of other silent films weren't about vanity or shock — they were an actor's alchemical surrender. He didn't wear characters. He channeled them. He distorted his body, concealed his face, and shaped pain into movement. Into breath. Into eyes that could weep without ever blinking.

Chaney built character from the outside in, but his externalities were never hollow. Behind the grotesque masks lived profound compassion. Tragedy. A desperation that pulsed through every hunched shoulder or trembling hand. He didn't wait for the Method to arrive. He found it, in the silence, in the solitude, in the crawlspace between horror and empathy.

Veidt, Garbo, Chaney — they each understood something we often still forget: the body, when pushed beyond comfort, beyond realism, reveals truths the mind alone can't fabricate. By embracing stylization, distortion, and extremity, they bypassed the intellect and went straight to the gut. These weren't exaggerated performances. They were clarifying. Primal. Physical. Psychic. This wasn't realism.

It was a truth of a different order.

The influence runs deep. Tim Burton's entire aesthetic. David Lynch's nightmarish vision-scapes. Christopher Nolan's Joker and Ledger's interpretation, with his predatory gait and fractured micro-expressions, owes as much to Veidt as to any comic book panel. Edward Scissorhands is Chaney's Phantom reincarnated in suburban drag. And Depp's performance, wounded, delicate, ghostlike — all of these— echo.

These performances remind us that what is strange is often what is most human, made visible through distortion, and made beautiful by what it costs to hold the pose.

Alexander Skarsgård's recent portrayal of Nosferatu draws directly from Max Schreck's original, understanding that some horrors are best conveyed through physical transformation rather than psychological subtlety. Willem Dafoe's entire career, from the demonic Bobby Peru in "Wild at Heart" to the tortured anxiety of "The Lighthouse", demonstrates an actor willing to distort his face and body to expressionistic extremes in service of deeper emotional truths.

For today's actor, German Expressionism offers a vital counterpoint to our Stanislavski-dominated landscape. It reminds us that externals — body, voice, physical form — aren't merely vessels for internal emotions but powerful tools of expression in their own right. In an era where naturalism reigns supreme, these films suggest an alternative approach.

What if the body itself becomes the primary instrument of meaning?

This doesn't require period-appropriate stylization. Contemporary performers draw from expressionist techniques without mimicking the aesthetic. The lesson lies in the physical commitment — a willingness to transform one's instrument completely, to find truth through the external rather than some internal recall. When Joaquin Phoenix contorts his shockingly emaciated body in "Joker," he's accessing an emotional state through a physical distortion that other approaches might never reach.

Filmmakers like Lars von Trier explicitly reference the expressionist tradition, creating contexts where heightened performance becomes not a stylistic choice but a necessary response to extreme circumstances. Charlotte Gainsbourg and Willem Dafoe in *Antichrist* engage with this lineage through physically punishing, emotionally volatile performances that externalize psychological disintegration. Their work isn't "naturalistic," but it achieves emotional truth by pushing beyond the comfortable limits of realism — into a realm where pain, grief, and desire rupture the frame. The film itself sparked intense controversy upon release, earning both accolades and outrage for its graphic violence, explicit sexuality, and bleak existential themes. For some, it was an act of cinematic bravery; for others, a provocation bordering on cruelty. Either way, *Antichrist* forced audiences — like its actors — to confront the unspoken and the unbearable, head-on.

For scenes requiring heightened reality, moments of extreme psychological pressure, supernatural elements, or abstract conceptual work, expressionist techniques offer solutions beyond psychological realism. An actor willing to explore grotesque physicality, exaggerated gesture, or distorted vocal quality gains access to expressive possibilities beyond conventional approaches.

Even in naturalistic work, carefully controlled elements of expressionist technique can elevate a performance. A fleeting distortion of the face during intense emotion — a tightening that doesn't quite match the line, a breath held too long, a hand that clenches as if anticipating something that never comes. Not "mugging" — that desperate, exaggerated telegraphing meant to ensure the audience doesn't miss the cued emotion. Mugging begs to be seen. It signals too loudly. But what we're talking about here lives just beneath that internal threshold. A subtle alteration in movement quality that hints at a psychological fracture disconnected from the scene's surface logic. A flicker that breaks pattern. A gesture that interrupts realism. Not for effect, but because something deeper is surfacing — something the character can't quite name. When used sparingly, with practice and discipline, these calibrated ruptures become markers of emotional authenticity. They leave a residue. They haunt. They expand the actor's palette not by abandoning naturalism, but by destabilizing it — briefly — to let something primal slip through. Something out of kilter. Singular. Memorable.

I often ask actors to explore an expressionistic physical vocabulary when they're feeling stuck. By temporarily abandoning their commitment to naturalism and embracing an over-stylized physical form, they are often able to access emotional states that verbal analysis or memory-based approaches can't reach. (Depp's dog, Walken's Bugs Bunny) The lesson isn't to perform the entire role in the expressionist style, but to recognize how a physical transformation, even momentary, can unlock emotional doorways that intellectual approaches often leave closed.

The legacy of German Expressionism reminds us that acting isn't always about being "real" — sometimes it's about being true. And truth, in its rawest form, sometimes requires distortion to be fully seen. In a world increasingly dominated by CGI spectacle, the human body — pushed to expressive extremes — still remains the most powerful special effect of all.

Why?

Because we've been reading bodies longer than we've been reading words. Long before language — before culture, before artifice — we watched each other's faces for twitch, breath, dilation, stillness. We learned to sense threat, grief, hunger, arousal, danger... not from language, but from flickers. Micro hints. From physical signals encoded into us across millennia. It's not training. It's ancestry. The actor who dares to contort, to unravel, to embody something *off-pattern* — they're not just performing. They're triggering something ancient in us. Some ghost-script of survival. A kind of bone-level recognition: *This is real. This is alive. This could mean something.*

No algorithm can fake that. No rendered avatar can approximate the full uncanny valley of a human being in rupture. Because what we're responding to isn't polish — it's inheritance.

Suggested Viewing – German Expressionism

For actors ready to explore performance as physical architecture — these films reveal how distortion, exaggeration, and precise physical control can unlock emotional truths realism often can't reach:

- **The Cabinet of Dr. Caligari** *(Robert Wiene, 1920)*
  Conrad Veidt's Cesare moves like a marionette trapped in a dream — a study in restraint, angles, and haunted precision.

- **Nosferatu** *(F.W. Murnau, 1922)*
  Max Schreck's Count Orlok is a performance of pure physical transformation — iconic, unsettling, unforgettable.

- **The Last Laugh** *(F.W. Murnau, 1924)*
  Emil Jannings communicates the slow collapse of dignity using only face, body, and breath — no dialogue required.

- **Metropolis** *(Fritz Lang, 1927)*
  Collective movement becomes metaphor. The worker shift sequence is performance as mechanized metaphor — a chilling dance of dehumanization.

- **M** *(Fritz Lang, 1931)*
  Peter Lorre's tormented child-killer externalizes internal chaos through twitch, breath, and bulging eye — a performance unraveling in real time.

Legacy Watch – Expressionism Lives On

Expressionist performance didn't vanish — it mutated. These modern works carry the movement's DNA, using physicality, exaggeration, and stylized distortion to unlock psychological truths:

- **Shadow of the Vampire** *(E. Elias Merhige, 2000)*
  Willem Dafoe channels Max Schreck's physicality with eerie intensity. A love letter to expressionism with an actor's body at the center.

- **Edward Scissorhands** *(Tim Burton, 1990)*
  Johnny Depp draws from silent-era monsters — expression through gesture, not dialogue. A gentle freak, rendered in physical metaphor.

- **Antichrist** *(Lars von Trier, 2009)*
  Charlotte Gainsbourg and Willem Dafoe push their bodies to emotional and physical extremes. Stylized agony, stripped of realism.

- **The Lighthouse** *(Robert Eggers, 2019)*
  Dafoe and Pattinson twist their faces, voices, and bodies into mythic contortions — madness as choreography.

- **Joker** *(Todd Phillips, 2019)*
  Joaquin Phoenix finds emotional depth not through method recall but through body distortion, facial tics, and disturbing grace.

- **The Northman** *(Robert Eggers, 2022)*
  Alexander Skarsgård channels primal myth through brute posture and guttural presence — expressionist scale inside a modern frame.

Italian Neorealism: The Poetry of Everyday Life

Then came the pendulum swing. The reaction.

Post-World War II Italy lay in ruins. No money. No studios. No professional actors available. From these limitations, a movement was born.

If German Expressionism distorted reality to reveal psychological truth, Italian Neorealism stripped away artifice to expose social truth. If Expressionist performers transformed bodies into grotesque manifestations of inner states, Neorealist actors often weren't performers at all but ordinary people captured in something approaching documentary reality. Two approaches — seemingly opposite — yet both reaching for authentic human experience beneath comfortable illusions.

Neorealism emerged from devastation. Cities bombed to rubble. Economy collapsed. Fascist film industry dismantled. In this environment, filmmakers like Roberto Rossellini, Vittorio De Sica, and Luchino Visconti found new approach — not by choice but necessity. They took cameras into streets of Rome. Found protagonists among working poor. Filmed in bombed-out buildings, on bustling sidewalks, wherever life was happening.

And the performances? Revolutionary in their ordinariness.

De Sica cast Lamberto Maggiorani, an actual factory worker, as lead in "Bicycle Thieves." His face wasn't handsome in any conventional sense. His movements lacked theatrical training. But when his bicycle is stolen — his lifeline to employment, to survival — the anguish that crosses his face needs no technique to communicate. It is raw. Real. Devastating in its simplicity.

Watch Maggiorani searching desperately through crowded market for stolen bicycle. No dramatic music underscores moment. No special lighting highlights his distress. No dramatic close-ups isolate his reactions. Just man moving through actual crowd with urgent purpose, documentary-like camera following his increasingly frantic movements. Performance emerges from situation itself — real desperation of character merging with actual physical exhaustion of nonprofessional actor navigating challenging filming conditions.

The boy who played his son, Enzo Staiola, was discovered on street. De Sica noticed how child walked — with particular gait, slightly bowlegged, utterly natural. No child actor could have manufactured that walk. No acting school could have taught unself-conscious way he ran alongside Maggiorani, occasionally glancing up at his father's face with genuine concern. The relationship feels lived-in because it was discovered, not constructed.

These weren't performances in traditional sense. They were captured moments of genuine human experience. Camera didn't create barrier between audience and subject — it dissolved it.

De Sica's direction was simple: "Don't act. Be."

This approach wasn't merely aesthetic choice but philosophical stance. After years of fascist propaganda films with their manipulative techniques and artificial heroics, these filmmakers sought truth as ethical imperative. They understood that conventional acting often creates barrier between audience and authentic human experience — layer of artifice that, however skillful, reminds viewer they're watching construction rather than reality.

Anna Magnani embodied this approach perhaps more than any other figure of movement. Watch her in "Rome, Open City," running after truck carrying her husband to execution. Her desperation isn't crafted — it's channeled. When she falls in street, shot by Nazi soldiers, there's no beautiful death scene, no careful arrangement of limbs. Just sudden, ungraceful crumpling of human body. Life stopped mid-sentence.

Compare this to stylized death scenes of conventional cinema — the graceful falls, the poignant last words, the carefully composed final images. Magnani offers none of these consolations. Her death shocks precisely because it lacks performative elements we expect. It happens with abrupt violence of actual death rather than choreographed beauty of theatrical passing.

Magnani wasn't just vehicle for neorealist philosophy — she was its embodiment. Her face — complex, lived-in, decidedly not conforming to classical beauty standards — became movement's most recognizable canvas. In "Rome, Open City," her Pina isn't character but presence. Her gestures aren't calculated for effect but emerge organically from circumstance. The way she adjusts her pregnant belly while climbing stairs. The casual manner she addresses her son. These moments weren't directed — they were inhabited.

71

This wasn't actor playing working-class woman — this was performer whose own life experience informed every gesture, every vocal inflection, every response. Magnani grew up in poverty, raised by grandmother in one of Rome's poorest neighborhoods. Her understanding of character's world wasn't intellectual construction but lived knowledge. The authenticity audiences responded to wasn't technique but recognition — the truth of someone portraying reality they themselves had experienced.

The lesson was clear and radical: truth doesn't require technique. Sometimes technique gets in way of truth.

This wasn't just aesthetic preference. It was moral stance. After war's propagandistic films with their polished lies, truth — however harsh, however unbeautiful — became ethical imperative.

Luchino Visconti's "La Terra Trema" took this approach to its logical conclusion. Shot in Sicilian fishing village, film used actual fishermen speaking their local dialect. Many viewers required subtitles to understand them — even Italian audiences. The fishermen moved through their daily routines with unconscious grace of those who have performed same actions thousands of times. They didn't need to learn how to haul nets or repair boats; these actions lived in their muscles, in calluses on their hands.

When protagonist, Antonio Arcidiacono, faces economic ruin after attempting to break free from exploitative merchants, his despair isn't portrayed through dramatic speeches or actorly breakdowns. Instead, we see him sitting silently at table, his weathered face mask of quiet defeat. The moment works precisely because it isn't performed — it's simply endured.

Visconti, despite his aristocratic background and formal training, recognized that conventional acting techniques often created barrier between audience and authentic human experience. By casting non-professionals in their own environments, speaking their own dialect, performing tasks they understood intimately, he achieved documentary-like immediacy while still crafting narrative with clear political perspective. The performances feel authentic because they emerge from genuine understanding rather than external research or technical construction.

The influence extended beyond casting. Rossellini directed his professional actors to strip away theatrical training. In "Paisan," he pushed performers to respond to circumstances as themselves, not as constructed characters. He often didn't provide complete scripts, preferring actors to discover moments rather than prepare them. Lines were sometimes given immediately before shooting, preventing kind of rehearsed delivery that characterized studio filmmaking.

This approach created performances of startling immediacy. Watch American soldier and Italian boy in "Paisan," navigating war-torn Naples together. Their connection transcends language barriers because it's built on genuine reactions to their environment and each other. The soldier's frustrated attempts to communicate, the boy's street-smart wariness — these qualities emerge from actors' authentic responses to circumstances, not from character analysis or technique.

In "Germany Year Zero," Rossellini worked with 12-year-old non-actor Edmund Moeschke to portray child navigating devastated post-war Berlin. The performance achieves heartbreaking authenticity precisely because Moeschke wasn't performing psychological complexity but responding directly to environments and situations Rossellini created. The boy's reactions feel genuine because they largely were — director elicited real emotional responses rather than teaching child to simulate them.

For trained actors, neorealism presented profound challenge: how to unlearn? How to strip away years of technical training to access kind of unmediated humanity these directors demanded? Some couldn't make transition. Others discovered that approach liberated them from performative habits, reconnecting them with core of human experience their training was supposed to access in first place.

The movement's performance philosophy contained implicit critique of traditional acting methodology. If ordinary people could create moments of profound truth without training, what exactly was theatrical training for? Was technique merely elaborate system for reconnecting actors with authentic responses they had suppressed through socialization and professionalization?

This question continues to challenge contemporary performance theory. Most acting training begins with premise that authentic human response must be recovered after years of social conditioning that teaches us to hide, control, or modify natural reactions. Children don't need acting classes to express genuine emotion — they need them to learn how to simulate emotion on cue. Neorealism suggested possibility of circumventing this technical reconstruction by finding performers who hadn't yet lost connection to authentic response.

For contemporary performers, neorealism offers crucial lessons. The approach reminds us that observation — deep, patient, non-judgmental observation of actual human behavior — forms foundation of truthful performance. Before method exercises or technical systems, there must be commitment to seeing people as they are, not as dramatic convention suggests they should be.

I often tell actors in my studio: "Before you can play human being truthfully, you need to become student of humanity." This means watching actual people — not other performances, not fictional representations — with anthropologist's eye for detail and pattern. How does elderly man with arthritis navigate crowded bus? What happens to teenage girl's posture when cute boy enters coffee shop? What physical adjustments does office worker make during long meeting as fatigue sets in? These observations provide raw material far more valuable than any technical exercise.

Neorealism challenges actors to examine whether their training enhances access to truth or creates additional barriers. Has technique become end in itself? Has virtuosity replaced authenticity? The factory worker playing Antonio in "Bicycle Thieves" didn't worry about his vocal placement or physical alignment — yet his performance remains devastatingly effective decades later.

I worked with actor trained in highly technical approach to voice and movement. His performances were precise, controlled, impressive in their technical execution. But something was missing — the sense of spontaneous life, of unpredictable humanity. I suggested exercise: spend week riding public transportation, observing how ordinary people moved, spoke, reacted. Then create character based not on technical principles but on specific person he'd observed. The resulting performance had life his previous work lacked — not because he abandoned technique but because he grounded it in observed reality rather than abstract principle.

Neorealism also reminds performers that physical circumstances create emotional truth. These films didn't rely on psychological exercises to generate emotion. Instead, they placed non-actors in concrete situations that naturally evoked authentic responses. The lesson: sometimes most direct path to emotional truth isn't internal recall but full commitment to physical circumstance.

Modern equivalent might be actor performing emotional scene while actually running up six flights of stairs, creating genuine physical stress that informs emotional state. Or rehearsing relationship scene in actual location — cramped apartment, noisy restaurant — rather than neutral studio space, allowing environment's specific qualities to shape interaction organically.

Perhaps most importantly, movement elevated dignity over dramatics. These films found profound meaning in ordinary gestures — father teaching son to shave in midst of desperate poverty, woman making coffee in bombed-out apartment. They recognized that human resilience often expresses itself not through dramatic declarations but through quiet insistence on continuing daily rituals amid devastation.

For today's actor, working in industry often obsessed with technique and training, Italian Neorealism stands as necessary corrective. It reminds us that beneath layers of method and system, performance must connect with fundamental truth of human experience. Sometimes most powerful choice isn't to transform into someone else but to be nakedly, vulnerably present — to trust that your unadorned humanity, fully engaged with circumstances, contains all drama necessary.

When working with highly trained actors stuck in technical display, I sometimes suggest "neorealist reset." Put aside training. Respond as yourself — not character you've constructed but human being you actually are — to imaginary circumstances. What would you — not character but you yourself — do if bicycle you needed for work was stolen? If child was ill and you couldn't afford medicine? If home was threatened with destruction?

This approach often cuts through technical clutter to core emotional truth that connects directly with audience.

In world of increasing artifice, radical simplicity of neorealism's approach to performance remains revolutionary. Its essential instruction — "Don't act. Be" — continues to challenge performers seven decades later.

Suggested Viewing – Italian Neorealism

For actors exploring how truth emerges through simplicity, circumstance, and raw human presence — these films demonstrate that performance doesn't have to be built. Sometimes, it only needs to be witnessed:

- **Rome, Open City** *(Roberto Rossellini, 1945)*
  Anna Magnani runs, screams, falls. No choreography, no buildup. Her death isn't played — it happens. And it stuns.

- **Shoeshine (Sciuscià)** *(Vittorio De Sica, 1946)*
  A story of innocence bruised by bureaucracy. The boys aren't actors — they're boys. Their performances ache with uncoached urgency.

- **Bicycle Thieves** *(Vittorio De Sica, 1948)*
  Lamberto Maggiorani's factory-worker face tells the whole story. Desperation, dignity, and love — without a trace of technique.

- **The Earth Trembles (La terra trema)** *(Luchino Visconti, 1948)*
  Real fishermen. Real dialect. Real labor. Performance emerges not from script but from the calluses on their hands.

- **Umberto D.** *(Vittorio De Sica, 1952)*
  Carlo Battisti, a retired professor with no acting experience, delivers one of cinema's most moving portraits of aging, poverty, and grace.

De Sica, Rossellini, and Visconti weren't looking for actors. They were looking for *people*. In postwar Italy, professional performers felt like a luxury — polished faces delivering rehearsed emotions. But these filmmakers wanted truth. So they went into the streets, the villages, the factories. They found workers, fishermen, old men, and boys who had never seen a camera.

When De Sica cast Lamberto Maggiorani in *Bicycle Thieves*, he didn't care that Maggiorani was awkward or hesitant. That *was* the character — a man out of his depth, clinging to dignity as poverty stripped him bare. Visconti went even further in *La terra trema*, casting Sicilian fishermen to play themselves. Their weathered hands, their dialect, their unstudied movements carried more truth than any script.

This wasn't just an aesthetic choice. It was political. Italy was broken, and these directors wanted to show the people who bore the weight of its collapse. By using non-actors, they captured raw, unfiltered humanity — gestures and silences too real to be faked.

It changed cinema forever. From Satyajit Ray's villagers in *Pather Panchali* to the French New Wave's street-cast rebels, and on to today's realist filmmakers like Sean Baker and the Dardenne brothers, the ripple effect is everywhere.

As De Sica put it:

"To capture life, one must work with life itself. The face of a man who has suffered is worth more than the finest makeup."

Legacy Watch – Neorealism Today

Neorealism didn't vanish. It changed clothes. These contemporary films continue the tradition — telling small stories with big truth, and asking actors to be present, not performative:

- **The Rider** *(Chloé Zhao, 2017)*
  Real rodeo rider Brady Jandreau plays a version of himself. The result: a performance so quiet and honest it barely feels like one.

- **The Florida Project** *(Sean Baker, 2017)*
  Non-actors and professionals collide in a motel on the edge of Disney World. Watch Brooklynn Prince — pure, unfiltered, alive.

- **Wendy and Lucy** *(Kelly Reichardt, 2008)*
  Michelle Williams gives one of her most restrained, vulnerable performances — the face of someone just trying to hold on.

- **Tangerine** *(Sean Baker, 2015)*
  Shot on iPhones. Real locations. First-time actors. An electric mix of grit and heart with no space for artificiality.

- **Gerry** *(Gus Van Sant, 2002)*
  Long takes, sparse dialogue, and physical endurance shape a meditative study in presence. Acting as *being*, not doing.

- **Nomadland** *(Chloé Zhao, 2020)*
  Frances McDormand blends into a cast of real nomads. The performance works because it listens more than it speaks.

French New Wave: Cinema as Personal Expression

"The camera is a pen."

The phrase *"La caméra-stylo"* — "The camera is a pen" — was coined by Alexandre Astruc, French film critic and director, in his 1948 essay "The Birth of a New Avant-Garde: La Caméra-Stylo."

Astruc argued that cinema should evolve into a form as flexible and personal as literature — filmmakers could use the camera to write in the same way a writer uses a pen. His idea laid the groundwork for auteur theory and helped inspire the French New Wave.

With this declaration, French critic-turned-filmmakers launched a revolution. Cinema shouldn't just be a way of telling stories — it should be a means of personal expression, as intimate and distinctive as handwriting.

This wasn't merely a theoretical position but a radical reimagining of what film could be. Until then, cinema had largely defined itself as either an entertainment industry (Hollywood) or an artistic tradition with established rules. The New Wave proposed something else: cinema as a direct extension of the filmmaker's consciousness, immediate as thought and as personal as a diary entry.

If Neorealism stripped away artifice in search of social truth, the New Wave dismantled conventional filmmaking in pursuit of personal truth. They broke rules not for rebellion's sake but because those rules constrained cinema's potential as an expressive medium. They asked: Why shouldn't film be as free, as subjective, and as individualistic as a novel or poem?

This philosophical shift transformed everything, including performance. Actors weren't just interpreters of a script but collaborators in the creation of cinematic reality that follows emotional logic rather than narrative convention, subjective perception rather than objective representation.

Jean-Luc Godard placed Jean-Paul Belmondo in "Breathless" and let him improvise, jump cut, and break the fourth wall. François Truffaut followed Jean-Pierre Léaud from adolescence to adulthood across his Antoine Doinel films, blurring the line between character and actor. Agnès Varda turned her camera on ordinary people with extraordinary empathy, finding poetry in faces that cinema had previously ignored.

The performances felt spontaneous, unpolished, and alive with the electricity of the moment. Actors didn't recite lines — they inhabited them, often changing them on the spot. The camera didn't dictate their movements — it followed them, sometimes struggling to keep up.

Look at Belmondo in "Breathless." His Michel doesn't behave like a conventional movie criminal but like a young man who's seen too many Hollywood gangster films and is half-playfully, half-seriously trying them on like a costume. He mimics Humphrey Bogart, makes gun noises with his mouth, and narrates his own actions as if simultaneously living and watching his life. This isn't method acting's deep psychological immersion but something entirely different — a performance about performance, about a gap between movie mythology and actual experience.

Belmondo's Michel thumbs his nose at convention — both narratively and performatively. Watch how he moves through a cramped apartment: touching objects, trying on hats, practicing expressions in mirrors. These weren't scripted moments. They were lived ones — actor and character discovering each other in real time. That sliding thumb across the lips? Iconic now. But in the moment? Just instinct — a gesture pulled from the ether of the scene itself. A flare of restless charisma, captured before it vanished.

I saw that same kind of physical authorship — the body writing what the script only sketches — in Cate Blanchett, recently, in *Disclaimer*. Watch her move through her kitchen: making espresso, lifting the cat from the table (twice), stirring a pot with one hand while spooling out dialogue with the other. She's not performing these actions — she's inhabiting them. They feel lived-in, as if they've been done a thousand times before, even if this is take three or seven, or twelve. Her ease recalls Belmondo's playfulness, but rechanneled — not through cigarette smoke and bravado, but through domestic rhythms and quiet control.

And that's no accident. Alfonso Cuarón — director of *Disclaimer* — understands this lineage. He's not mimicking the French New Wave, but inheriting it. Expanding it. The way he lets the camera linger, drift, observe — it's Godard's handheld intimacy reimagined with modern restraint. Cuarón doesn't direct traffic. He invites atmosphere. He allows his actors to find the scene in movement, not in monologue. In Blanchett, he's found a collaborator who, like Belmondo before her, lets character bloom not from psychology, but from behavior.

This is the long thread — from Nouvelle Vague to now. From a man in a mirror with a hat and a cigarette, to a woman with a coffee spoon and a cat she keeps gently shooing. Same spirit. Same alchemy. Different moment.

This approach to character — built through the accumulation of behavioral detail rather than psychological architecture — created performances that felt less constructed and more discovered. Actors weren't portraying predetermined characters but helping to invent them through a collaborative process that valued spontaneity over consistency, authentic moments over narrative logic.

Jean-Pierre Léaud's collaboration with Truffaut created something unprecedented — a character aging in real time across multiple films, with the boundaries between actor and role increasingly blurred. In "The 400 Blows," fourteen-year-old Léaud wasn't merely playing Antoine Doinel; he was co-creating him, infusing the character with his own adolescent awkwardness and intensity. By the time of "Stolen Kisses" and "Bed and

Board," where did Léaud end and Doinel begin? Performance exists in the liminal space between autobiography and fiction.

The famous final shot of "The 400 Blows" — Antoine running to the sea, then turning to face the camera in freeze frame — wasn't just a cinematic innovation but a performance breakthrough. Léaud's expression in that moment — uncertain, questioning, challenging — wasn't directed in any traditional sense. Truffaut created circumstances and trusted the young actor's instincts. The result? A gaze that still haunts viewers decades later.

What made this performance revolutionary wasn't technical virtuosity but its fundamental honesty. Léaud wasn't demonstrating adolescence but embodying it, bringing his own lived experience directly to the screen without a conventional actorly filter. This approach required a different kind of courage than technical performance — a willingness to reveal rather than represent, to be seen rather than to show.

Watch Anna Karina in Godard's "Vivre Sa Vie," sitting in a theater watching "The Passion of Joan of Arc" — tears streaming down her face as she watches Falconetti's performance. It's a moment of perfect meta-cinema: an actor watching another actor, both revealing truth through artifice. Karina isn't performing emotion but experiencing it; her response to Falconetti's suffering is genuine rather than manufactured.

This scene illuminates the New Wave's approach to performance: creating conditions where authentic emotional response becomes possible, then capturing that response rather than simulating it. The line between documentary and fiction blurs. Karina isn't "playing" a character watching a film; she's actually watching a masterpiece and responding genuinely while the camera captures her real emotion. Yet this moment exists within a fictional framework — layer upon layer of reality and representation collapsed into a single powerful image.

In *Cléo from 5 to 7*, Agnès Varda doesn't follow her protagonist — she trails her like a thought that won't settle. A pop singer, Cleo wanders through Paris awaiting biopsy results, her mind as restless as her steps. Corinne Marchand doesn't perform transformation — she *leaks* it. Frame by frame, her presence shifts. The self-absorbed glamour fades. Awareness, awkward and slow, starts to press in. There are no "big" scenes. No fireworks. Just the way she holds her purse. The way her pace changes. The way her silence lands.

What Varda knew: performance isn't what you do in the close-up. It's how your body *lives* inside the time and space — how it resists, adapts.

This demanded a different kind of actor. Not someone building a character from the girding, outside-in. But someone willing to let the world sculpt them in real time. No emotional beats to "hit." No rehearsed transitions. Just a radical presence — alert to "*a*" moment, and willing to be altered by it.

This wasn't just a technique. It was a *stance*. A belief that cinema should catch life before it postures — raw, stumbling, full of contradictions.

And yes, the tech helped. Lightweight cameras could move with actors instead of anchoring them. Sound could be recorded as it happened — no need for dubbing booths to "fix" feeling. Fewer crew members meant fewer eyes watching, which meant more truth. These weren't just production upgrades. They redefined what acting could *be*.

But philosophy mattered more. These films — stolen on the streets of Paris without permits or polish — weren't aiming for realism. They were chasing life *as it unfolds*. Uncontrolled. Observed. Full of risk.

Check out Belmondo and Seberg in *Breathless*. They're not blocking a scene — they're navigating crowds. People glance at them. Bump into them. React in ways that aren't part of the "script." And that becomes the performance.

Claude Chabrol — often called the French Hitchcock — twisted the blade a little deeper in *Le Boucher*. His then-wife, Stéphane Audran, plays a repressed schoolteacher circling a man who might be a killer. But she doesn't signal judgment. Doesn't offer us clarity. Instead, she hovers — quietly — in the space between knowing and denial. Her performance isn't driven by answers. It lives in the *not knowing*. No resolution. No safety. Just the body of a woman trying to balance on an emotional fault line.

There's a moment — simple, devastating — where she notices blood on his coat. A lesser performer might push fear to the surface. Or retreat into denial. Audran does neither. She registers it... then suppresses it. Her face stays still, but something beneath it flickers — trembles — a private shift we're not entirely invited in to see, but *feel* it just the same. *That's the work.* Holding two or three contradictory truths at once... and letting the camera catch whatever leaks through. It's not performance *as display* — it's presence under pressure.

I've watched that film both with subtitles and without. And strangely — maybe beautifully — I found it easier to see Audran's performance when I *didn't* understand the words. Without language getting in the way, I could actually feel her choices. Her hesitations. Her unspoken terror. The nuance wasn't in the lines — it was in the silence between them.

Rohmer asked something different — quieter, but no less demanding. In *My Night at Maud's*, Jean-Louis Trintignant moves through conversations dense with theology and philosophy — Pascal's wager, Catholic morality, the fragile scaffolding of belief — yet he delivers them with the ease of small talk. It's not intellectual performance. It's breath-level thinking. The brilliance of the performance isn't in the cleverness, but in what unravels underneath. His principles begin to feel more like armor than truth — convictions clung to not because they're right, but because they protect something unspoken. That's where the performance lives. Not in the delivery, but in the rupture between what the character believes he's doing and what the audience sees him actually doing.

And that takes a particular kind of actor. One willing to play both the mask and the face beneath it. One willing to lose their footing mid-line — and not recover.

New Wave cinema reminds us that acting doesn't happen in isolation. It's a collision — actor, camera, environment, noise, unpredictability — all pressing in at once. Preparation matters. Of course, it does. But too much of it can kill the thing you're trying to catch. Sometimes the most honest work doesn't come from control, but from surrender. From a crack in the plan. Being *inside* the scene, not executing it. Feeling it rather than performing it.

When actors become too calculated — too locked in — I try to disrupt it. "Forget the script. Just be here, present, respond with your own words or subtext." I might introduce a new piece of business or a prop. Add an unexpected comment or disruption. Anything to break up the grip of what they rehearsed.

And in that break? That moment of jumble? That's where I can see the real actor show up. Not the one they've prepped — the one they *are*.

That, to me, is the greatest gift of the New Wave. It gave actors back their agency. Their artistry. It treated them not as deliverers of only the director's vision, but as collaborators and co-authors of the work. Léaud, Karina, Seberg — they weren't simply cast. They shaped the films. Their instincts, their missteps, their raw moments weren't cleaned away in post. They were honored. The work bent around them, not the other way around.

And that model still matters. Today's actor can wait for a role... or they can build one. Not just by writing their own material — though yes, do that too — but by stepping fully into their own creative authority. Bringing something to the table no one else can. Letting the work reflect their personal gravity — their rhythm, their contradictions, their humanity.

And the polish? Let it go. Completely throw it away. Let it die.

The New Wave found its beauty in what wasn't planned. The stumble, the hesitation, the gap between the intention and the execution. A flubbed line might stay in if it revealed something honest. A moment of real confusion might say more than five pages of perfect craft. Authenticity, not precision, is what the camera craves.

I often work with very experienced commercial actors whose techniques are immaculate — every choice clean, every beat hit. But the performances for film leave you cold. A homework assignment might be to watch Karina — a scene where her voice breaks unexpectedly, where something slips through she didn't mean to show. In that space where control gives way to something real, that's the deeper truth.

Acting isn't about hiding your flaws behind technique. It's about revealing yourself through it. The New Wave wasn't just a style. It was — and still is — a revolution. A reminder that cinema, at its best, doesn't imitate life. It *becomes* it. New Wave wasn't just a French experiment. It was — and still is

— a reminder that cinema isn't life *reflected*. It's life *becoming*. Study it. Watch films endlessly of this era.

Suggested Viewing – French New Wave

For actors exploring how spontaneity, authorship, and emotional risk redefined screen presence, these films show what it means to perform like a person discovering themselves in real time:

- **Breathless (À bout de souffle)** *(Jean-Luc Godard, 1960)*
  Jean-Paul Belmondo doesn't act Michel — he *becomes* him through movement, gesture, and improvisation. The cool that cracks.

- **The 400 Blows (Les Quatre Cents Coups)** *(François Truffaut, 1959)*
  Jean-Pierre Léaud's Antoine Doinel is a boy seen, not performed. His final stare into the lens still speaks volumes.

- **Cleo from 5 to 7** *(Agnès Varda, 1962)*
  Corinne Marchand transforms across real-time. No dramatic arc — just shifts in body, breath, and gaze as her interior cracks open.

- **Hiroshima Mon Amour** *(Alain Resnais, 1959)*
  A poetic study in memory and intimacy. Emmanuelle Riva and Eiji Okada embody longing through presence and silence.

- **Vivre Sa Vie** *(Jean-Luc Godard, 1962)*
  Anna Karina doesn't perform Nana — she offers her piece by piece, gesture by gesture. Her stillness is its own rebellion.

Legacy Watch – The New Wave's Ripples

The French New Wave didn't end — it fragmented into everything. These films carry forward its spirit of cinematic and performance freedom, where actors are co-creators, not just interpreters:

- **Before Sunrise** *(Richard Linklater, 1995)*
  Julie Delpy and Ethan Hawke improvise presence, not lines. A love story made of listening, walking, discovering.

- **Frances Ha** *(Noah Baumbach, 2012)*
  Gerwig *is* the New Wave's heir — dancing, stammering, folding performance into personality and vice versa.

- **La Vie d'Adèle (Blue is the Warmest Color)** *(Abdellatif Kechiche, 2013)*
  Adèle Exarchopoulos gives a raw, sustained performance of emotional discovery, captured with intimate realism.

- **The Dreamers** *(Bernardo Bertolucci, 2003)*
  French cinephilia, rebellion, and sensuality echo through Eva Green's layered, volatile performance.

- **Cold War** *(Paweł Pawlikowski, 2018)*
  Joanna Kulig channels Karina-level magnetism in a story of fractured connection. Expressive eyes, expressive silence.

- **Portrait of a Lady on Fire** *(Céline Sciamma, 2019)*
  The gaze replaces dialogue. Noémie Merlant and Adèle Haenel give masterclasses in restraint, friction, and subtext.

American New Wave: Method in the Madness

America was watching. Not imitating — *absorbing*. Taking in the revolution across the Atlantic and metabolizing it into something messier, louder, darker. Something uniquely its own.

The 1970s — that brief, volatile golden age of American cinema — didn't just borrow from the European New Wave. It *fused* it with myth, muscle... and Method.

Actors in this moment combined the interior depth of Strasberg's training with the raw spontaneity of truth. They weren't just playing characters. They were *collapsing into them* — melting structure to impulse. The result was a kind of controlled detonation. And it worked. Because the system was already falling apart.

The old studio model — polished, profitable, predictable — was crumbling under its own weight. Television had stolen a mass audience. The big-budget musicals and epics were misfiring. Nobody trusted the formula anymore. Which, ironically, created the perfect opening for this evolving, organic cinema. With less to lose, the gatekeepers got out of the way. Directors took risks. Studios let things get weird. And actors — finally — were handed the matches.

But none of this came out of nowhere. The fuse had been laid decades earlier. A build-up of such talent had been ready, waiting for someone to give them wings.

The Actors Studio 1947. A quiet revolution in a brownstone. Stanislavski refracted through Strasberg, Adler, Meisner — a hundred voices arguing over what truth meant, and how to summon it under lights and lens. Then came Kazan, bringing it west with *On the Waterfront*, *East of Eden*. Brando. Dean. Clift. Men who didn't perform their feelings — they *boiled in them*. They twitched. They mumbled. They disintegrated on camera. And audiences leaned in.

For the first time, American film didn't ask for heroes. It allowed contradictions. Vulnerability. Shame. Method acting carved out space for interiority on screen — the half-thought, the unsaid, the pause that reveals more than the monologue. It gave permission for actors to not be beautiful, or even likable, but *real*.

By the late '60s, the cultural temperature had shifted. Vietnam. Civil rights. The assassinations. Watergate. A generation disillusioned — turned inward, tuned out. The old myths — of victory, virtue, manifest destiny — no longer hold. Hollywood, still clinging to outdated tropes, suddenly felt irrelevant.

Into that vacuum stepped a new kind of performer. Trained in the Method, yes. But more importantly cracked open by the influence of European art cinema, documentary realism, improv theater, and countercultural experimentation. These actors didn't seek emotional truth — they questioned what truth was.

They improvised. They resisted clean arcs. Broke scenes open from the inside.

Watch Hoffman in *Midnight Cowboy*, Pacino in *Panic in Needle Park*, De Niro in *Taxi Driver*, Burstyn in *Alice Doesn't Live Here Anymore*. These performances don't resolve. They spiral. You don't watch them *act* — you watch them *endure*.

This wasn't about performance as control. It was about discomfort. Risk. The performance wasn't polished — it was *compromised*, in the best way. And we couldn't look away.

The American New Wave didn't just expand what acting could be — it exploded it. Suddenly, vulnerability was marketable. Complexity could be sexy. A stammer or silence might say more than a monologue ever could.

It was a moment when craft met chaos — and for a while, the screen felt *honest* again.

Case Study: Robert De Niro in Raging Bull

De Niro didn't just play Jake LaMotta — he absorbed him. The physical transformation was extreme (gaining sixty pounds to portray LaMotta's decline), but it was only the surface. Beneath it was an excavation into violence, shame, and identity built entirely around the body.

He trained with LaMotta, fought in real matches, and studied not just the boxer's technique but his rhythms — the volatility, the vulnerability, the emotional decay. Early scenes show De Niro prowling through space, coiled and alert. Later, the body bloats, and so does the rage. What was once a weapon becomes a cage.

This wasn't mimicry. It was embodiment. The performance lives in physical specificity — how the body speaks when the voice no longer can. De Niro's LaMotta is a man coming apart from the inside, and every frame makes you feel it.

Case Study: Jane Fonda — Klute

Fonda's Bree Daniels isn't a role — it's a mirror. A woman split between performance and self, survival and vulnerability. As a high-end call girl, Bree moves fluidly between control and collapse. Fonda doesn't play her as a victim or a cliché — she plays her as a strategist, constantly negotiating how much of herself she can afford to show.

The therapy scenes are masterclasses in layered performance. Bree is speaking, revealing, confessing — but also performing. For the therapist. For herself. For us. Fonda lets that ambiguity linger. She's not emoting. She's calculating. And beneath that calculation — flickers of fear, of longing.

Watch how she shifts. A change in posture. A clipped voice softening. The way she recalibrates in real time, depending on who's watching. This isn't technical virtuosity — it's lived complexity. A portrait of a woman who has made her survival a performance, and is slowly forgetting where the mask ends.

These weren't performances you could teach. They came from somewhere deeper — from actors' willingness to strip away not just artifice but identity itself, to become vessels for characters that were neither wholly invented nor wholly real, but something in between.

This was method pushed to its logical extreme. Not just emotional recall but total immersion. Not just understanding character but becoming them. The line between actor and role dissolves, sometimes at great personal cost.

Case Study: Gene Hackman — The Conversation

Hackman's Harry Caul isn't performed — he's revealed through absence. A surveillance expert obsessed with privacy, Harry is defined not by what he expresses but by what he withholds. Hackman plays him with exquisite restraint — triple-locking his doors, avoiding eye contact, sitting apart from others at his own party. Nothing is exaggerated. Everything is deliberate.

The paranoia doesn't come in outbursts. It builds through details — the transparent raincoat, the way he disassembles his phone, the silence that stretches too long. Even his body seems to retreat from the frame.

And then there's the saxophone scene. Alone in his apartment, Harry plays not to impress, but to release. No dialogue, no exposition — just a man grasping for connection through sound. It tells us everything. Hackman's performance is a study in subtraction. The more he holds back, the more we feel.

Case Study: Sissy Spacek — Badlands

Sissy Spacek turned emotional detachment into performance architecture. In *Badlands*, her narration floats above the violence — flat, affectless, disquieting. It's not emptiness. It's dissociation. She plays a young girl numbed by disconnection, watching her life unfold as if from the outside.

That vacancy? It's not a lack of skill. It's precision. Spacek refuses to perform traditional emotion. Her deadpan delivery becomes its own kind of commentary — more revealing in what it withholds than in what it expresses. The result is quietly radical. A study in trauma told not through screams, but through the absence of response.

Case Study: Ellen Burstyn — Alice Doesn't Live Here Anymore

Burstyn's Alice is a woman in motion — between identities, between lives, between what she wants and what she's allowed to want. Scorsese gave her space to explore, not execute. The result is a performance full of risk, awkwardness, and aching truth.

The restaurant scene says it all. Alice tries to sing while taking food orders — slipping between performance and survival, glamour and grit. It's not polished. It's not planned. And that's why it lands. Burstyn doesn't "play" a woman struggling to hold onto herself — she *inhabits* that struggle, moment by unsteady moment.

This is the New Wave approach at its most personal: discovery over design. Burstyn isn't showing us who Alice is. She's finding it, in real time — and we're invited to find it with her.

Case Study: John Cazale and the Art of Ensemble Depth

John Cazale didn't need screen time to create impact. In just five films — all nominated for Best Picture — he became the soul of the American New Wave. His work exemplified what made the movement revolutionary: the elevation of supporting roles to deep vessels of psychological truth.

As Fredo in *The Godfather* films, Cazale didn't play the concept of weakness. He inhabited it. Shame, longing, a desperate need to matter — all communicated in glances, pauses, silences. He didn't reach for emotion. He became its residue. Even in stillness, every moment felt loaded.

His genius was restraint. Ensemble scenes didn't diminish him — they sharpened him. He brought the same intensity to five minutes that most actors couldn't sustain for two hours. In doing so, he redefined what it meant to "support" a film — proving that a story's emotional center might come from its quietest corner.

Cazale never headlined a film. But he never faded. His influence lives on in actors like Daniel Day-Lewis, Joaquin Phoenix, and Meryl Streep — performers willing to disappear so completely into character that their own identities become irrelevant. His spirit echoes in the work of directors like Paul Thomas Anderson and David Fincher, who continue creating the kind of textured, actor-driven environments where this kind of truth can still be found.

The American New Wave reminded us that acting at its most profound isn't about showing but becoming — not demonstration but transformation. In era of increasing technical sophistication, this commitment to raw human truth remains its most enduring contribution to art of performance.

Case Study: Jack Nicholson — One Flew Over the Cuckoo's Nest

Nicholson's R.P. McMurphy is built on contradiction. He's a provocateur, a rebel, a manipulator — but is any of it real? Or all of it? The brilliance lies in the ambiguity. Nicholson never settles McMurphy's motivations. He plays the tension between con and conviction, performance and impulse.

The character isn't stable — he morphs. One moment charming, the next volatile. He tests boundaries not just to break rules, but to see what they're made of. And Nicholson never explains him. He leans into the unpredictability, keeping both the audience and the institution guessing.

It's that refusal to clarify that makes the performance electric. You're not watching a strategy. You're watching a man constantly rewriting himself in response to a world that doesn't know what to do with him.

What united these disparate performances was commitment to a psychological truth over technical display. These actors weren't interested in showing their skill but in revealing human complexity — often messy, contradictory, and unresolved. They approached characters not as collections of traits to be demonstrated but as living consciousnesses to be inhabited.

Case Study: Al Pacino — Dog Day Afternoon

Al Pacino didn't just perform in *Dog Day Afternoon* — he unraveled. The iconic "Attica!" scene wasn't in the script. It erupted in the moment, a spontaneous cry born from Sonny's desperation. Pacino wasn't reciting choices; he was *discovering* them. Each line, gesture, stammer felt like a man thinking in real-time.

What makes the performance radical isn't just the charisma. It's the contradiction. Sonny is impulsive, deeply flawed, at times incompetent — yet still achingly sympathetic. Pacino doesn't resolve that tension. He lives inside it. Watch him shift from threatening the bank manager to apologizing to the hostages — and meaning both. This wasn't calculated modulation; it was moment-to-moment survival. Pure presence.

The Directors — American New Wave

Scorsese, Coppola, Altman, Lumet, Malick — these directors didn't just shoot films. They built environments. Spaces where discovery could eclipse design. Where control was loosened just enough for something unexpected — and alive — to happen.

They understood that performance didn't need to be "delivered." It needed to *emerge*.

Sidney Lumet favored minimal takes to preserve risk. He wanted spontaneity on screen, not polish. Coppola created immersive sets where actors could lose themselves entirely in the world of the film. Scorsese pushed improvisation, letting the camera chase something real rather than stage something safe.

But no one redefined the actor-director dynamic like Robert Altman. His overlapping dialogue, multi-camera setups, and ensemble chaos invited actors to listen, react, exist — not perform. In *Nashville*, *McCabe & Mrs. Miller*, and *The Long Goodbye*, characters weren't blocked into scenes — they wandered through them. No perfect cues. No clean coverage. Just texture, noise, truth.

Altman's genius was in showing that background behavior could carry as much emotional weight as front-of-frame dialogue. Every actor, lead or not, had to show up fully formed — with a backstory, a rhythm, a voice. There were no "minor" roles. Only partial glimpses of complete people.

This freedom came at a cost. The line between character and self could blur. De Niro's weight gain for *Raging Bull* had lasting health effects. Pacino admitted feeling physically ill after immersing in Michael Corleone's psyche. Brando, famously, wouldn't learn his lines for *Apocalypse Now* — nearly halting the production altogether.

It wasn't elegant. It was messy. Demanding. Dangerous. And what came out of that crucible changed acting on screen forever.

The directors of this era didn't treat actors as vessels for vision. They treated them as co-creators — collaborators whose instincts could reshape a scene. Their sets weren't governed by obedience to script or structure. They were laboratories. The work wasn't to capture something polished. It was to catch something *true*.

For contemporary actors, the legacy is clear: the most enduring performances come not from decoration but from *depth*. Not from method alone, but from trust — in circumstance, in instinct, in contradiction. This era proved that character is more than posture and accent. It's behavior under pressure. Belief under scrutiny. A living, breathing consciousness pressed into a frame.

I still show scenes from this era to my students — not as nostalgia, but as a challenge. De Niro talking to his mirror in *Taxi Driver*. Hackman tearing his apartment apart in *The Conversation*. Gena Rowlands unraveling in *A Woman Under the Influence*. These aren't period pieces. They're seismic. And they still shake the room.

Suggested Viewing – American New Wave

For actors exploring how raw psychology, behavioral specificity, and emotional exposure redefined performance in the 1970s — these films offer a map of risk, restraint, and revelation:

- **Taxi Driver** *(Martin Scorsese, 1976)*
  De Niro's Travis Bickle is a powder keg of isolation and rage — a haunting monument to psychological disintegration.

- **Dog Day Afternoon** *(Sidney Lumet, 1975)*
  Pacino doesn't deliver lines — he detonates them. Improvised desperation turns a botched robbery into protest and poetry.

- **The Godfather Part II** *(Francis Ford Coppola, 1974)*
  John Cazale's Fredo is heartbreak distilled, a masterclass in silence, shame, and slow collapse.

- **One Flew Over the Cuckoo's Nest** *(Milos Forman, 1975)*
  Nicholson's McMurphy walks the razor's edge between rebellion and madness — unpredictable, dangerous, alive.

- **The Conversation** *(Francis Ford Coppola, 1974)*
Gene Hackman doesn't perform Harry Caul — he retreats into him. A quiet study in paranoia and behavioral detail.

- **Badlands** *(Terrence Malick, 1973)*
Sissy Spacek floats through violence with eerie detachment — a chilling portrait of innocence gone sideways.

- **Klute** *(Alan J. Pakula, 1971)*
Jane Fonda's Bree Daniels flickers between control and collapse — a character both self-aware and emotionally exposed.

- **Alice Doesn't Live Here Anymore** *(Martin Scorsese, 1974)*
Ellen Burstyn captures the whiplash of surviving while dreaming — grace, grit, and real-time emotional recalibration.

- **Nashville** *(Robert Altman, 1975)*
A symphonic ensemble with no central lead. Every performer builds a private world barely holding itself together.

- **Five Easy Pieces** *(Bob Rafelson, 1970)*
Jack Nicholson's Bobby Dupea is a man always running — from himself, from comfort, from knowing what he wants.

Legacy Watch – Aftershocks of the American New Wave

The revolution never ended. These later performances carry the emotional volatility, behavioral truth, and unvarnished humanity born in the 1970s — where acting stopped performing and started breaking open:

- **The Master** *(Paul Thomas Anderson, 2012)*
Joaquin Phoenix's Freddie Quell is animal need in human form — instinct, contradiction, and trauma in constant collision.

- **The Wrestler** *(Darren Aronofsky, 2008)*
  Mickey Rourke bleeds autobiography into performance — a body aging in real time, holding onto dignity by its fingertips.

- **Blue Valentine** *(Derek Cianfrance, 2010)*
  Ryan Gosling and Michelle Williams improvise love and ruin — performances built from long takes, real-time tension, and unraveling.

- **Boyhood** *(Richard Linklater, 2014)*
  Twelve years of lived performance. Patricia Arquette and Ethan Hawke don't build characters — they become them, quietly and completely.

- **A Woman Under the Influence** *(John Cassavetes, 1974)*
  Technically from the era, but still unmatched. Gena Rowlands gives the template for emotional risk — raw, unrepeatable, volcanic.

- **You Were Never Really Here** *(Lynne Ramsay, 2017)*
  Joaquin Phoenix again — minimal dialogue, maximal subtext. Performance as psychological residue.

- **Marriage Story** *(Noah Baumbach, 2019)*
  Adam Driver and Scarlett Johansson dig deep into rupture and regret. Nothing flashy. Everything earned.

- **Zero Dark Thirty** *(Kathryn Bigelow, 2012)*
  Jessica Chastain burns slow and steady — emotional containment as performance strategy, until it finally breaks.

- **The Florida Project** *(Sean Baker, 2017)*
  Willem Dafoe blends professional control with documentary immediacy. Every gesture feels both deliberate and accidental.

- **The Rider** (*Chloé Zhao, 2017*)
  Brady Jandreau doesn't act — he reinhabits his own trauma. Stillness, silence, and uncoached truth.

Dogme 95: The Vow of Chastity

By the 1990s, cinema had grown sleek. Expensive. Protected. Special effects dominated. Emotional risk took a back seat to technical polish. Performances? Often processed, protected — glossed to perfection.

Into that landscape walked Danish saboteurs.

Lars von Trier and Thomas Vinterberg issued the *Vow of Chastity* — a manifesto, a provocation, a dare. No lights. No sets. No score. No props. No genre. No director credit. No tricks.

Just people. And a camera. Nothing else.

It wasn't an aesthetic preference — it was a rebellion. A rejection of cinema as spectacle. A refusal to let performance drown beneath production. Von Trier and Vinterberg weren't just reinventing style. They were trying to rescue the *soul* of acting from its growing dependency on post-production, control, and illusion.

Performance Under Pressure

In Dogme, there are no safety nets. No flattering light. No ADR to fix the moment. No visual grammar to prop up a weak choice. Acting in these films isn't supported — it's exposed. Which is exactly the point.

Look at Emily Watson in *Breaking the Waves*. There's no retreat. No filter. Her face — relentlessly close, even during breakdowns. Especially during breakdowns. She isn't "performing" Bess. She *is* Bess — desperate, fragmented, divine.

Watson had to carry sexual degradation, religious ecstasy, and mental collapse — sometimes in the same scene. But without the usual cues — no swelling score, no lighting change, no slow dolly in — she carried it through *physical truth*. Her posture. Her breath. Her eyes. You don't see technique. You see surrender.

What made it work was her willingness to look foolish. To speak to God, aloud, and answer as Him. Without irony. Without winking. The performance lives in that risk — the choice to believe so completely that the audience has no option but to follow.

Von Trier's direction? "Don't act. Be." And she was.

In *The Celebration*, Vinterberg created a living set — cast and crew housed together, actors unaware of when certain revelations would occur. Ulrich Thomsen's accusation of abuse — a toast turned confession — arrives like a gut-punch. Not a monologue. A rupture.

Henning Moritzen, playing the accused father, doesn't "react." He *fights not to*. Watch his face. It's not technique. It's a man trying to hold onto his reality as it shatters.

The Freedom of Limits

Dogme's harsh constraints — no lights, no props, no sets — weren't just formal exercises. They liberated actors. No marks to hit. No eyelines to match. No camera tricks to time. The only rhythm was the one *they* found inside the moment.

Long takes couldn't be rescued in the edit. Emotions had to sustain themselves in real time. And without stylized set pieces or constructed worlds, actors had to interact with real environments. Not just inhabit them — respond to them.

In *Mifune*, Anders W. Berthelsen plays a man caught between city performance and rural memory. His body tells the story. Watch how he stiffens on the farm, how his voice shifts. He's not playing an idea. He's trying to *remember* how to move through a world he once left behind.

This is physical acting as memory retrieval.

Dogme required actors to **reconceptualize preparation**. They couldn't plan beats. They couldn't anticipate cues. What they needed was *responsive readiness* — not knowing what would happen, but knowing who they were when it did.

I've used this approach with actors stuck way too much in intellectual planning. "Forget your choices. Just be in it... feel the space, as this person would. Then toss all the mechanics." What emerges isn't always clean. But it's always alive, true, and real.

Beyond Denmark

Dogme's influence didn't stay in Scandinavia. Harmony Korine, in *Julien Donkey-Boy*, followed the ethos. Ewen Bremner's portrayal of schizophrenia doesn't explain, doesn't ask for understanding. It immerses. His performance isn't clinical — it's experiential. It invites us inside a consciousness where coherence has been rearranged.

Bremner doesn't indicate symptoms. He *lives* a rhythm where reality and imagination slide into each other. You don't analyze the character — you inhabit his frame.

Lone Scherfig's *Italian for Beginners* softened the edges, but kept the soul. Anders W. Berthelsen (again) and Ann Eleonora Jørgensen build a love story not through cinematic chemistry but *behavioral honesty*. Awkward silences. Misdirection. Emotional misses.

The haircut scene? It's disastrous. But it's real. And because it's real, it's tender. They don't play for charm. They *find* it — in discomfort, not in design.

Lessons That Remain

Dogme showed that when you strip everything away, what's left *must* be real. No framing to save you. No cutaway to cheat. Just performance — raw, unstable, human.

It reminded us that perfection isn't the goal. Truth is.

It asked what acting becomes when the scaffolding is gone — when you're naked to the lens, forced to respond without control.

And that question still matters. Because we now live in a time where digital safety nets are everywhere. When performances can be re-timed, re-lit, re-scored. When spontaneity can be simulated in post.

Dogme still whispers: *Don't simulate. Don't decorate. Just tell the truth.*

Suggested Viewing – Dogme 95

For actors exploring what performance looks like without polish or protection — these films showcase Dogme's commitment to raw, immediate, human truth:

- **The Idiots** *(Lars von Trier, 1998)*
  The second official Dogme film — controversial, confrontational, and relentless in its commitment to emotional risk.

- **The Celebration (Festen)** *(Thomas Vinterberg, 1998)*
  The first Dogme 95 film. Ulrich Thomsen's performance turns a family toast into an emotional rupture that still stuns.

- **Mifune** *(Søren Kragh-Jacobsen, 1999)*
  A businessman returns to his rural past. Anders W. Berthelsen's body tells a story his dialogue avoids.

- **Julien Donkey-Boy** *(Harmony Korine, 1999)*
  The first American Dogme film. Ewen Bremner dissolves into the psyche of a schizophrenic with raw, disorienting truth.

- **Italian for Beginners** *(Lone Scherfig, 2000)*
  A gentler Dogme film. Intimate, understated, and full of behavioral nuance rather than dramatic punctuation.

- **Breaking the Waves** *(Lars von Trier, 1996 – pre-Dogme but spiritually foundational)*
  Emily Watson's performance is unflinching — religious ecstasy, emotional devastation, and spiritual surrender without cinematic cushion.

- **The King Is Alive** *(Kristian Levring, 2000)*
  A group stranded in the desert stages *King Lear*. Dogme's constraints create claustrophobic psychological terrain for ensemble performance.

Mumblecore (2000s-present)

The pendulum swung again toward intimate naturalism. Films like *Funny Ha Ha* and *The Puffy Chair* embraced lo-fi production values and improvised dialogue, creating performances that felt like eavesdropping on real conversations. Actors weren't performing emotions—they were living through awkward pauses, fumbled words, and the ambient confusion of becoming a person. This movement's influence spread far beyond its original films, teaching a generation that authenticity could be more compelling than spectacle.

Suggested Viewing – Mumblecore

For actors seeking to experience this performance style firsthand — in its raw beginnings and evolving forms — these films and series trace the movement's quiet but powerful arc, from lo-fi intimacy to the structured chaos of streaming-era realism.

- **Funny Ha Ha** *(Andrew Bujalski, 2002)*
  The film that quietly started it all. Kate Dollenmayer's performance is a masterclass in behavioral subtlety.

- **The Puffy Chair** *(Jay and Mark Duplass, 2005)*
  A road trip, a relationship, and the emotional weight of a piece of used furniture. Naturalistic and deeply felt.

- **Baghead** *(Jay and Mark Duplass, 2008)*
A mumblegore hybrid. Realistic relationship drama wrapped in a lo-fi horror setup.

- **Quiet City** *(Aaron Katz, 2007)*
A tender, atmospheric story of connection between strangers. Minimal drama, maximum resonance.

- **Humpday** *(Lynn Shelton, 2009)*
Male friendship, boundary testing, and the tension between intention and follow-through — all in a hotel room.

- **Your Sister's Sister** *(Lynn Shelton, 2011)*
A tighter, more polished version of mumblecore with improvisational roots and emotional honesty intact.

- **Jeff, Who Lives at Home** *(Jay and Mark Duplass, 2011)*
Post-mumblecore with broader narrative sweep — still grounded in natural dialogue and lived-in characters.

Evolution & Mainstream Infusion

- **Drinking Buddies** *(Joe Swanberg, 2013)*
Professional actors meet mumblecore minimalism. Olivia Wilde and Jake Johnson bring nuance to everyday choices.

- **Tangerine** *(Sean Baker, 2015)*
Shot entirely on iPhones. Raw, fast, and intimate — captures life on the edge with radical empathy and immediacy.

- **The Florida Project** *(Sean Baker, 2017)*
Naturalistic performances from both professionals and non-actors. Finds wonder and heartbreak in the margins of American life.

- **The Big Sick** *(Michael Showalter, 2017)*
  A mainstream evolution of the movement — improvisational tone, grounded emotion, and real-world awkwardness.

Streaming as a Movement: The Contemporary Era

And now... here we are.

We've passed through Mumblecore's handheld intimacy and into something sharper, more complex, hungrier. The camera hasn't stopped shaking, but has refined the jitter into choreography. This shift is more than stylistic. It's systemic.

Streaming isn't just a platform anymore — it's a movement in its own right. A living, breathing evolution of storytelling with its own rules, rhythms, and rituals. Part algorithm, part instinct. Part chaos, part curation. A hodgepodge of everything, everywhere, all at once — yet somehow coalescing into new lanes of taste and tonality.

The result? Not just a broader playing field, but stove-piped expectations. Viewers aren't sampling everything. They're locking into distinct ecosystems. Call them aesthetic tribes. A flavor of production value here, a cadence of delivery there. What once belonged only to the "Art House" crowd, in terms of stylized performance and experimentation, now stretches across the full breadth of the streaming landscape, embraced by viewers who might never have stepped inside an art-house theater.

The streamer audience isn't just following story anymore — they're following style. Not just what's being told, but how it's being delivered. They're responding to the full production language — the visual texture, the pacing, the tone, the emotional temperature. What kind of performance it invites. What kind of truth it traffics in. Whether it leans into polish or deliberately leans away. Whether it dares to linger in discomfort — be it tender, awkward, painful, or quietly indifferent.

And for actors? That changes the game. Dramatically.

Episodes aren't episodes anymore — they're chapters, essays, sometimes poems. Pacing bends. Some moments stretch, others collapse in an instant. A single glance might linger too long, too awkwardly, or flash by without a beat. Structure melts. Performance does too. Everything's in flux. Except the lens. The lens is closer. Tighter. And always less forgiving... only now, that false intention the actor might show, has become part of the game.

Shows like *The Bear*, *The Studio*, aren't just well-shot — they're quietly revolutionary. Not with spectacle, but with structure. Specifically in *The Studio*: the one'er — that single, unbroken shot, a gauntlet thrown at the actor's feet. A ritual. A pressure cooker. Five, ten, fifteen minutes of uninterrupted presence.

But the revolution runs deeper.

We can find its quieter mutations in shows like *Tires* on Netflix. It's not that audiences have rejected refinement — they haven't. They still want craft, the precision. But alongside it, something rougher, more raw has taken hold. A taste for what feels unguarded and unfinished, seeded years ago by Dogme 95, later Mumblecore — where the acting wasn't polished to a shine, but cracked open.

Tires inherits that spirit. Built out of rough cuts and shrugged-off lighting, it leans into hesitation, misspeaks, awkward stalls. What *The Office* began — Ricky Gervais flinching his way through in the U.K., Steve Carell perfecting

110

it in the U.S. — Shane Gillis now drags into the garage, battered but still breathing.

This isn't just realism. It's anti-performance. Characters not playing the part, but stalling inside it. Flailing a little, even.

Tires carries forward what Dogme and Mumblecore hinted at: the performance of barely performing at all.

And yet — is it really new?

Or is it something older resurfacing? A return to the Silent Era's unbroken takes. To theatre's relentless now. When performance wasn't captured in fragments, but lived continuously, bodies and breath carried the weight of the story without respect or rescue.

This new era — the Streaming Era — demands more. Not just muscle or technique. But absorption. Presence without self-watching. Truth under imaginary circumstances, held taut within a 4K close-up.

Station Eleven. Beef. Reservation Dogs. Euphoria. The Rehearsal. All pushing performance past the line where technique can follow. Requiring actors to stay alive inside the unbearable intimacy of the moment.

The actor's role has evolved again. Not vessel. Not translator. Co-creator. Emotional technician. Equal parts muscle, memory and radar.

Scary wonderful, I'd say.

Scary because the safety net is gone.

The old techniques — hit the mark, find your light, deliver the line. These don't protect you anymore. Now, the actor has to live inside a moment that isn't entirely theirs. They have to co-create it, react to it, bleed with it — all without over-controlling it.

It's dangerous. Vulnerable. Every take is a tightrope without a net.

But wonderful because that's where the real magic happens. When it's not rehearsed — when it's alive — the camera catches something you can't manufacture: truth. Small, unspeakable truths that make an audience lean in closer, hold their breath, believe in the illusion yet again.

This movement isn't even a movement at all. It's a state of readiness. Always listening. Always one breath away from the line.

A return — not forward, but inward.

And in this way, it echoes something far older than cinema — something alchemical. The camera, like the ancient furnace, becomes a crucible. Presence is the element. The moment? Fire. What survives is no longer the raw material of the actor's intent, but something transmuted. Purified. Not gold from lead — but truth from posture. Soul from technique.

We're living in a moment where the performance style has changed gradually, then suddenly. The shows above didn't just shift audience taste. They rewired the actor's job. Dialogue-driven scenes gave way to micro-behavior, emotional leakage, and thought arriving before speech. Across these series, you'll see it — actors learning to do less, and in doing so, giving more. Presence has replaced projection. Listening has replaced signaling. And silence — finally — has earned its seat at the table.

Yes... if I can quote myself here, *"Learn to love the pause."*

So what does that mean for you — the working actor trying to adjust in real time? Let's talk about what that shift actually feels like in the room.

You know the feeling. The same preparation, the same instincts, the same energy you've brought to a dozen scenes before. And yet... it doesn't land. Not this time. Something's off — but it's not you. Not entirely.

The ground has shifted under your feet, and the old rhythms — what once worked so well and carried you into a scene with confidence — now feel a little too much. A beat too long. A thought too late.

This is where we are. Not because actors have lost their way, but because the camera, the style, and the era have found a new language. It's whispering to you. Not asking you to perform, but to live quietly, microscopically. To let the thought hit before the word does. To feel the shift between intention and impulse, and trust the lens will catch it.

I've worked with actors who felt this unease — the subtle sense that the room changed, but no one told them the new rules. What once read as raw now feels overly loud. What once worked is now working against them. They're not wrong. The evolution is real. It's not just technical — it's biological, neurological. The audience's awareness has changed. Their sensitivity to truth, real truth, is unnervingly sharp. And if you're still acting like it's 2002, you're already behind.

But this isn't cause for panic. It's a reason for adaptation. Because while the medium may change, the craft — the deep work, the honest work — remains. It just demands a different touch. A different kind of stillness. And a different type of bravery.

High-definition cameras have changed the game — not just because they're sharper, but because they bring the audience closer. Audiences don't sit back anymore. They lean in. The work isn't performed at them — it happens internal. A viewer watches sometimes from six inches away, phone in hand. Or on a seventy-five-inch 8K flat panel. They don't want to be impressed.

They want to be invited. And if you fake it, even a little, they feel it. And you lose them.

The performance space has collapsed. No longer a proscenium. No longer a medium shot, safely framed. Now, it's the trembling of an eyelid, the hesitation behind a blink, the breath caught before a word.

The work happens not in dialogue, but in the spaces between the words. Not in action, but in the moment before the action — the decision to act, or not act.

Watch *Moonlight* — the 2016 American coming-of-age drama by Barry Jenkins. In the diner scene between Chiron and Kevin, the most powerful moments live not in the dialogue but in the silence. A glance. A slight shift in posture. An entire history of fear and longing wrapped tight beneath the surface.

Or take Elisabeth Moss in *The Handmaid's Tale*. The camera holds her face hostage. She can't safely express her thoughts, but it betrays her anyway — recording the resistance, the compliance, the rage just under the skin.

Phoebe Waller-Bridge in *Fleabag*? Her looks to camera aren't cheeky winks. They're ruptures. Three layers of consciousness in a split-second glance: what she shows others, what she shows us, what she hides from both.

Across the best work of today, the performance isn't shown. It's lived. Not emotional display, but a deep, internal quiet dialogue. A cognitive presence. We're not watching characters act. We're watching them think. And that's what makes it real.

In a recent coaching session, an actress shared her sides with me from a new project she'd been cast in.

"I'm playing anger underneath here." She pointed to the script. She'd done her prep, made strong choices, and rehearsed them to precision. The problem? When we ran it, it read as preloaded. Intended. As performed. She was preparing to feel, rather than preparing to *realize*.

So I tried to shift the framing.

"Is your character discovering anything new at this exact moment? Does something change in her understanding? And if it does — besides anger, what other kind of reaction could that provoke?"

At moments like this — especially with actors who are well along in their process — I have to choose my words carefully. Say too much, and they can interpret it as a line reading. Say too little, and you risk introducing a layer of cognitive fog — a subtle self-consciousness that interrupts the flow. Another actor might've been completely thrown by my question. But I knew her — knew how she would likely translate that note.

"Don't try to play anything. Just step into her circumstance. Let what happens, happen."

And when she did — when she stopped intending and simply lived in the beat — an authentic response emerged, on its own terms, in the very next take. From there, as we worked it, her performance bloomed. Not neat. Not overly polished. Raw. Real. Responsive. Lived.

Actors don't evolve in a vacuum. The most powerful performances today are built on layers of performance DNA — generations of artists responding to their moment in culture, in technology, in truth. Brando revolutionized screen acting, but he stood on the shoulders of John Garfield. Garfield's work in *Body and Soul* and *Force of Evil* was already breaking away from the stage-bound, toward something looser — something lived.

Every great revolution in acting carries echoes of what came before. Mumblecore borrowed from the French New Wave. The New Wave drew from Neorealism. And so it goes.

Understanding this lineage isn't about carrying the weight of those traditions — it's about loosening their grip. Knowing where a technique came from frees you to use it for what it was meant for... or to set it aside entirely, in favor of something fresh. Something brave. Something never seen before.

The goal? Not imitation. Not allegiance. Truth — however, and wherever, it arrives.

And in this new era of close-up intimacy, razor-sharp fidelity, audiences who can smell the false intention a mile away — truth doesn't whisper anymore.

It breathes deep... and beautifully.

Legacy Watch – Echoes of Today in the Craft of the Past

For actors tracing the roots of modern realism, these landmark performances offer early echoes of the demands now resurfacing in the streaming era. Each title reveals how presence, stillness, and raw emotional clarity have always been part of the actor's deepest arsenal — even before the technology caught up.

Silent Era Precision & Physical Presence

- **The General** *(Buster Keaton, 1926)*
  Physical timing as poetry. Keaton's stone face conceals high-stakes choreography — every gesture precise, earned, and narratively vital.

- **The Passion of Joan of Arc** (*Carl Theodor Dreyer, 1928*)
  Renée Jeanne Falconetti's performance is all eyes, breath, and tremor. No dialogue — just presence, pressure, and soul laid bare.

Golden Age Intensity & Emotional Constraint

- **A Streetcar Named Desire** (*Elia Kazan, 1951*)
  Brando's performance marks the birth of modern screen realism. Watch his silences. His listening. His simmer. Method meets lens.

- **On the Waterfront** (*Elia Kazan, 1954*)
  Brando again — now more internal, more broken. "I coulda been a contender..." lives forever in the pause before he says it.

- **The Misfits** (*John Huston, 1961*)
  Monroe and Clift stripped bare — emotionally exposed in ways that would feel at home on *The Bear* or *Beef*. The camera lingers. They hold.

New Hollywood & Early Verité Grit

- **Midnight Cowboy** (*John Schlesinger, 1969*)
  Hoffman and Voight disappear into character — awkward, flawed, human. Scenes feel found, not staged.

- **Five Easy Pieces** (*Bob Rafelson, 1970*)
  Nicholson's kitchen-table stillness. The diner breakdown. The long drive into silence. Restraint as rebellion.

- **Wanda** (*Barbara Loden, 1970*)
  Lo-fi, handheld, heartbreakingly real. A woman drifts through America, and the camera doesn't rescue her. It just watches.

European Influence & Behavioral Depth

- **L'Avventura** *(Michelangelo Antonioni, 1960)*
  Long, lingering takes. Minimal dialogue. Emotional truth unfolds not in what's said, but in what's avoided.

- **Scenes from a Marriage** *(Ingmar Bergman, 1973)*
  Raw. Close. Relentless. Liv Ullmann and Erland Josephson pull each other apart in long takes that feel almost improvised.

- **The 400 Blows** *(François Truffaut, 1959)*
  A boy stares into the camera at the end — and that look tells the whole story. Behavior over plot. Emotion over exposition.

Modern Predecessors to the Streaming Aesthetic

- **Secrets & Lies** *(Mike Leigh, 1996)*
  Improvised structure. Painful honesty. Performances that unravel in real time — often without a cut to hide behind.

- **Before Sunset** *(Richard Linklater, 2004)*
  Essentially one long conversation in real time. Watch how the actors breathe. How the city passes. How tension builds *between* the lines.

- **Elephant** *(Gus Van Sant, 2003)*
  Long Steadicam shots follow students through hallways, aimless until they're not. Actors must hold tone through stillness and dread.

—THE FIERY CROSS OF THE KU KLUX KLAN—

D.W. GRIFFITH'S MIGHTY SPECTACLE

THE BIRTH OF A NATION

FOUNDED ON THOMAS DIXON'S 'THE CLANSMAN'

PART II

THE INDUSTRY
& THE INDIVIDUAL

The Art of Being Chosen — The Work of Staying Ready

Craft alone isn't enough. A brilliant performance means nothing if it happens in an empty room.

This section confronts the dual reality every actor faces: you are both artist and entrepreneur, both soul and commodity.

Here we explore the business landscape surrounding creative work — how to navigate industry structures, build essential relationships, sustain your career through inevitable ups and downs, and understand the concept of *champion-building*. This is a strategic reinvention of practical approaches to your life in the entertainment business.

Rather than viewing business demands as separate from artistic development, discover how understanding industry realities can actually enhance creative choices. Art and commerce need not be enemies. Approached with integrity and strategic thinking, they become powerful allies in building a sustainable career.

The industry doesn't care about your technique, your training, or your artistic integrity. Not because it's cruel, but because it's a machine with its own logic and demands. Learn to speak its language while preserving what makes you unique as an artist.

Your work exists within a system. Ignoring its realities doesn't make you pure; it makes you unprepared. Champions — those industry figures who advocate for your talent — don't materialize through wishful thinking. They emerge through strategic relationship-building, solving problems others create, and persistence that outlasts rejection.

The business of acting isn't a distraction from craft; it's the context that gives craft purpose. It's the container that allows art to reach audiences, and the bridge between artistic impulse and professional opportunity.

Learn to build this bridge. Cross it with confidence, and return to your artistic core stronger for understanding both worlds you inhabit.

CHAPTER 3

WHY ACTORS NEED TO UNDERSTAND THE INDUSTRY

Talent Isn't a Strategy

You're doing the work. You've mastered the Meisner repetition exercise. You can recall emotional memories at will. You've got three or four monologues in your back pocket that, on a moment's notice, can bring audiences to tears. And yet... you're not booking.

This scenario plays out daily across Los Angeles, New York, London, and now — with the explosion of regional markets — Georgia, Atlanta, New Mexico, Texas, Utah, Nevada, Toronto, and dozens of other regional markets that, through aggressive tax incentives, siphoned off what was once LA's production dominance.

The industry no longer revolves around a handful of power centers but sprawls across a complex geography of opportunity and competition. Actors everywhere find themselves facing the same fundamental challenge:

extraordinary talents languishing in obscurity while mediocre performers with sharp, aggressive business acumen build successful careers. Is it fair? No. Is it reality? Absolutely.

Geographical shift isn't a minor footnote — it's a fundamental restructuring of how the industry operates.

Atlanta, once seen as an outlier, now routinely outpaces Los Angeles in total productions during key seasons. With robust infrastructure and aggressive tax incentives, Georgia has become the new default for countless major projects. New Mexico, meanwhile, has carved out its identity as an epicenter for prestige television, fueled by Netflix's expanded presence in Albuquerque and some of the most generous incentives in the country. Vancouver continues to double for dozens of U.S. cities with seamless efficiency, and Louisiana — long bolstered by its competitive tax credits — remains a formidable player, though recent legislative changes may affect its long-term dominance.

And at the time of this writing, Texas has entered the conversation in a serious way. A major new entertainment incentive bill just passed — signaling a likely production boom, especially given Taylor Sheridan's already sprawling footprint across the state. Expect more projects heading there.

An actor who doesn't understand these shifting market dynamics — where productions are happening, why they're happening, and how to position themselves within these evolving ecosystems operates at a severe disadvantage, no matter how talented.

I've watched brilliant actors remain stubbornly anchored to traditional markets while opportunity migrates elsewhere. A performer who insists on staying exclusively in Los Angeles may find themselves in the unemployment line, while a less polished peer who established a presence in New Mexico might book a recurring role on a prestige drama. Geography itself has become a strategic consideration no serious actor can ignore.

This decentralization creates both challenges and opportunities. Established actors face new competition as regional performers gain access to major productions. Newcomers may find their "type" suddenly in demand in less saturated markets. Everyone, no matter their level, must begin factoring geography along with the flexibility to move often into their equation of success. It's not about where you live. It's about where you can be seen.

The uncomfortable truth is that acting exists at the intersection of art and commerce. The most brilliant performance means nothing if it happens in an empty room. The most profound character work is invisible if casting directors don't know you exist. And the deepest emotional truth won't pay rent if you can't achieve, day-job or not, a living wage.

This creates a fundamental tension many actors are never able to resolve. They want to believe talent alone ensures success — that exceptional skill will be recognized on its merits. That the industry is a meritocracy. That the best performer wins the role.

That comforting fiction allows them to focus solely on the craft while ignoring the business — which feels, to them, inauthentic or beneath the art.

I have mentored many actors who are reluctant to learn how the industry truly operates — including deal structures, decision-making processes, and the importance of relationships, or "champions," as I like to call them. Understanding the business side of acting does not compromise the integrity of the craft; rather, resisting this knowledge leads to marginalization.

The industry is relentless. It does not adapt to your preferences; it moves forward, with or without you. Those who appreciate both the artistry and the business will find their place.

The Dual Path of the Actor

Great actors must train in their craft — that much is obvious. They study technique, develop their instrument, and hone their artistic sensibilities. But equally important, and less discussed in most acting programs, is the business of *career longevity*.

As the saying goes, "It's not a sprint; it's a marathon."

Navigating the industry is not a secondary concern to artistic development; rather, it is a parallel priority that demands just as much attention.

These paths aren't separate but interconnected, each informing and enhancing the other. Artistic growth without a professional strategy leads to brilliant performances that go unnoticed. Business acumen without artistic substance results in an empty career that collapses when trends shift. The integration of both establishes the foundation for a sustainable artistic life.

Consider actors like Bryan Cranston, Laura Dern, or Samuel L. Jackson. Each spent decades being typecast or overlooked before finding roles that showcased their full capabilities. Their persistence wasn't just artistic but strategic. They understood that longevity requires reinvention — moving from perceived lead roles to supporting character work as the industry shows its willingness to accept them in different capacities.

Cranston spent years as a sitcom dad in "Malcolm in the Middle" before his transformation into Walter White in "Breaking Bad." This wasn't an accidental pivot but a strategic transition based on careful cultivation of relationships with producers and directors who could see beyond his established image. He didn't merely wait for the perfect role to find him — he actively positioned himself to be considered for opportunities outside his previous casting pattern.

Laura Dern navigated an even more dramatic evolution — from ingenue roles in films like "Blue Velvet" to character-driven work in "Enlightened" to prestigious supporting performances in "Big Little Lies" and "Marriage Story." Each phase required not just artistic adaptation but strategic recalibration — new relationships with different filmmakers, deliberate choices that expanded the industry's perception of her range, and careful selection of roles that built upon each other rather than merely repeating previous successes.

Such careers don't happen through talent alone. They emerge from a sophisticated understanding of how the industry operates, how perceptions are managed, and how strategic choices at critical junctures can open or close entire categories of opportunity. These performers recognized that artistic growth must be matched with industry awareness — understanding when to push boundaries and when to build credibility, when to take financial risks for artistic growth, and when, how, where to secure commercial stability.

Adaptability has become even more crucial in today's decentralized production landscape. With Georgia now hosting Marvel blockbusters, New Mexico becoming synonymous with prestige television, and states like Louisiana and Massachusetts aggressively competing for studio projects, an actor's strategic territory has expanded dramatically. The question isn't simply what kind of career you want, but where you'll pursue it. Many successful actors now maintain bases in multiple regions or develop specific market strategies for different types of projects.

Regional production hubs have their own distinct ecosystems, their own casting relationships, and their own specific needs. Atlanta productions often seek different performer types than those in Los Angeles. New Mexico series require different skill sets than New York theater-influenced television. Understanding these regional variations — and strategically positioning yourself to leverage them — can transform a struggling career into a thriving one.

I advise actors to consider regular *market analysis* of their careers — examining where their specific (yet ever-evolving) type, skills, and connections might yield the greatest opportunity. This isn't cynical calculation but pragmatic recognition that different markets value different qualities. An actor who reads as *too theatrical* for Los Angeles casting might be perfectly suited to another region's aesthetic. A performer struggling to be noticed among thousands of similar types in New York might be a standout in Austin's growing production scene.

But many resist this kind of self-inventory. Some because it feels too business-minded — as though art should transcend strategy. Others because they've been seduced by the fantasy: that just being in L.A., walking under that sign, soaking in the Hollywood air, somehow means they've *arrived*. They post a few filtered photos from Runyon Canyon, wait for the phone to ring... and weeks turn to months. The reality hits hard: they're not just one of many — they're one of *too many*. Surrounded by actors with better resumes, sharper tools, deeper connections. The dream gets heavy. The sparkle dulls. And still, they resist leaving, as if stepping away would mean giving up on the dream, when in truth... it might be the first step toward actually living it.

Understanding where and how your specific talents are *valued* doesn't dilute your integrity. It *creates conditions* where that artistry can finally be seen. The most brilliant performance means little if it's given in the wrong room. Or worse — a room that never opens its door.

Market Selection and Reinvention

Choosing where to build your career is as important as how. Each market offers different opportunities and challenges. A strategic actor doesn't just pursue work everywhere but identifies markets where they can not only fit in but thrive given the competition. Find your groove and choose low-hanging fruit — markets where your specific type, skills, and background give you a competitive advantage.

This might mean starting in a smaller regional market where you can build credits and relationships before tackling more competitive territories. It might mean focusing on markets that cast your ethnic background more frequently. It might mean leveraging regional connections or training that gives you credibility in specific territories. The path isn't identical for everyone — it's about aligning your specific attributes with the right opportunities.

Besides acting sessions and training, career consulting and mentoring are a big part of what I do — which occasionally means talking actors off the ledge of bad decisions dressed up as ambition. Case in point: a smart, talented actor with deep Southern roots and a burning desire to relocate to Los Angeles. (*Insert dramatic sigh here.*)

He had the accent, the cultural fluency, hometown connections — everything casting directors in Atlanta look for. But in his mind, if he wasn't struggling in a West Hollywood studio apartment and sipping bad coffee between shifts at the Cheesecake Factory, was he even a real actor?

I advised him — bluntly — to stay put. To build where he already had leverage. He did, and lo and behold... within a couple of years, he started to book consistently. Recurring roles on network shows. Paychecks. Resume credits. All without having to blow his life savings trying to "make it" in a city where even Starbucks baristas have agents.

That foundation didn't just pad his resume — it helped create the foundation of a career. When and if he chooses to finally make the move to a larger market, he will have some momentum at his back.

Sometimes, the smartest career move isn't moving at all. Especially when the fantasy is more expensive than the opportunity. Hollywood will still be there. And if you play it right... it might even be waiting for *you* — once you've built enough traction somewhere that actually sees you.

Of course, geography isn't the only thing worth reevaluating. Sometimes, what needs to move... is *you*. Not just your location, but your entire presentation.

You will likely go through multiple iterations over the life of a long career. That's not failure — it's professional evolution. New headshots, shifts in representation, physical transformation, or even a fresh reel built around a new tone or archetype — all of these can change how the industry sees you.

An actor who clings too tightly to a single identity risks becoming irrelevant. But those who adapt, who experiment and lean into their own changes, tend to open up lanes that others miss. The industry is always shifting — and smart actors shift with it.

These pivots aren't admissions of failure — they're strategic recalibrations. The industry evolves constantly: what it needs, what it values, how it labels performers. An actor who clings too tightly to a single identity risks fading into irrelevance. Those who learn to shift, stretch, and reframe their presence open up new lanes for momentum and longevity.

Sometimes, that shift means changing your home base. As trends migrate and personal needs evolve, so too must your positioning. An actor who once thrived in Atlanta's action-driven ecosystem may find deeper resonance — and richer roles — in New Mexico's prestige dramas. A seasoned New York theater veteran might suddenly find their classical chops in demand on a regional streaming series looking for depth and credibility.

But let's be clear: this isn't about selling out or faking it. It's about surfacing different facets of your talent to meet the moment. A decades-spanning career isn't one long, unchanging performance — it's a series of carefully chosen iterations. A dynamic evolution that honors your artistry while tracking with the rhythms of the marketplace.

And this kind of professional evolution isn't just reactive. Sometimes, it's the only way to break through. An actor stuck in the "always the best friend, never the lead" category might rework their physical presence, train up in an unexpected discipline, or create their own project that reframes how they're seen entirely. Without such bold, deliberate transformation, the industry will default to the last thing it saw — and box you into it.

Because the uncomfortable truth? When it comes to casting, nobody has much imagination. You are, in their eyes, whoever you were *last time*. Unless you show them something new.

I worked with an actor who was the "nice guy." Best bud. Never the romantic interest and breaking through to more significant leading roles. Rather than continuing the same approach, we began to evolve a reinvention strategy — a physical transformation through diet, fitness, and new material emphasizing a darker, more complex emotional range. Creating a completely

131

different visual presentation. Within a year, he began receiving auditions for anti-hero, bad guy, character roles — a category previously closed to him despite tons of talent that was always there invisible to the industry in his previous incarnation.

Understanding the business landscape isn't a distraction from artistry but an essential foundation for creating sustainable conditions where your art can flourish. The most brilliant actors balance unwavering commitment to their craft with a strategic understanding of how the industry operates. They know when to make purely artistic choices and when commercial considerations must factor into decisions. They recognize which relationships need development and which markets offer the greatest opportunity for their specific attributes.

This isn't selling out. It's creating circumstances where your artistic contribution can actually reach audiences. The most profound performance means nothing if industry structures prevent it from being seen. By understanding and strategically navigating these, you don't compromise your art — you create conditions that allow it to flourish.

But knowing where to work is only half the game. The rest? It's about who's willing to bet on you when it counts.

Creating Champions: Your Career Advocates

Beyond skill and strategy, successful actors grasp a quieter truth: talent alone rarely breaks through — not without advocates.

I believe in *Creating Champions* for your work and talent. That means finding agents who genuinely think you're brilliant — not just marketable. Cultivating relationships with casting directors who call you back again and again because they want to be the ones to "discover" you. Champions aren't just people who like you. They're the ones willing to stake their own reputation on your name. They fight for you in rooms you'll never enter. They remember you when the right opportunity opens. They push decision-makers to take chances on you. Without these advocates, even exceptional talent can remain unseen.

I advise actors to consider regular *market analysis* of their careers — examining where their specific (yet ever-evolving) type, skills, and connections might yield the greatest opportunity. This isn't cynical calculation but pragmatic recognition that different markets value different qualities. An actor who reads as *too theatrical* for Los Angeles casting might be perfectly suited to another region's performance aesthetic. A performer struggling to stand out among thousands of similar types in New York might become a distinctive presence in Austin's rapidly expanding scene.

But many resist this kind of analysis. Some because it feels too clinical — as though weighing strategy somehow pollutes the purity of the craft. Others because they've been seduced by a quieter fantasy: that simply being in Hollywood means you've arrived.

I worked with a brilliantly talented actor who couldn't understand why her career wasn't advancing, despite strong training and consistently excellent auditions. Taking a closer look, it became clear — she was floating in what I deemed as the **Recognition Nebula**. Glowing with potential. Surrounded by praise. But never coalescing into anything solid. Plenty of admirers. No champions.

Understanding where and how your particular talents are *valued* doesn't compromise your integrity — it creates the conditions for your art to be seen. Most brilliant performances have no impact if they occur in a market that doesn't *see* them in every sense of the word. Visibility alone is not enough. The light has to focus. The orbit has to shift. And sometimes... the artist has to make the first move.

CHAPTER 4

BUILDING A CHAMPION ECOSYSTEM

"A champion is someone who believes in you
more than you believe in yourself."

Beyond Networking

The industry runs on talent. But it survives on belief — often someone else's, before your own.

The mythology of the entertainment industry loves the overnight success story — an unknown plucked from obscurity and catapulted to stardom through a single audition, chance encounter, or moment of serendipity. These narratives make for compelling interviews, but obscure a fundamental truth: sustainable acting careers aren't built on lucky breaks but on methodically cultivated relationships with industry advocates who genuinely believe in your talent and potential.

I call these advocates "champions" — agents who pitch you passionately rather than merely submitting you, casting directors who remember you months after an audition, directors who fight to cast you against the studio's reluctance, and producers who create opportunities specifically for your abilities. These champions form the infrastructure of a successful career, providing not just access to opportunities but crucial advocacy that transforms access into bookings.

The myth of meritocracy — the idea that the most talented performer always wins the role — keeps many actors from developing this essential network of advocate champions. They believe that excellent auditions alone should secure opportunities and that the industry naturally rewards superior talent. This misconception leads to frustration when seemingly less skilled performers advance while their careers stagnate. What they fail to recognize is that those advancing often possess robust champion networks actively advocating for them in decision-making environments the actor never sees.

I've seen this dynamic play out more times than I can count — first as an actor, then as a coach, and briefly during a stint inside a top casting office in LA. I watched strong auditions — smart, grounded, fully prepared — get quietly passed over. Not because the actor missed the mark, but because someone else had a passionate advocate in the room.

I've sat in casting sessions with what used to be the Big Four agencies — now the Big Three — where roles were discussed, reshaped, and slowly molded around specific actors before a single audition went out. And these weren't stars. These were working actors whose reps pushed hard, made calls, and put weight behind their names at just the right time.

I've seen directors hesitate on a choice — unsure, second-guessing — until someone who's trusted, leaned in and said, *"You need to take a serious look at this person."* Suddenly, the "risky" option became the right one.

These moments — invisible to actors — steer careers more decisively than anything that occurs during an audition.

Building a network of champions is fundamentally different from traditional networking. While old-school networking focuses on volume — handshakes, business cards, thank-you cards, postcards, networking mixers, polite smiles, websites, new headshots, and follow-up emails — the goal is often to meet as many people as possible, hoping at least one remembers your name. It's a numbers game with countless moving parts that can become overwhelming and, all too often, very expensive.

Building champions? That's something else entirely. It's deeper. Slower. Personal. Fewer relationships, but stronger bonds — forged through shared effort, not shallow interactions. Champions don't emerge from small talk and forced smiles. They emerge from interactions where people *witness* you. A teacher who's watched you grow over months or years of scene work. A casting director who's seen how you think on your feet in a workshop. A director who has observed you on set — prepared, professional, quietly elevating every moment. Ready when it's your time. And out of the way when it's not.

These people don't back you because you sent them the right postcard. They back you because your work *helps* theirs. A great agent champions you not just because you book — but because your bookings and who you are make them look good. A casting director becomes your advocate because your performance makes their tastes look keen and insightful. A director wants you back because your presence lifts the cast and crew.

This isn't about asking for favors. It's about offering extended value. Shared value. Strategic alignment. You're not just saying, "Hey, would you help me, please." You're saying, "Here are the things I do, not just my talent, that's a given, this is the way I comport myself, and the whole package makes *you* and *us* look better. And that's how we win together."

Agent Champions

Agent Champions don't just add you to the roster. They think long-term. They help shape how the industry sees you — and more importantly, how you see yourself. They pick up the phone when it matters. They push when it counts. And they tell you the hard truths — the ones that sting a little but save you a year.

The good ones aren't just negotiating deals. They're tracking your arc. They're working toward something sustainable. A path that builds, holds, and evolves.

Finding the right agent isn't about chasing prestige. It's about finding the person who actually sees you — who knows where your work fits and believes in where it can go. Sometimes that means choosing the mid-tier rep who's hungry, honest, and fully in your corner... over the big-name agency that signed you as a courtesy favor and promptly forgot you existed.

I had an actress come to me torn between two offers. One from a top-tier agency with serious brand recognition. The other from a scrappy, sharp young agent at a strong mid-level shop. The former looked great on paper. The latter looked her in the eye and actually talked about her work.

Everyone around her — friends, family, even fellow actors — said take the name.

We sat down. Talked it through. Where she was in her career. What she really needed. And in the end, she went with the champion. The one who was already acting like she mattered.

Within a year, she was booking the kind of work her colleagues with fancier reps weren't even being seen for.

That's what advocacy looks like.

But there's no one-size-fits-all answer here.

I had another client — a seasoned actor with a long list of credits, great relationships in every major market, and a résumé that included recurring roles and meaningful supporting parts in studio films. She'd hustled for years, self-submitting, flying out at her own expense, doing the grind.

It was time for something else.

She didn't need another rep who'd "work hard for her." She needed someone whose name opened doors before she even walked in. She needed a major. Not for ego — for leverage. To command better rates, better billing, and better treatment on jobs she was already getting.

Different needs. Different strategy.

That's what a real career plan looks like — built around where *you* are, not where someone else thinks you should be.

And a real agent champion? They're not just chasing what's trending. They're aligning with who you are and what you're ready to become.

Casting Director Champions

Casting Director Champions work differently than most industry advocates. They don't just remember your name. They remember your choices. Your instincts. They call you in for roles that stretch how the industry sees you. They pitch you in creative meetings you're not even aware of. The ones that matter. The ones where real decisions get made.

But those kinds of relationships aren't built overnight. They're built slowly — one audition at a time. One moment of real presence. A good audition doesn't disappear just because it didn't book. It leaves a breadcrumb. Something specific. And if your work solves a casting problem — cleanly, honestly, without drama — they remember you. Not as a hopeful. As a resource.

I once mentored an actor who went to every industry event he could find — trying to meet everyone, hand out as many headshots as possible, hoping that desperate actor energy would show how badly he wanted it. I advised him to pull back. That kind of chasing — with the smell of desperation on you — doesn't work.

Instead, we got specific. We identified three casting directors in his represented geography whose work might actually align — not just in genre, but in tone, energy, and type.

He took a workshop with one of them. We prepped him for it. Kept it clean. No pitch, no overexplaining — just show the work and leave that lay. He was ready for that new reinvention. The new image of himself that he wanted to present as a professional, talented actor who's earned his right to be in the room. His choices were sharp, his instincts were specific. He let his scenes carry the weight. No need to sell it or himself.

It landed.

Within a few months, that casting director started calling him in — and kept calling him in. Even for projects his agent hadn't submitted him for. Not because he followed up aggressively with her. Not because he pushed his agent and the casting director. But because the work made an impression. And the impression stuck.

That's the shift. From generic awareness to targeted belief. From name on a list — to name on someone's lips... in the room.

Champions notice patterns. Not one good read. Not one polished self-tape. Patterns. Consistency. A history of walking into a room and doing the job — clean, distinct, on point. Adjusting on the fly. Handling notes with ease. Elevating the scene without taking it over.

They remember the actor who makes their job easier. And they forget the ones who don't.

Strong choices — even if they don't book — stick longer than safe ones. Bland auditions get erased. But the bold ones, the usable ones, the ones that offer something real? They leave a trail.

I always tell actors: know the room you're in. A casting director known for risk-taking will respect courage. One with a network TV focus might value precision and efficiency more than originality. Don't pander. But don't walk in blind, either.

And when it comes to follow-up? Keep it professional. A thank-you note, a short email, a heads-up about a show — all fine. But never push. Never beg. Let the relationship build over time, through the work itself. Respect the boundary. That boundary is part of what builds trust.

Casting director champions aren't built on charm. They're built on evidence. Repeated. Reliable. Undeniable.

Show up that way — and eventually, someone will fight for you when you're not in the room.

Director and Producer Champions

Director and Producer Champions will matter more as your career shifts and matures. These are the people who build things, and can build things around *you*.

Director champion relationships usually start small. You nail a three-line role. You take something thankless and turn it into a moment. Directors notice that. They remember. They begin to consider you for bigger things.

Producers are different. They're not watching the scene in the same way. They notice who shows up prepared. Who solves problems without creating new ones. Who delivers on time, under pressure, and helps save the budget.

Directors are looking for artistry — someone who elevates their vision, who brings unexpected textures without going rogue. Producers are looking for reliability — someone who hits the mark and doesn't crack when the clock and budget start bleeding and the day is going long.

Balancing both demands — that's the trick. You have to maintain artistic integrity without being precious. Directors love actors who surprise them but still serve the story. Producers love actors who are solutions, not liabilities.

I worked with one actor — intense, instinctive, interesting on camera. But his process? It created friction. Performances were undeniable. But collaboration? Not so much. His instincts were dead-on for the character work. He wanted to discover the performance *in the moment* — but he hadn't earned the right at that point in his career to ask for an extra take or to adlib the scene on the fly. Not yet. That "Can I have one more?" request only comes after you've proven you can deliver — reliably, efficiently, without adding unnecessary drama.

The problem was he was swinging for the fences on take one. Acting in his own private movie. And he wasn't the lead. He hadn't earned the leeway that comes with a long-standing career — where a director gives you the extra rope to find something special. He was trying to pour it all out — what he thought he had in the tank and what might improve the scene — without permission. Without the context of a career or relationship.

I told him flat out: "All that great work we do in our sessions? We needed to retool your approach."

Going forward, whenever he got a role, we'd rehearse multiple interpretations before he even set foot on set. Then the job — his *only* job — was to deliver the clean, by-the-book read on the first take. Give them exactly what's on the page. Solid. Professional. Executable. Humble even — he had history to revise.

Then — and only then — listen. Wait for notes. Wait for the room to open up. Once you've hit the mark and shown you're there to do the job — *then* you stretch. *Then* you flex the muscles you've trained so hard for. *Then* — if you get the chance — *Then* you can "Release the Kraken," as I like to tell my actors.

"Read the room," as they say — and by take four or five, you might get the nod. That quiet greenlight to stretch a little, explore more, go deeper. But that moment has to be earned. It's never your right to take over. It's not your place to decide the scene needs something extra. It's not your movie. It's the director's.

If the director invites you to "give me something else," that's not just a note — it's a compliment. It means they trust you enough to explore. But until then? Stay in the scene as written. Deliver what's on the page, clean and clear.

You don't get to show them how brilliant your different interpretation might be... unless they ask to see it.

It took some drilling for sure, as he desperately wanted to give everything he had — every scene, every line — to make it unforgettable. For the good of the project, sure. But also, if we're being honest, to showcase his talent driven by ego.

But after a few hard lessons — and some uncomfortable feedback from his agent — he finally understood. The work wasn't the problem. The process was. No matter how talented or charismatic he was on screen, he'd be labeled "difficult" if he didn't learn how to read the room.

The good news is he's in a reinvention place now — and it's paying off. He's hitting his marks. Staying inside the lines (literally) until he's invited to color outside them. Directors who once hesitated are calling him back. Producers who once crossed him off their lists are giving him another shot.

Because talent opens doors.
But managing relationships — the *right way* — keeps them open.

Champion Cultivation: Find the People Who Actually Need You

Building your champions network isn't about collecting contacts. It's strategic. Deliberate. Focused.

Not every powerful person is your person. Not every handshake is worth chasing. You don't need *any* advocate — you need the *right* ones. Champions whose professional focus matches your strengths.

Start with the facts. Study the agents who consistently rep actors who look like you, move like you, book like you. Look at casting directors whose projects naturally fit your energy, your type, your skill set. Find directors whose sensibilities line up with the way you approach the work.

Because here's the hard truth: misalignment wastes time. No matter how good you are, an agent who specializes in ingénues, models, print work, commercials, background actors won't fight for you if you're a character actor. A casting director living in the world of procedural dramas won't see your comedy chops — even if you're brilliant. It's not about *you*. It's about what they need.

This kind of alignment takes three things: honest self-assessment, serious market research, and shoe leather. Look at what's been cast in your target markets over the last year. Who consistently hires actors with your general look, type, vibe? Who keeps going back to performers who work the way you work? That's your map. Follow it.

Earn It First: Show Your Work Before You Ask for Support

One of the biggest mistakes actors make? Trying to build champions before they've done the real work. Champions don't show up because you're charming. They show up because you're valuable. You don't get advocacy because you ask for it — you get it because you're *useful* to what they're building.

And that starts long before the coffee meeting. Before the elevator pitch. Before you're even a blip on their radar.

Get the basics right: training that sharpens your instrument. Headshots that aren't vanity projects — they're market-aware and honest. Reels that don't just show you acting — they show you solving casting problems. Handle the logistics — clear your day-job conflicts, set your geographical availability, sort out your union status if it's a hurdle. Champions aren't just looking for talent — they're scanning for *readiness*.

And don't just talk about what you can do. *Show* them.
Indie shorts. Theater showcases. Workshop performances.
Have your three best monologues locked and ready — tight, lived-in, no warm-up needed. If the opportunity arises — even if it's across from them at a Starbucks — *be ready* to show them who you are.

Champions want evidence.
Something real they can point to when they make the call on your behalf.

Nobody champions potential.
They champion proof.

Approach With Caution: Protocol Matters

A word of warning here — because this is where many actors quietly blow it.

Protocol matters. In this business, boundaries aren't just etiquette — they're survival. Cross them, and you leave a mark. A bad one.

No one likes the desperate actor. And there are far too many who veer into near-stalker territory chasing connections. Agents getting unscheduled office visits. Casting directors cornered at coffee shops. Producers ambushed in public spaces. It happens every day — and it doesn't impress anyone. It kills your shot before you've even had one.

Industry professionals build walls for a reason — to keep out the noise. An actor who tries to climb over those walls doesn't look resourceful. They look clueless, as if they don't understand the very business they're trying to break into. And no one champions someone who doesn't grasp the basics.

I've counseled more actors than I can count who meant well but tanked potential relationships because they didn't respect the rules.
— An actor interrupting a casting director's family dinner at a restaurant.
— A performer sending an elaborate, unsolicited gift to an agent after one good meeting.
— An actor messaging a producer on their personal Instagram after tracking down their info online.

Each of them thought they were showing initiative. What they really showed was poor judgment — and just like that, doors closed.

If you want to build real champions, you have to move through the right channels: industry events designed for professional connection — workshops, showcases, sanctioned mixers, festivals. Spaces where interaction is expected — and even then, it's about *building rapport*, not begging for a job.

When direct communication does become appropriate — maybe after a strong audition or a good workshop — keep it brief, professional, and useful.
— A quick note letting a casting director know about a new project you're in.
— A heads-up to an agent about a stage performance that showcases a different side of your range.
Keep it about *giving* information, not *asking* for favors. That's the difference.

Digital communication? Even trickier. Just because you can find them doesn't mean you should message them. Blind DMs to casting directors you've never met? Friend requests to agents who don't represent you? It's rarely appropriate. And when the connection *does* happen naturally, treat it the same way you would in person — professionally, respectfully, with no pitches.

The actors who build real champions know patience matters. Timing matters. They understand relationships aren't forced — they're earned. Slowly. Through professionalism. Through readiness. Through respect for the protocols that signal you actually belong here.

Create Legitimate Points of Contact

Initial connections should happen where they're supposed to happen — not forced. Not awkward. Not desperate.

Workshops. Showcases. Referrals from mutual colleagues. Properly submitted materials. These are the right doors — the ones that stay open once you walk through them the right way.

Think of it this way: a casting director teaching a workshop isn't there to discover clients — they're there to teach. But if you do exceptional work in that room? They remember. An agent accepting submissions isn't likely to sign you on the spot. But strong, polished materials might keep you on their radar when the right showcase invite hits their desk.

Legitimate contact points extend beyond formal setups too — panels hosted by actor organizations, networking events at festivals, post-show introductions when industry people attend your play. These aren't "networking hacks." They're natural, professional spaces where introductions happen without crossing lines.

I always advise actors to develop an annual strategy — not a random hustle, a *plan*.

— Target a few key workshops with casting directors you're aiming to work with.

— Build showcase performances and ensure the right agents are invited.

— Get your face and work into the right rooms at the right festivals.

This isn't spray-and-pray networking. This is methodical champion cultivation. And it works.

Convert Initial Contact to Ongoing Consideration

The gap between initial contact and active championship requires bridge-building — converting one-time interactions into ongoing professional relationships. This delicate process requires patience, appropriate follow-up, and continuous development of your craft and materials.

Appropriate follow-up varies by industry role and relationship context. An agent who expressed interest following a showcase might welcome a quarterly update on significant professional developments. A casting director who responded positively to your audition might appreciate a brief thank-you note without the expectation of a response. A director who worked with you on a small project might value an invitation to subsequent performances.

The consistent element: communication should provide professional value rather than seek immediate opportunity. Updates should focus on meaningful developments (new skills, significant credits, professional transformations) rather than generic check-ins. The goal isn't to maintain constant contact but to demonstrate ongoing professional growth that makes you increasingly valuable to potential champions.

I recommend that actors maintain a detailed contact management system to track interactions with potential champions, appropriate follow-up timeframes, and specific developments worth sharing with particular industry segments. This systematic approach prevents both over-communication that becomes intrusive and under-communication that allows promising connections to fade.

Recognize and Nurture Emerging Champions

Champions rarely announce themselves as such — they demonstrate advocacy through actions rather than declarations. Learning to recognize these signals allows you to nurture emerging champions appropriately:

- An agent who provides detailed feedback on your materials rather than generic encouragement
- A casting director who brings you in for projects beyond your existing credits
- A director who mentions future projects during current work
- A producer who discusses your range beyond your immediate role

These behaviors indicate a professional who sees not just your current value but your potential — the foundation of a champion relationship. When these signals emerge, nurture developing championship through exceptional reliability, consistent artistic growth, and professional reciprocity. Champions invest in talent that consistently rewards their advocacy with excellent work. They withdraw support from actors who prove unreliable, stagnant, or ungrateful regardless of talent.

Professional reciprocity doesn't mean transactional exchanges but genuine mutual support. When a champion's advocacy leads to an opportunity, deliver work that validates their judgment. Express appreciation specifically and sincerely without excessive effusiveness. Demonstrate that their investment in your career produces tangible professional benefits for them as well — better performances, smoother production experiences, and successful creative outcomes.

Maintaining Your Champions Network: The Long Game

Building your network is just the beginning — maintaining these advocacy relationships requires ongoing attention and reciprocity:

Champions invest in potential as much as current capability. Demonstrate ongoing development through training, creative projects, and expanding your range. Update champions appropriately on significant growth without overwhelming them with details of every workshop or class.

This growth should respond to champion-specific professional contexts. For agent champions, development might focus on expanding marketable skills that increase bookable categories. For casting director champions, growth might emphasize a range that qualifies you for broader consideration. For director champions, development might explore creative approaches that align with their artistic sensibilities.

The most effective professional development responds directly to feedback from existing champions. When an agent suggests a specific skill would expand your marketability, prioritize that development and document your progress. When a casting director notes a limitation that prevents broader consideration, address that specific area. This responsive growth demonstrates both professionalism and authentic interest in building mutually beneficial relationships.

Practice Reciprocal Advocacy

When appropriate, become a champion for your champions. Recommend exceptional agents to colleagues seeking representation. Express appreciation for casting directors when speaking with directors and producers. Support projects involving your director champions even when you're not personally involved. These gestures of reciprocal advocacy strengthen professional bonds beyond transactional relationships.

Reciprocity extends beyond verbal support to substantive professional contributions. Actors with producing capabilities can create opportunities for directors who have championed them. Performers with teaching platforms can invite casting champions to conduct workshops. Established actors can suggest promising emerging talents to agents who have supported their careers. These substantive exchanges transform purely self-interested connections into a genuine professional community.

Recognize When Championship Evolves

Championship naturally evolves throughout careers. An agent perfectly suited to launching your career might not be ideal for its next phase. A casting director who championed you for co-star roles might not see you in leading parts despite your growth. Evaluating these relationships periodically allows you to recognize when certain champions no longer serve your evolution or reinvention and when new advocacy relationships need development.

These transitions require careful handling. Leaving a former champion who launched your career for more prestigious representation without appropriate acknowledgment and gratitude creates an industry reputation for disloyalty that can undermine future championship development.

Strategic actors manage these transitions with transparency, genuine gratitude, and appreciation for the foundational support while clearly communicating your professional needs that necessitate change.

I advised an actor contemplating leaving a longtime agent who had secured his initial breakthrough opportunities but now seemed unable to advance his career to the next level. Rather than an abrupt departure, we developed a professional transition strategy. It began with an open conversation acknowledging the agent's crucial early advocacy while honestly and respectfully discussing current limitations, exploring supplementary representation options before a complete separation, and crafting appropriate industry messaging emphasizing the agent's value and importance to his career growth. This careful transition preserved a valuable industry relationship and friendship while allowing the actor his needed career evolution.

The Ultimate Outcome: A Self-Sustaining Career Ecosystem

A fully developed champions network doesn't just open doors; it builds something larger. It creates a self-reinforcing ecosystem of opportunity.

Your agent champions secure auditions with casting director champions, who recommend you to director and producer champions, who in turn begin to create roles with you in mind. Each successful collaboration strengthens these relationships while attracting new advocates — people who notice and want to get involved. Over time, what began as isolated professional connections becomes an interconnected network, a career architecture that supports itself.

But none of this happens overnight. It's built over years — through consistent excellence, strategic relationship development, and, above all, professional integrity. Once established, though, it creates a level of sustainability that transcends the randomness of individual bookings. Your career no longer hinges on a single job, a single season, or a single agent. It becomes about the system you've built — a living ecosystem of people invested in your continued success.

The actors who build this kind of ecosystem live a different career reality than equally talented actors who do not have one. They're not endlessly chasing auditions. They receive calls directly — projects shaped around their strengths, offers made without auditions. Their agents aren't just submitting them into the chaos; they're creating opportunities before the breakdowns even go out. Their champions work *with* them — not just for them — and that changes everything.

But it's important to understand: this isn't about making your success someone else's responsibility. Real champions don't sign up to carry you. They sign up to build *with* you. They want to be proud they recognized you early — proud they brought your talent to the table, that they helped launch something real. It's a co-creative relationship. They invest their influence and reputation in you — not out of charity, but because your success reflects back on them. When you make good on that early belief — when you deliver, when you grow — they don't just support you; they *share* in your victories. And if you understand that, you treat the relationship differently — with respect, with gratitude, and with the work ethic that shows you're aware of what it cost them to bet on you in the first place.

The champion-building approach ultimately transforms how you experience the profession itself. Acting stops being a solitary hustle and becomes a collaborative, reciprocal ecosystem. Your wins fuel their goals. Their advocacy advances yours. It stops being about scarcity — about fighting for scraps — and becomes about building mutual value. Not just a more sustainable career, but a more fulfilling professional life.

I've watched this transformation happen again and again across decades of industry work. Actors who see their careers as isolated pursuits — one audition, one project, one shot at a time — usually end up stuck. Anxious. Frustrated. No matter how talented they are, they can't build momentum because they're always starting over.

The ones who build champion ecosystems — deliberately, strategically — transition over time. They stop being perpetual applicants. They become collaborators. Partners. Their careers aren't just more stable; they're more interesting, more creative, and more alive. Because the champions around them create space for the actor's specific strengths, rather than forcing them to squeeze into the mold of what's already been done.

And none of it replaces craft. None of it diminishes the work. In fact, it's the opposite — it creates the conditions where the work can actually *matter*. Where your talent isn't just admired but employed. Where your voice isn't just heard but sought out. Where your career can absorb the inevitable shocks and changes of this business — because you're not standing alone.

This isn't selling out.
This is how art survives.

PART III

THE CRAFT
& THE CREATION

Blueprint to Living Character

Now that we've laid the historical foundation and acknowledged the realities of the industry, we turn toward the heart of the actor's journey — the craft itself. This is where aspiration becomes discipline, and inspiration gives way to method.

This section offers a comprehensive set of tools and techniques designed to sharpen your instrument, build dimensional characters, create authentic relationships on screen or stage, and prepare for the uniquely high-stakes environment of auditions. But more than that, it offers a roadmap for navigating the evolving landscape of modern performance, where internal life must be made visible, where the camera now captures thought itself, and where audiences possess an almost uncanny ability to detect falsehood.

The demands of contemporary acting have shifted. It's no longer about projecting emotion — it's about revealing thought. The actor's task today is to make the invisible visible, to show the thinking behind the intention, and to embody characters in a way that feels spontaneous yet precise.

The techniques shared in the chapters ahead adapt classical methods to meet these modern expectations. They emphasize a granular, thought-based approach to acting — one that builds each choice from the inside out, while grounding it in physical truth. Each chapter builds upon the last, creating a layered toolkit designed to support truthful human behavior under imaginary circumstances.

This is not about tricks. It's not about shortcuts. It's about the disciplined development of a responsive, flexible instrument — one that can meet the demands of any scene or story with nuance, clarity, and depth. It's about creating characters so thoroughly inhabited they feel as if they've broken free of your conscious control. About forging relationship dynamics so real, the audience forgets they're watching fiction.

This is where mechanics meet mystery. Where the technical meets the transcendent. Where preparation enables spontaneity, and spontaneity becomes inevitable. Where truth arrives not from planning alone, but from living fully in the unrepeatable now.

Every concept presented here is grounded in application. These are not theoretical musings, but practical, trainable principles. Each technique is paired with exercises — ones you can do immediately, either solo or with a partner. Because theory without practice is a closed loop. These chapters demand implementation. They ask you to risk. To fail. To get messy. And to grow.

Welcome to the work.

CHAPTER 5

THE ACTOR'S INSTRUMENT & THE TOOLKIT

Author's Note:

Beginning in the second half of the book, I'll occasionally pause the narrative to offer specific tools or exercises that have proven useful to the actors I've worked with. These aren't assignments or checklists. They're practical suggestions — things you can try if they serve the work.

They're not all mine. Many are drawn from other teachers, disciplines, and rooms I've learned in along the way. Take what's useful. Leave what isn't. They're here if you want them.

The Complete Arsenal

E very carpenter has a box of tools. Every surgeon arranges instruments with ritual precision before the first cut. Painters don't guess which brush will hold the line; they reach instinctively for the right one, without thinking, without hesitation.

And you? What's in your kit?

What do you carry into the audition room, into rehearsal, onto the set when the cameras roll and the silence thickens? What do you bring when the room gets small and the lens comes closer than you expect?

Here's the question most actors never ask: Are your tools built for now? Or are you still hauling around implements of another era — polished, familiar, but outdated? A style forged for prosceniums and projection, not for pixels and tight frames.

The lens has changed.

The camera of 2025 doesn't see the way the one your teachers trained on did. It reads the smallest flicker of doubt in your eye, the breath that catches in your chest before a decision, the slight shift in tempo when your thoughts change course.

It captures thought itself. That's the new stage.

Today's lens doesn't crave performance. It craves presence. It doesn't reward demonstration — it rewards discovery.

The tools themselves haven't changed — your body, voice, emotional access, imagination. They remain the core of the craft. But how we use them has evolved dramatically. It's like comparing a surgeon from the 1950s with a contemporary counterpart. Both use scalpels. But the modern surgeon uses that same basic tool with a different understanding, a different precision, informed by decades of technological advancement and a deeper knowledge of the human body.

The same is true for actors. The fundamental instruments — body, voice, emotional life — haven't changed, but the way we apply them must reflect the medium's current demands. Actors who haven't updated their application find themselves at a disadvantage, no matter how much raw talent or classical training they bring with them.

I've seen incredibly skilled actors — deeply trained, fully committed — come up against unexpected resistance in modern productions. Not because they lacked talent. Not because their training was wrong. But because the tools they were using hadn't been recalibrated for the medium.

The actor with extraordinary stage vocal technique finds that same power reads as overbearing in a close-up. The performer trained in beautifully composed stage movement suddenly feels stiff under the lens. The emotionally immersive actor who thrives in long, uninterrupted scenes has to adjust when the shot is tight, the pacing fragmented, and the performance needs to reset with mechanical precision, again and again.

It's not failure. It's friction.

Same instruments. Different context.

Same tools. Wrong application.

As mentioned earlier, we are living in the age of micro-expression. Performances must be granular, internal, alive beneath the surface of the skin. If your toolkit still leans on the tricks designed for the back row, you're shouting in a library.

The medium has shifted. You have to shift with it.

Think of yourself as a fighter — not in a cage, but under a lens. You need tools from multiple disciplines: the calm internality of Strasberg, the instinctive reactivity of Meisner, the embodied presence of Hagen, the spontaneous freedom of Spolin. You're not choosing one — you're training them all. Because when it matters most, the camera doesn't care what method you studied — it only captures what is real.

The Mixed Martial Arts analogy isn't casual. It's deliberate. Early MMA fighters were single-discipline purists — boxers, wrestlers, jiu-jitsu specialists — and it eventually became apparent that most could be beaten by fighters who blended these disciplines. Fighters who took the best from everywhere and discarded the rest. The ones who adapted endured.

Actors are no different. We sure as hell are fighters — and we've got the scars and bruises to prove it.

Those trained exclusively in a single methodology — pure Strasberg, orthodox Meisner, strict Adler — often find themselves outshone by actors who have synthesized multiple traditions. The psychological depth of Strasberg, the immediacy of Meisner, the sociological insight of Adler, the physical economy of Lecoq — each tradition offers tools for different challenges.

The versatile actor doesn't pledge allegiance to a method, a guru, or a lineage. They gather what's useful, let the rest go, and shape a toolkit built on practice, not religion. They don't cling to dogma. They adapt. Because they know that every role requires something different, and the tools must often adapt to meet the moment.

Over time, my approach has become deliberately mixed — what I call the Mixed Martial Arts of Acting. The goal is simple: to give you the most effective tools in the quickest, clearest way possible, so you can deliver when it counts.

The tools haven't changed — body, voice, emotional access — but their application has.

The volume has been turned down. The externals have been restrained. What is loud now *is the interior life* — the thing you almost say but don't, the breath you hold, and why.

We are no longer performing for the rafters. We are inviting the lens inside.

What we often call traditional training tends to break the work into silos — each skill set developed in isolation, without considering the larger question: how does it all come together when the camera rolls? The result? Technically strong actors who struggle when it counts. Not because they lack ability, but because no one showed them how to adapt the tool to the medium. Effective training integrates instrument development along with application awareness.

Voice training must go beyond projection and articulation — it must include microphone technique and the conversational immediacy required for close-up work. Movement training must go beyond stage presence and broad gestures — it must build the subtle, micro-movements that read on screen. Emotional work must do more than unlock feeling — it must teach the precision necessary to calibrate those feelings to different shot sizes and performance demands.

So again — what's in your kit?

What do you actually bring to the role, beyond instinct and hope?

An actor without a toolkit leans on luck. And luck is lovely — until it isn't.

Talent might get you through the door. But tools — sharpened, reliable, repeatable tools — are what will keep you there.

And nothing serves you longer, or better, than *range*.

Range is what lets you pivot — from drama to comedy, from stillness to volatility, from the tight frame of a two-camera sitcom to the intimacy of a streaming close-up. It's the difference between being cast in one kind of role... and being called back for ten more, each one a little further from the last.

The more instruments you master, the more lives you can inhabit. The deeper your control, the wider your range. And over time, that range becomes your creative freedom — and your career insurance. It keeps the work from going stale. It keeps *you* from being boxed in.

This isn't about technique for technique's sake. It's not polish. It's not perfection. It's about problem-solving — in real time, under pressure, with no margin for error.

Can you hit the emotional beat on cue?
Can you find the pivot in the scene without pushing?
Can you do it again — and again — while staying connected, spontaneous, true?

That's what craft does. That's what builds range.
Not inspiration.
Preparation.

The industry constantly presents technical challenges that untrained actors can't reliably solve. An actor might be asked to summon tears on command across multiple takes and angles. The untrained performer may find the emotion once, but struggle to replicate it. A trained actor with emotional access techniques can deliver steady emotional truth, again and again, giving the editor the coverage needed to construct the scene.

Or consider a scene requiring precision — hitting marks, coordinating business, maintaining pace — all while sustaining an authentic emotional state. I still remember a scene early in my career: in the middle of a long dialogue, I casually unwrapped a piece of gum, popped it in my mouth, spit it out, lit a cigarette. It felt so natural. I remember thinking how cool it was going to look on screen — right up until the director yelled, *"Cut!"* "Nice work," he said. "Now can you do that fifteen more times, at the same dialogue point, so we can get all the coverage?"

I believe the words running through my head were, *"Oh, shit."*

Needless to say, all my interesting, natural business never made the final cut.

The undertrained actor — as I was then — might deliver authentic moments, but miss the technical marks that make a scene usable. A fully trained actor, equipped with both emotional access and technical precision, delivers both.

These aren't hypothetical challenges. They are the daily realities of the craft.

The most authentic performance means nothing if it doesn't meet technical requirements. The most technically precise performance is hollow if it lacks emotional truth. An effective toolkit must address both — simultaneously.

As I've said endlessly, every great actor has great range. But don't mistake range for variety alone. It isn't just the ability to play ten different roles — though that's part of it. It's the ability to play one role with ten different layers, each integrated with your sharpest tools.

You work to broaden your range not just to serve the role — but to serve your own growth. Even to deepen the role you play in life.

Range isn't about showing off. It's about showing up — fully, deeply, truthfully.

It's not luxury. It's necessity.

The Body — Your First Instrument

Mastery begins with the first tool.
Your body.

Physical transformation doesn't happen through guesswork. It requires structured exploration — a consistent, principled approach to expanding your expressive range. Several methodologies offer this kind of roadmap: Laban Movement Analysis, Michael Chekhov's Psychological Gesture, Lecoq's movement dynamics, and the Feldenkrais Method. These aren't theoretical or abstract techniques — they are practical systems designed to move you beyond your habitual gestures and into a more nuanced, embodied craft.

One of the most effective ways I've found to begin this process is by working through a series of core physical oppositions — contrasting qualities that exist along a spectrum. These oppositional forces form the foundation of physical characterization. When explored intentionally, they reveal a wide array of physical states and movement styles that open the door to deeper, more truthful transformations.

Here are six foundational continua I introduce when building a character from the body outward:

Vertical vs. Horizontal — Does the character lift and contain their energy upward through the spine, or do they spread laterally into space with grounded, open movement?

Central vs. Peripheral Initiation — Is movement generated from the core — the chest, pelvis, and spine — or does it spark from the extremities, like fingers, toes, or head?

Bound vs. Free Flow — Are gestures tightly controlled and measured, or loose, relaxed, even chaotic?

Advancing vs. Retreating — Does the character lead into space assertively, or do they yield and withdraw, minimizing their presence?

Sustained vs. Quick Tempo — Do movements unfold slowly and thoughtfully, or arrive in sharp bursts of rapid action?

Strong vs. Light Weight — Is the character heavy in their impact, grounded and firm, or light in their step, drifting, buoyant?

By exploring these contrasts — not just once but as an ongoing physical practice — you begin to build a wider range. You break free from your default physical identity. Character work moves beyond superficial gestures and becomes a coherent, embodied reality. The broader your range, the more detail and variation you can bring to every role. Even when playing close to type, your previous physical explorations enrich your performance — subtly, unconsciously. They live in your breath, in the weight of your stillness, in the way you inhabit space.

Even performances that appear effortless or "natural" benefit from this kind of training. Take Jennifer Lawrence in *Winter's Bone*. Her character is shaped by poverty, hardship, and rural isolation — a life very different from her own. Yet nothing feels put on. The authenticity of her performance emerges from grounded, specific physical choices: the way her shoulders are set, the measured rhythm of her walk, the rooted tone of her voice. These are not gestures. They are traces of a lived-in physical life — fully integrated.

Think of a cat stalking a bird. Every movement is precise, efficient, and committed. There's no waste — no separation between thought and action. That's what we're after in performance. Not behavior that's performed, but behavior that is physically inevitable.

That level of integration — where the body is no longer performing the character, but *has become* the character — is the true aim of physical training. You're not showing a physicality. You're inhabiting it so completely that transformation becomes unconscious. Look at Daniel Day-Lewis in *There Will Be Blood* or *Lincoln*. His physicality changes not only his posture and gesture, but the very rhythm of how he moves through space. He's not just playing someone different — he's living inside a new physical identity. And we feel it.

But this isn't limited to overt transformations. Frances McDormand in *Nomadland* barely shifts physically, yet every motion carries the weight of a lifetime of quiet labor. Mahershala Ali in *Moonlight* crafts three versions of the same character at different ages — not through costume or makeup, but through minute, precise modulations in how that body holds presence. These aren't performance tricks. They're physical truths, embedded in the work.

What all of these performances share is this:
The physical choices have disappeared.
What's left is presence.
A fully realized body shaped by history, belief, trauma, memory, and time.

That's your goal. Not to show a character, but to become one — from the inside out, and from the ground up.

The Voice — Your Second Instrument

You've heard them. Voices that stop the air cold. James Earl Jones, rumbling like distant thunder. Meryl Streep, with that precise, almost musical cadence. Alan Rickman — velvet and menace wrapped around each syllable.

These voices didn't just happen. They weren't gifted and left untouched. They were trained. Tuned. Refined over time.

And yet, something's changed.

The camera no longer wants the same vocal performance it once did. We're in a new era — one where whispers carry more weight than declarations. Where the space before the line often means more than the line itself. Dialogue today has to feel necessary, not theatrical. It has to emerge, not announce.

That doesn't make voice work less important. It makes it more exacting.

The tools remain the same — pitch, tone, rhythm, articulation, resonance. But how those tools are used has changed. Modern work asks for intimacy. It asks for vocal detail that doesn't sound like technique. The craft hasn't loosened — it's sharpened.

Listen to the actors shaping this moment. Jeremy Strong as Kendall Roy — halting, broken, thoughts arriving mid-sentence. Ayo Edebiri's Sydney in *The Bear* — clipped, tightly modulated, always holding something back. Or Barry Keoghan in *Saltburn* — Dominic's voice constantly edging between apology and threat, saying more in his pauses than in his lines.

These actors have tuned their voices to the intimacy of the lens. They understand the audience is often just inches away — watching on laptops, phones, through headphones. Performance today lives in the smallest shifts. Not the stage. Not the projection. Not the performance of voice, but the internal ripple behind it.

Still — the moment you speak, your voice reveals worlds.

One breath can betray everything — background, education, emotion, trauma. That regional sound you thought you'd outgrown? It slips back in under stress. That vocal fry that creeps in when you're tired? It speaks a vulnerability you didn't mean to share. The voice leaks information constantly.

These vocal patterns run deeper than habit. They're tied to physiology, region, identity. Real voice work begins with awareness — not general impressions like "I'm articulate" or "I speak well," but a more honest scan of what your voice actually does when you're not monitoring it.

One of the more useful practices I ask actors to work with is a personal vocal inventory. It's not about judgment. It's about clarity. Specific awareness of how your voice moves when you're not trying to shape it. That includes:

- **Pitch** — your default speaking range, whether you live high in your register or too low, and how easily you shift up or down
- **Resonance** — where your sound naturally sits (head, chest, mask, throat), and how flexible that placement is
- **Articulation** — common tendencies in how you form words, including any regional shapes or muscular tightness
- **Rhythm** — how you pace thought and speech, where you naturally pause, and how you handle emphasis

- **Breath** — where it lives in your body, whether you push or collapse under stress, and how you manage support

You can't change what you can't feel. This kind of mapping gives you a starting point — a personal blueprint for transformation.

Because like the body, your voice contains far more potential than you use day to day.

It begins with pitch. Pitch is emotional. A subtle lift can turn certainty into insecurity. A drop can close the conversation. Watch political speakers — they lower pitch to claim authority. Watch animated characters — pitch is used like color to draw out feeling. And in between these poles is a nuanced world of emotional range.

But most actors operate inside too narrow a slice. Not because of physical limitations, but psychological ones. Fear of sounding too soft, too assertive, too emotional. Men often avoid their upper register. Women avoid dropping too low. And entire characters — full worlds of possibility — get lost in those avoidances.

Volume matters too, but not the way most people think.

It's not about being louder. It's about control. Can you whisper and still be heard? Can you raise your voice and still hold the truth? Can you change the room without raising your pitch? That's where volume becomes story — not volume as power, but volume as intimacy, tension, release.

Too many performances fall into a single default volume — safe, even, forgettable. Real range requires intention. And training.

Modern film and television are merciless in their demands. They require quiet control. Volume that doesn't distort. Clarity under tight acoustic conditions. Performances that feel like secrets — not announcements.

Pace is thought in motion.

Quick speech suggests panic, uncertainty, impatience. Slower pace can signal control — or hesitation. It depends on the weight behind it. Consider Mamet — dialogue that fires out in fragments, colliding mid-thought. Now contrast that with Tennessee Williams — slow, drawn, sentences that feel like they've been carried a long way before being spoken.

Pace reveals how the character thinks — not just how they talk.

And then there's tone.

Tone isn't decoration. It's subtext. It's meaning. The line "I love you" can be delivered as fact, threat, sarcasm, plea — all without changing the words. That's tone. And the camera hears it before the audience does.

Great film actors understand this. They don't just speak the line. They shape the moment before it. The intention behind the intending. The hesitation behind the breath.

Timbre adds even more. The texture of your voice. Its physical character. You can shift it. You've heard it — the husky voice, the soft vocal fry, the tightened throat, the nasal resonance of irritation. Christian Bale shifts timbre across *Batman*, *Vice*, *American Psycho* — same actor, same voice, applied differently.

Michael Caine once said, "Stage acting is talking loud and moving large. Film acting is thinking loud and barely moving at all." It's not about size. It's about compression. Intensity pulled inward.

The voice doesn't just deliver lines. It carries thought. It reveals tension, history, control. It tells us what the character won't say.

So when we work with the voice, it's not just about polish. It's about opening access. Building a bridge between sound and emotion. Breath and impulse. Word and wound.

And on camera — that's what we're really watching.
Not the performance.
But the thought just before it.

Simple Vocal Exercises for On-Camera Presence

These aren't warm-ups for the stage. They're short, targeted behaviors to tune the voice — not perform it. Use them to build awareness, range, and clarity without losing the grounded tone modern film and television demand.

1. The Breath Drop

Purpose: Ground the breath and release unconscious tension.
Sit or stand tall without stiffness. Inhale gently through the nose. Exhale with a relaxed "hah," like fogging a mirror. No push, just release. After a few rounds, add a soft "ah" to the exhale. Let the voice ride the breath without effort.

2. Pitch Slide Humming

Purpose: Unlock range and resonance awareness.
Hum a comfortable note. Glide up and down slowly, like a siren. Let the vibration move — chest, mask, forehead. Don't force pitch. Just feel where the sound naturally wants to go.

3. Text on the Exhale

Purpose: Connect breath to thought to speech.

Take a short, simple phrase — "I don't know," "That's not true," "You sure?" Inhale. Speak the line in one full, natural exhale. No pushing. Repeat it with slightly different internal intentions. Same words — different truth underneath.

4. Consonant Clarity

Purpose: Sharpen articulation without jaw tension.

Try phrases like "bad blood builds boundaries" or "she sells sea shells." Speak slowly, clearly. Keep the jaw loose — let the lips and tongue do the shaping. Go half-speed. Then again at a natural pace. Clear, not crisp.

5. Volume Dial

Purpose: Develop calibrated dynamic control.

Choose a word — "listen" or "wait." Speak it barely audible. Then gradually increase volume in 5–7 steps. Keep emotional tone steady. Don't perform it louder — just own it more fully each time. Stay present, not projected.

Movement and Business: "Doing" Reveals Character

Always begin with movement. Always start with what we call *a piece of business*.

Theory can paralyze. Overthinking kills impulse. You don't need to tell me who your character is. Show me what they do. What they reach for. How they hold things. What they're not even aware of doing. These specific, physical actions say far more than any line of dialogue ever could.

At the foundation of this work is a simple but powerful principle: external behavior reveals internal truth. Not sometimes — always. A character is not who they claim to be, and certainly not who they believe themselves to be. A character is what they do, especially in the moments when no one's watching and the mask is down.

Even something as routine as making a cup of coffee reveals endless variation. A precise, ritualistic character will measure out the beans, time the water, and follow the same steps every morning as if it were a sacred ceremony. Another might forget the water entirely, spill the grounds, change mugs three times, distracted by internal static. One pours to control the world. The other, to survive it. The coffee isn't the point — it's the behavior around the coffee that tells the story.

Uta Hagen called it *The Moment Before*. It's not just an acting theory. It's a lifeline. If a character enters a scene with no history, no residue, the audience senses it. They won't be able to explain what's missing, but they'll feel it — a kind of hollowness, like something got cut from the reel just before the first line. No matter how well delivered that line may be, it falls flat when it isn't built on something that came before it.

This idea extends beyond the first moment of a scene. It applies to the entire physical structure of performance. Characters don't blink into existence when the scene starts. They've been living before we meet them — reacting, hurting, thinking, breathing. That pre-life, whether we see it or not, carries into every gesture, every pause, every adjustment they make in space.

Watch James Dean. In *Rebel Without a Cause*, he walks into the station holding that wind-up monkey. He doesn't make a big show of it. He's not using it as a prop in the theatrical sense. He just holds it. Like it's an extension of whatever turmoil is moving through him. In *Giant*, he enters with a lasso — doesn't twirl it, doesn't perform with it. He just lets it hang, runs it through his fingers, piddles with it like he's working something out in his mind that he can't quite verbalize. These are not actor choices designed to communicate anything to us. They're lived-in behaviors. They carry character.

Brando understood this. In *The Godfather*, when Don Corleone sits behind his desk and rubs his fingers before he speaks, it's not decoration. He's not fidgeting. It's something internal being made physical — almost like he's kneading the thought before releasing it. That tiny moment tells you everything. Power doesn't need to rush.

Philip Seymour Hoffman brought this kind of subtlety to a more modern rhythm. In *The Master*, and again in *Capote*, he creates characters who do almost nothing — on the surface. But then you notice the hands. The breath. The way he presses his fingertips together, or touches an object as if it has weight no one else understands. Often, these behaviors come just before a line. Not by accident. They prepare the body for truth. He doesn't announce internal life — he lets it tremble through.

This is the kind of continuity that creates authenticity. The audience doesn't need to consciously track the details. They don't need to know why a gesture feels right. But they absolutely notice when something feels wrong — when a movement seems borrowed, or disconnected from the truth of the moment.

Think about watching someone slam a car door and stride across a parking lot. You know what just happened. You know what they're carrying. Whether it's rage, heartbreak, urgency, or fear — it's already in their spine. Their trajectory says it all before they even reach the next line of dialogue.

These aren't broad emotional states we're talking about. This is the totality of the character's relationship to their environment. Someone raised with scarcity handles objects differently than someone raised with abundance. Someone raised with violence will scan a room before they speak. They'll angle their body toward the exit. A person trained in ballet won't sit the same way as someone trained in boxing. And they shouldn't. These distinctions don't come from performance. They come from physical biography — from understanding what shaped this body long before page one.

Stillness matters too. But stillness must be earned. Stillness must be charged.

Look at *The Thinker* — that iconic Rodin sculpture. Yes, it's frozen, but it isn't passive. Every muscle is activated. The weight in the pose is deliberate. It vibrates with thought, with internal tension. Stillness like that tells a story.

Same with Anthony Hopkins in *The Silence of the Lambs*. Lecter barely moves, but the stillness is alert. His body is hunting, even while seated. It's not the absence of motion. It's a kind of readiness — stillness as precision, as focus, as danger.

This is where business comes in — the real kind, not the theatrical "add a gesture" kind. The handling of objects, the way characters perform tasks, these things speak volumes. An anxious person doesn't simply pour coffee. They grip the pot too hard. They overfill the cup. Or they clean obsessively. Someone at ease? They move economically, without apology. Same task — wildly different psychology.

What matters is not the action, but the relationship to the action. Two anxious characters can both clean a desk. One might straighten every item obsessively. The other may start the task and then abandon it midway. Both are anxious. But one seeks order, and the other gives up. That's character.

One of the more revealing practices I ask actors to work with outside of our sessions involves performing everyday tasks — folding laundry, cooking a meal, packing a suitcase — while thinking entirely in character. At first, without any lines. Just behavior. No commentary. Let the body lead. Let the nervous system reveal what the character does when no one's watching. That's where the truth begins to surface.

Then, slowly, we begin to integrate the dialogue — layering the lines into those same natural, physical activities. Not for effect, but to uncover how the words live inside the body. You start to find rhythm. You start to find resistance. The lines become organic — not memorized, not performed — but released through action, as they would be in real life.

This is where actors begin to move beyond playing emotional generalities. They begin to discover who the character actually is — not through analysis alone, but through lived behavior. Through how they stand. Through what they reach for. Through the pause that happens before the hand moves.

Don't play it safe. Be specific. Be bold in your prep. The more lived-in the moment before, the more natural the first line becomes. And the less likely you are to fall into that dreaded cold start — the moment when nothing has happened yet and the words come out flat. A rich physical life eliminates that dead space.

And this specificity requires research. Not just understanding your character's backstory, but physically learning the world they inhabit. If you're playing a surgeon, it's not enough to study the script. You need to hold a scalpel correctly. If you're playing a welder, it helps to know how to grip the torch. It's in the body, not the words.

Which is why I encourage actors to develop a physical biography. Not just what the character thinks or wants — but how they move, where they come from, what trained their nervous system. What jobs they've done. What injuries they've carried. What tools feel natural in their hands. Whether they lead with their chest or their hips. Whether they make themselves small when they sit, or take up space instinctively. These aren't embellishments. These are the architecture of believability.

Because character isn't made from dialogue.
It's made from behavior.
And behavior begins — always — with the body.

Internal Dialogue vs. External Expression

Every human being lives two lives at once — the life they speak aloud and the one they keep hidden. The gap between these lives is where drama, irony, and complexity are born. Yet too many actors focus only on what is spoken, leaving the interior landscape undeveloped.

A character's inner monologue runs continuously — evaluating, questioning, judging, reacting. It may contradict the spoken dialogue, elaborate on it, or reveal tensions the words conceal. This internal dialogue creates the rich, subterranean life that makes characters feel three-dimensional.

Modern performance — especially on film — depends on this internal life being visible, even if unspoken. The camera reads thought as easily as it reads action. It captures the slightest flicker of internal conflict — the breath before a lie, the hesitation behind a smile. Audiences may not consciously articulate it, but they feel the presence or absence of a living inner world.

Developing this inner life isn't merely an intellectual exercise. It is imaginative. What is your character thinking that they won't say aloud? What memories are triggered by this conversation? What judgments are they making about the other characters? These thoughts — invisible but persistent — manifest as micro expressions, shifts in breathing, and subtle changes in focus.

Turning internal dialogue into usable performance technique requires methodology. Some effective practices include:

- Scripting precise internal monologues for key moments, creating a word-for-word track of what the character is thinking beneath the dialogue.
- Practicing *parallel awareness* — maintaining real-time attention to scene partners while tracking an internal line of thought.
- Developing *thought triggers* — physical or sensory cues that instantly call up specific thinking patterns.
- Training micro expression control — allowing authentic facial reactions without breaking character or tipping too much to the audience.

The camera captures these details whether you intend it or not. It sees the thinking — or the lack of it — behind your eyes. This is what separates a merely adequate performance from a compelling one: the sense that something real is happening under the surface.

The difference is immediate in a close-up. The actor with an active inner monologue creates the impression of genuine cognition — thoughts forming, emotions rising, decisions being made. The actor without it looks like they're waiting for their next line.

Film acting thrives in this space — between thought and expression. The smallest shift, the slightest hesitation, tells volumes. You don't have to *show* it. You only have to live it. The camera will find it.

This demands a shift in preparation. It's not enough to know what your character wants. You must also know what your character is *thinking* in each moment — and how those thoughts ripple through your body and voice in ways the camera can catch.

Because in film, as in life, what you say is only part of the story.
It's the unspoken — the internal dialogue — that gives the story depth.

Subtext: What Runs Beneath the Words

Harold Pinter understood — perhaps better than anyone — that what characters *don't* say often matters more than what they do. His plays vibrate with menace, tension, and hidden agendas lurking beneath seemingly mundane conversations about tea and the weather.

Subtext — the meaning beneath the text — generates the emotional electricity that drives compelling scenes. It's the unstated current powering exchanges that, on the surface, appear ordinary. Characters may speak about dinner plans while the subtext screams betrayal, longing, or threat.

This dynamic operates far beyond obviously subtext-heavy writers like Pinter. Nearly all dramatic writing carries layers of meaning below the literal. Contemporary performance demands actors who can communicate these multiple layers simultaneously — delivering the surface conversation while revealing the deeper currents through precise vocal inflection, physical choices, and micro expressions.

Finding subtext begins by asking simple but essential questions:
What does my character truly want in this scene?
What are they afraid to reveal?
What past experiences color this present interaction?

The answers build the underground river flowing beneath the words. They generate not a general emotional tone but specific psychological content — the kind that manifests through physical detail. A character avoiding a painful topic might consistently break eye contact, fiddle with objects to distract themselves, or shift their body to create psychological distance. These small, specific behaviors communicate subtext far more effectively than generalized emotional displays.

When you play the subtext rather than just the text, dialogue gains dimension.

"Thank you for coming" might mean:

- I'm relieved you finally showed up.
- I'm surprised you had the nerve to come.
- I wish you'd stayed away, but I'm being polite.
- I've been desperate to see you, but I'm hiding it.

Same words — completely different scenes. The subtext lives in *how* it's said — in tone, timing, stance, glance — not in the words themselves.

Effective subtext work depends on integration. Subtle vocal stress patterns that suggest ironic meaning must align with micro expressions revealing contradictory emotions, supported by physical choices that position the character psychologically. Authentic subtext feels organic because all the performance elements — voice, face, body — are aligned in revealing it without overt demonstration.

Learning to layer subtext without indicating it is the mark of sophistication. The audience should *feel* the undercurrents without seeing you paddle. It's the art of revelation through concealment — showing the truth while the character tries to hide it.

This becomes especially important on camera, where the lens catches the slightest dissonance between what is said and what is meant. In theater, larger physical and vocal choices can externalize subtext; on screen, calibration must be microscopic. The audience watches not only what you say but what you suppress.

Agenda: The Engine of Character Action

Every character wants something. Always.
Agenda — the pursuit of something specific — drives everything a character says and does. Without a clear agenda, characters drift through scenes aimlessly, creating neither conflict nor connection.

Focusing on agenda transforms performance from passive recitation to active pursuit. Traditional character analysis often emphasizes emotional states — he's angry, she's confused, they're in love. Agenda shifts the focus to objectives and strategies — he wants her to confess the affair, she needs him to leave before discovering the evidence, they're competing for the same promotion while pretending to be friends.

Your character's agenda might align with their dialogue or contradict it. They might openly state their objectives or conceal them under social niceties. Regardless, the agenda must be specific, actionable, and have high enough stakes to create tension.
"To be happy" is not an agenda.
"To make him admit he lied about last night" is.

Specificity changes everything. An actor preparing a scene with the vague objective of "seeking approval" delivers a different performance than one who is pursuing "getting this person to acknowledge a particular achievement that validates a deep insecurity." The precise agenda generates tactical choices, clear obstacles, and defined outcomes — all of which drive the performance forward.

Agendas produce active verbs: to persuade, to seduce, to threaten, to comfort, to expose. These verbs energize performance. They push the character into action rather than leaving them passively delivering lines.

And these verbs must be tailored. Not simply "to seduce" but "to regain romantic control after feeling rejected." Not just "to threaten" but "to reestablish dominance without crossing professional lines." Specific agendas create textured, nuanced behavior.

Importantly, agendas shift within scenes. A character who enters wanting forgiveness might, after being rebuffed, pivot toward revenge. These evolving agendas create dynamic, living performances. Static agendas create static scenes.

I train actors to map scenes with possible agenda shifts based on whether the character's initial objectives are met or blocked. This prepares them to respond to the reality of the moment rather than following a rigid emotional arc. It builds *prepared spontaneity* — the readiness to adapt tactics in real time.

The intersection of conflicting agendas creates drama's heartbeat. When two characters pursue incompatible goals, tension arises naturally. There's no need to manufacture conflict — it's baked into the collision of desires.

This approach changes the preparation process. Rather than general emotional mapping, actors break down scenes tactically:
What does my character want right now?
What will they do to get it?
What happens if they don't succeed?

These questions generate playable, specific choices — the kind that create living, breathing human beings on stage or screen.

Caution: The Traps That Swallow Good Actors Whole

Actors sometimes conflate revealing strong emotional depth with being unhinged or angry. They chase the high of a demonstrative release, mistaking its volatility for truth. This isn't the bravery they think it is — rather, it's laziness. The work can't survive if the actor isn't grounded enough to carry the contradictions that we as humans suffer in desperate situations.

...Actors can fall victim to these shortcuts — easy tricks that look like emotion but have no root. The danger is that once these habits set in, they become invisible to the performer. What feels like craft is really just camouflage.

Take one of the most seductive traps: the confusion between showing vulnerability versus playing it. Actors often think fragility means simply exposing weakness — slumping the shoulders, letting the voice break, attempting to hold back a tear. But the strongest choice isn't in revealing emotion too openly. It's in abandoning the logic that underpins the character's goal.

The strongest actors don't perform *collapse*. They play the mission that holds them upright against the tide even as their character falters. It's the sunk cost of their identity — the logic and strategy beneath a trembling surface that keeps the scene thriving. When an actor stays committed to the argument, to the reason their character must press forward, the audience feels the tension of complexity of the two forces colliding: a death grip of control and barely teetering above a point of complete collapse.

When the moment finally arrives to let the emotions flood through, it doesn't dissipate into indulgence — it lands with a devastating impact. Precision in timing, balance of logic and feelings, makes the release of it, unforgettable.

Not because rage lives under the emotion itself, but because the emotion untethered from the character's goal becomes a trap for the actor, who often defaults to weakness and courts self-indulgence. The actor who plays the character's personal logic, the goal, the mission — activates empathy in the mind of the audience, who then leans in... not out.

And that's the point: traps aren't always obvious. They don't always look like "bad acting." Sometimes they feel like effort, intensity or even courage. Which is why you have to guard against this as fiercely as you guard your technique. Because once the trap closes, it narrows your range — and that's the hardest thing for an actor to see from the inside.

Traps don't always announce themselves. Some are loud, blurting out in visible collapse. Others creep in quietly, invisible until the scene is already lost. If collapse is the obvious danger, anticipation is its subtler cousin but just as destructive.

You've seen it.

That moment when a promising scene faulters — not with a bang but with a whimper. The actor who was alive and truthful a moment ago, suddenly stiffens and becomes the "actor" *acting*. The audience drifts. The magic evaporates.

What happened?

False intention, self-awareness — the silent killers of authentic performance.

False intention emerges when the actor's awareness of the scene's structure intrudes on the character's reality. The character doesn't know what happens next. They experience events in real time, responding without foreknowledge. But the actor knows. They've read the script, rehearsed the scene, and this knowledge creates a subtle anticipatory tension. The body betrays it — a slight shift of weight, a microsecond of bracing before the shocking news, a tension that says, "I know what's coming."

This anticipation ruins authenticity.
It feels scripted.
It feels false.

We're trained from a young age to anticipate — to prepare our responses while others are still speaking. It's polite in conversation, deadly in performance.

False intention creeps in especially during emotionally charged moments. Actors brace for the big reveal or prepare the emotional response before the event that should cause it. The audience feels the disconnect instinctively — they may not know why the scene falls flat, but they know it does.

Self-awareness is its twin assassin. It creeps in when the actor's gaze turns inward — not into the private life of the character, but into their own reflection. Instead of being inside the moment, they begin watching themselves perform it. A flicker of thought — *How did that look? Is this the right choice? Was that believable? Here's that line I like. I'll really sell this one.* — and the organic truth of the scene collapses under the weight of all this self-monitoring. The character no longer breathes freely; they are being steered, adjusted and polished in real time. To no avail and to their detriment.

What should be instinctive becomes calculated. What should be alive becomes observed. The body tightens, the voice constricts, the eyes dim with observer evaluation. And the audience feels it. They don't see a human being caught in a moment — they see an actor worried about how the moment plays.

Why does this happen to even skilled actors?

Script-consciousness.

Even with all the training and talent in the world, the temptation to anticipate the next moment can override presence. Rehearsal breeds familiarity; familiarity breeds bad habits.

Tom Hanks probably put it best:

"My job, I figured out a long time ago, was to get beyond self-awareness, because it's the death of acting."

When the actor becomes aware of their own performance, all authenticity dies.

The irony is cruel — as technical skill increases, so does the risk of self-monitoring. Beginners often stumble into truth through naïveté. Experienced actors must work even harder to protect their presence. True mastery is not just technical proficiency — it's the ability to use that technique without becoming self-aware.

The antidote is ruthless presence. **Learn. Practice. Let go.**

True listening is not waiting to speak — it's being surprised by what your scene partner says, even after a hundred rehearsals. It's cultivating *beginner's mind* — approaching each moment as though you don't know what happens next, even though you do.

Practical techniques to avoid false intention/self-awareness syndrome include:

- Focusing deliberately, listening to your partner rather than on yourself
- Locking into immediate sensory reality rather than anticipated dialogue
- Practicing genuine receiving before responding
- Using improvisational exercises with unpredictable outcomes
- Building detailed thought content that fills your focus instead of self-monitoring

Focus on subtext, not delivery.

When your mind drifts to how you'll deliver the next line — that clever pause, the meaningful look you've practiced in the mirror — you've already left the moment. Stay rooted in what your character wants and let the *how* emerge organically from the *why*.

Train yourself to resist anticipation. Wait for the genuine impulse before speaking. Sometimes it means stepping on your partner's line; sometimes it means *leaning to love the pause* — a beat of processing before responding. Let the character's mind, not the actor's memory, dictate the timing.

Technically, this demands full command of your material — it needs to live in you so fully that it becomes automatic. Psychologically, it demands discipline — the ability to remain present in the fictional moment, immune to the pull of self-consciousness.

These are only two examples, but the pattern runs deeper and wider. Every shortcut that masquerades as craft. Whether its anger mistaken for depth or anticipation mistaken for presence, it shares the same root problem: the actor drifting from truth into performative intention. The traps change shape, but the cost is always the same. Once you lose the living moment, the audience knows it... even when they don't know why. Guarding against that loss isn't just about avoiding mistakes — it's about preserving the spark that makes it craft.

Art instead of an artifice.

The Approval/Disapproval Syndrome: The Fear That Kills Creativity

Viola Spolin named it plainly — *The Approval/Disapproval Syndrome*.
The constant internal dialogue of the actor asking: *Am I doing this right? Do they like me?*

This self-evaluation fractures focus.
You become performer and critic at the same time — a divided consciousness that sabotages authenticity.

Physically, it shows up as hesitation, tension, guardedness.
Instead of inhabiting the character's world, you shrink inward, worried about being judged.

This isn't just a beginner's problem.
Even seasoned actors fall into it — especially as careers advance and external pressures mount.
Reviews. Expectations. Comparison to past performances. All of it feeds the approval loop.

The only way out is a fundamental shift — from outcome to process. From impressing to inhabiting.
From self-judgment to full immersion.

Practical techniques for breaking the cycle include:

- Training attention toward your scene partner, away from internal monitoring

- Task-focused improvisation that forces attention onto objectives, not appearances
- Movement-based disciplines like Viewpoints or Lecoq work that anchor attention in physical reality
- Sensory awareness exercises that ground you in the moment rather than in imagined judgment

It's not about abandoning technique.

It's about embedding it so deeply that it disappears. You train endlessly so that in the moment of performance, you forget the training and simply live.

Integration: The Complete Actor

Body. Voice. Business. Internal dialogue. Subtext. Agenda.
These are your tools.

But no single tool makes a performance. Integration does.

True range requires not just strength in one area but mastery across all. Some actors lead with physicality, others with voice, others with emotional accessibility. Complete actors can shift among all these — flexibly, fluidly, invisibly.

Integration doesn't happen by accident. It demands conscious effort, cross-disciplinary training, and the courage to confront your weaknesses.

The complete actor commands all these tools — and yet appears to use none.
The technique becomes invisible. The craft disappears.
All that remains is a living soul, navigating real circumstances.

When the audience forgets they are watching a performance — when they believe completely in the life unfolding before them — then the actor has done their work.

That forgetting — that suspension of disbelief — is what we are always, always after.

Actor-Type Archetypes

This isn't about typecasting. It's about self-awareness and the business side of your product. You.

Understanding the kinds of roles you most naturally gravitate toward — and the kinds you stretch into — isn't limiting. It's strategic. It helps you prepare better, position better, and pivot when the industry shifts under your feet. And it will.

Every actor has patterns. Rhythms. Strengths. Sensibilities. Learning to recognize those in yourself doesn't trap you — it *frees* you. It gives you language for your strengths and insight into how others might perceive you before you even walk into the room. Directors may not always know what they're looking for — until they see it. Your job is to help them see it more clearly.

Below are a few archetypes I've seen emerge again and again in actors with long, varied careers. You may fit one. You may float between a few. Or you may be working toward expanding beyond the one you've always defaulted to. All of that is useful.

The Chameleon

Perhaps the pinnacle and very definition of *craft*. Actors who disappear completely into each role. Physically, vocally, and psychologically unrecognizable from project to project. They live within the transformation.

Examples, to name a few: *Gary Oldman, Cate Blanchett, Daniel Day-Lewis, Johnny Depp, Christian Bale, Meryl Streep, Tilda Swinton.*

The Anchor

Provides emotional gravity and subtlety. Often not the flashiest in the scene, but holds the whole thing together.
Example: John Cazale, Toni Collette

The Disruptor

Brings chaos, unpredictability, and sometimes danger. They break the rhythm of a scene — in the best possible way.
Example: Willem Dafoe, Benicio del Toro

The Everyperson

Relatable. Accessible. The lens through which an audience sees the story. Never "too much." Just human.
Example: Paul Giamatti, Frances McDormand

The Provocateur

Draws attention with intensity — often walking the line between charisma and confrontation. Thrives in friction.
Example: Adam Driver, Viola Davis

The Outsider

Lives just outside the edges of the world — slightly offbeat, haunting, unknowable. Thinks differently, moves differently.
Example: Tilda Swinton, Ezra Miller

The Heartbeat

Connects everything emotionally. Feels everything. Makes others feel it, too. Deeply expressive — even when silent.

Example: Joaquin Phoenix, Claire Foy

None of these types are fixed identities — they're tools. Starting points. Mirrors for reflection. Knowing which you lean toward can help you choose material, sharpen your auditions, and understand your place in an ensemble.

Knowing where you're not, as well as where you are, can show you where to grow.

Self-Assessment: What Type Are You (For Now)?

This isn't a branding exercise.
It's a compass.

Forget typecasting. Forget what your résumé says. Forget the last ten roles you've played. This isn't about externals — this is about your core. Your gravitational pull. The energy you bring into a scene before you even speak. What kind of presence do you have? Not what you want to be. Not what your mind says you *should* be. But what you genuinely bring into the room — naturally, instinctively, involuntarily.

We all have a default charge.
Sometimes it shifts. Sometimes it grounds us.
This is about locating yours.

A Few Questions for You to Consider...

Before you memorize another line... before you hit record on your next self-tape... stop for a moment.

Set the script aside.

Because none of it matters — not really — until you know *what* you're bringing into the room. Into the role. Into the silence between someone else's line and your breath.

So here are a few questions. Not for judgment. Not for branding. Just for *noticing*.

Answer them honestly. Privately. Out loud, even. Don't perform for yourself. Just pay attention to what stirs when you ask:

When you walk into a room — real or imagined — what kind of energy do people pick up on first?

Don't over-analyze. Just feel into it.

- Do people lean in... or take a step back?
- Do you settle the air — or stir it?
- Do you invite trust? Disrupt it? Do you slip under the radar completely, then suddenly reshape the room from the inside out?

Are you calm, magnetic, guarded, volatile, radiant, unknowable?

Not who you perform as — who you *are*, when unguarded.

This is not about charm. It's about charge.

In scenes, do you find yourself pulling focus — or grounding it?

This isn't about stealing attention. It's about *mass*.

- Do you center the moment — or destabilize it?
- Are you the still point... or the spark?
- Do you draw others toward coherence — or do you fracture expectation?

Some actors create gravitational pull. Others create friction. Both are valuable. But which do *you* default toward?

What kinds of roles are you most often cast in — and which ones leave you aching for more?

Be honest.

- What shows up again and again in your auditions or bookings?
- What feels easy? What feels flattening?
- And which roles — even if you've never booked them — make you sit up straighter, feel something electric, something dangerous or intimate or expansive?

There's no shame in patterns. But patterns don't define you. They're just weather. What you ache for — that's geography.

Who are the actors you most admire — and is that admiration aspirational (who you want to be) or familiar (who you already are)?

Look at your idols.
Now separate the admiration.

- Is it awe — or recognition?
- Do you admire their craft... or feel a kinship with their presence?
- Are you chasing their range — or finding a mirror?

The distinction matters. One shows your horizon. The other, your foundation.

When you're not trying to be anything — when you're just present — what kind of character naturally emerges?

Not the one you prep. The one who shows up when you stop pushing.

- Are they careful? Observant? Restless? Aloof? Warm?
- What's their default tempo? Do they fill space... or leave it open?

Sometimes the truest version of your acting self arrives when you stop acting entirely.

That's the core you work from — even when you're building far from it.

Revisit the archetypes

Don't reach. Don't rationalize. Just notice:

- **Which one feels closest to home?**
- **Which one feels like a challenge — or a stretch that excites you?**

This isn't about choosing a brand.
It's about learning your *gravity*.
Knowing where you're strongest — and where you're curious to grow.

You're not stuck in one role forever. But knowing your center gives you something to push off from.
A place to stand, a vector to pivot.
So when the scene begins, or the character pulls you elsewhere — you're not just floating.

You're flying — with purpose.

Different Arenas, Different Rules

But wait, we need to have this conversation...

Truth is, not every acting job demands or should have the same approach. The techniques we've been exploring serve storytelling, character development, and emotional truth — but they're not universal tools for every performance.

Let's be clear about something. Day player work? That's its own animal. So if you're playing "Waitress #2" with one line, or "Security Guard at Door"— production doesn't need your deep character exploration or moment-to-moment emotional vulnerability. They need reliability. Efficiency. Technical precision. Again and again. They need you to hit your mark, deliver your line clearly, match your performance, blocking, timing across takes, and get out of the way of the other characters providing the story being told.

This isn't less valid work. But it's different work.

Same goes for commercials. Commercial acting isn't inferior — it's specialized. Consider Stephanie Courtney's "Flo" from Progressive Insurance... over a decade playing the same character with precise, consistent energy. Or consider Dean Winters as Mayhem for Allstate—same intensity, same timing, same physical vocabulary commercial after commercial. Think about Dennis Haysbert's authoritative voice for Allstate or Jonathan Goldsmith's "Most Interesting Man in the World" for Dos Equis. These performers aren't exploring new emotional terrain each time. They're delivering technically precise, repeatable performances that have become valuable branded intellectual property.

The skills that make these brilliant commercial performers (consistency, technical awareness, ability to deliver identical takes, understanding product messaging) most often interfere with the process we've been discussing for film and television drama.

Commercial directors need performers who can reproduce exact readings and physical movements with machine-like precision. They need actors who understand that the product — not their character's journey — is the star. When Jake from State Farm says, "Uh... khakis?" the delivery needs to be identical every time. When the GEICO Gecko speaks, that specific accent and timing must remain consistent across years of campaigns.

Is this "acting"? Absolutely. Is it the same process I'm advocating for dramatic work? No. Not at all.

The error many actors make is applying dramatic process to commercial work (making themselves difficult and "artsy" in an environment that needs technical efficiency, only.) I've called this out as "acting in their own movie, one that no one cares to see." Or, perhaps worse, give the career stakes, applying their commercial technique to dramatic roles (delivering safe, identical performances when the material begs for risk and discovery).

So, discern which arena you're in. Adjust accordingly.

CHAPTER 6

THE ART OF
CHARACTER CREATION

Building a Living, Breathing Role

A compelling performance is never just about learning lines or hitting marks. It's about building a living, breathing human being with a rich internal world. Not a puppet strung up by craft — but a creature animated by breath, by contradiction, by the pulse of a private unknown desire. Perhaps unknown even to the characters themselves. An accomplished actor doesn't *imitate* the character — they *become* the character by layering psychology, physicality, voice, and personal truth into the role.

This distinction between a false imitation and authentic embodiment separates effective portrayal from superficial performance. Imitation focuses on external indicators — how someone speaks, moves, or expresses emotion. Embodiment creates an internal reality from which authentic behavior *naturally* emerges. The audience doesn't see an actor demonstrating character traits, but witnesses a character existing — made visible through complete behavior.

Consider Daniel Day-Lewis as Daniel Plainview in "There Will Be Blood." The performance isn't a collection of mannerisms or technical choices but complete psychological and physical transformation creating the impression of a human being with specific history, drives, and worldview. Plainview's distinctive speech patterns, physical carriage, and behavioral tendencies emerge not as bolted-on technique but as integrated aspects of the character's absolute being.

But the nature of this transformation has shifted dramatically in recent years.

Where actors once built characters through external indicators — distinctive walks, vocal patterns, physical mannerisms — today's most compelling work happens beneath the surface. The camera no longer needs signposts to understand a character's journey; it reads the microscopic shifts in thought, the private moments between declarations. It sees what you're thinking, *priori*, not what you're doing *posteriori* — which changes everything.

This evolution corresponds directly to changes in both technology and audience sophistication. Ultra high-resolution digital cameras capture detail invisible to previous generations of filmmaking equipment. Viewing platforms bring performances inches from audience's face rather than projected on distant screen. Viewers raised on increasingly complex storytelling have developed heightened sensitivity to performance authenticity, immediately registering false notes or indicated emotion.

The paradox at the heart of contemporary performance: characterization requires more detailed preparation than ever, yet must appear completely unconstructed. The extensive research, physical exploration, and psychological analysis can't become visible as technique but must dissolve into seemingly effortless authenticity. More work, less visible effort.

Contemporary character creation requires an almost archaeological precision in preparation, then given over to absolute spontaneity in execution. It demands all your research, all your choices, all your technique dissolve completely into a seamless being.

As we explore the art of character creation, remember: the end goal isn't to show the audience a perfect construction but to exist so truthfully within it that they forget they're watching a performance. Complete and total suspension of disbelief. And when it works, it's as if the actor has vanished, leaving behind only the pulse of another life — utterly singular, and yet instantly recognizable.

The transformation from actor to character doesn't happen by accident — or by inspiration alone. It begins, always, with questions both big and small. Not the kind that live in your head, but the ones that pull at your body, haunt you a little. The right questions open doors the script only hints at — and the character's life begins. She walks through them, uninvited, unannounced. This is how you provoke something internal — underneath the emotion. This is how you begin to carry around a soul that isn't your own.

The question-based big questions/small questions approach transforms abstract character concepts into a very specific human being. Rather than general character traits ("she's ambitious," "he's insecure"), effective characterization emerges from answers to precise questions generating specific behaviors. Not "What kind of person is this?" but "What exactly does this person want right now? What did they want before this moment? What might they be holding back? What are they willing to do to get it?" Not

"What's their emotional state?" but "What is the specific subtext running through their mind at this moment, and how does that thought physically manifest itself, the moment before the *words*?"

I've emphasized *words* here because, minus Shakespeare and the poets, words are largely the bane of an actor's performance. And nearly every actor becomes burdened by them. Most especially those not as yet skilled enough in their *craft*.

Words are the **final and last** expression of subtext and your internal dialog — not the other way around. If you learn nothing else from this book:

"Words are the residue. The echo. The last thing that happens. Not the first.
Subtext speaks long before the mouth opens.
Learn this —
Find the pause.
The hush.
That strange, electric stillness before the thought has shape —
where the soul waits in the wings.
That's where the work begins.
Not with the line...
— but with the life behind it."
— Jim Blumetti, The Alchemy of Acting

We don't begin with speech. We begin with stillness.
Before the line, there's a flicker — an impulse, a memory not our own.
It trembles beneath the ribcage, behind the eye, just at the edge of breath.
This is the actor's true entry point.
Not the words... but what's beneath them.
That restless thing unsaid.

When you learn to dwell there — to let it churn before it surfaces — you stop performing.

You begin being.

Questions. They create avenues for exploration rather than fixed outcomes. They generate possibilities rather than predetermined conclusions. They encourage discovery rather than implementation of a preconceived idea. This open-ended approach creates space for character to emerge organically rather than imposed through forced technical decisions.

Emotion. What is it anyway? It's not just a feeling — when we look deep, it's a physiological storm, an embodied response to stimulus that bypasses intellect and courses through the bloodstream. Psychology identifies it as a set of primary emotions: joy, sadness, fear, anger, disgust, and surprise. Others expand that into gradients — serenity to ecstasy, annoyance to rage, interest to vigilance. These aren't just words. They're temperatures that shift the body. They change the breath, the skin, the voice. And they show up — uninvited and unannounced — That is, when the work is honest, truthfully.

This physiological understanding transforms emotional performance from conceptual to embodied. Effective character building includes specific attention to how particular emotions manifest physically in this specific person. Some people express anger through immediate verbal aggression, others through physical stillness containing barely controlled tension, others through passive-aggressive behavior that disguises hostility beneath friendly surface. These aren't arbitrary acting choices but expressions of character's particular psychology and history — their learned patterns for processing and expressing emotional states.

Most actors rush straight to emotion — desperate to feel something, anything that might pass for authentic experience. They dive into scenes without maps, without compasses, without the faintest idea of the territory they're meant to inhabit. Then they wonder why their performances feel generic, untethered, floating in theatrical limbo.

Premature emotional focus creates superficial characterization. Without specific understanding of who this person is, what drives them, what they're fighting for or against, emotional choices become generalized and non-specific. The audience sees actor emoting rather than character experiencing authentic response to specific circumstances.

The questions change everything.

Not the intellectual exercise of asking them — that's just the beginning — but the visceral exploration they initiate. Each question opens a door to lived experience, to specific choices, to the thousand details that make a character breathe rather than merely speak.

Every character carries history. Desires. Flaws. Contradictions. Lives within specific world — surrounded by specific people, shaped by specific wounds. Your job? Not to play an idea. To become them. Know them better than they know themselves. This demands preparation... Mental investment. Physical commitment. Emotional archaeology. Digging until knuckles bleed.

The archaeological metaphor isn't just colorful language but precise description of character development process. Like archaeologist uncovering artifact, actor must carefully remove layers of generalization and assumption to reveal specific human being beneath. This requires patience, precision, and willingness to discard preconceptions when evidence suggests different truth than initially assumed.

Finding the Character Through Autobiography

Start with the character autobiography — not as a rote exercise, but as ritual embodiment. Write it in the first person. Let them tell you who they are, in their own voice. Don't just list facts — listen for what they emphasize, what they skip, where they fumble. The omissions often reveal more than the confessions. Then speak it aloud. Let their rhythm find you. Do they speak in short, clipped bursts? Or ramble nervously? Do they pause to choose words — or do the words spill out faster than thought? Listen for the music underneath the meaning. That's where you begin to hear the soul.

The first-person approach transforms intellectual understanding into embodied knowledge. Writing as the character rather than about them creates experiential shift from analysis to identity. The rhythm, vocabulary, syntax that emerges in this exercise reveals aspects of character psychology that intellectual analysis might miss. Speaking the autobiography aloud makes this understanding physical — breath patterns, vocal placement, physical impulses that accompany specific content all provide embodied information beyond purely mental comprehension.

Cover major life events, relationships, fears, dreams, motivations. Include sensory details — what sounds, smells, textures, and tastes have shaped this person? When writing, don't think like a writer crafting a character. Think like the character crafting their own narrative — with all their blind spots, self-deceptions, and deeply held truths. What would they emphasize? What would they avoid discussing? These choices reveal as much as the content itself.

The autobiography becomes more valuable for what it reveals between the lines than direct statements. Character who spends three paragraphs justifying behavior that requires no justification reveals defensive psychology regardless of content. Person who describes traumatic event in clinical, detached language demonstrates specific coping mechanism more significant than event itself. Individual who emphasizes external achievements while avoiding any mention of emotional life reveals specific relationship with vulnerability more telling than accomplishments listed.

Autobiography transcends backstory. Foundation of living consciousness. First step toward seeing through different eyes... breathing through different lungs. Some actors resist. Too intellectual, they claim. Too removed from instinct. Wrong. Dead wrong. Autobiography isn't literary exercise — it's doorway. Portal into embodiment. Not writing... becoming. As you write, you'll find yourself adopting the character's thought patterns, their emotional responses, their way of framing experience. The writing itself becomes an act of transformation.

The Method's Inner Exercises: Finding Truth in Stillness

While this external exploration lays crucial groundwork for your character, the true power of performance emerges from the stillness between actions — from the quality of thought that precedes speech, from the internal life that animates every gesture and choice. This is where many actors struggle most: accessing the internal subtext and quiet consciousness that naturally lives within us all.

Many actors struggle with accessing internal subtext and the stillness that naturally lives within our consciousness. They rush. They fill. They do — often out of fear. Fear of forgetting the words. Fear of the void. Fear of what might emerge if they simply... wait.

Yet when we truly speak — when actual human beings form thoughts into language — our words bubble up from a quiet place within us. They aren't manufactured. Aren't forced. They rise to the surface only after we give them permission to escape.

These micro-moments, just before handing thought over to voice, contain everything. The hesitation. The search. The decision to speak or remain silent. This is where truth lives. Where performance dissolves into being.

Some of the most compelling actors command attention with little to no movement. Think of Anthony Hopkins in "The Silence of the Lambs." Meryl Streep in "The Devil Wears Prada." Daniel Day-Lewis in "There Will Be Blood." Their stillness creates gravitational pull. Draws us in. Forces us to lean forward, to search their faces for hints of what churns beneath.

This presence, this gravitas, comes from something deeper than technique. It emerges from subtext and focus — from the thoughts that precede words, from the decision to withhold rather than express.

Try this: Stand completely alone. In front of a mirror. Begin to perform your favorite monologue.

It's wise to have at least three strong monologues in your back pocket — ready to perform at any moment should opportunity present itself. And seek out these opportunities when you can as often as possible, in front of situations that put you under pressure or can open doors to new possibilities.

Now take exceptionally long pauses wherever and whenever you can. Fill these with what we call "business." And when doing so, search for something deep from within your character's past. Not your past — your character's. Something you need to discover and fit within this pause before you speak.

Learn to embrace the pause.

Find an internal stillness before you speak. When you are ready to deliver your line... don't. Not yet. Stutter. Breathe. Scratch. Move. Grind your teeth. Learn to be comfortable in discomfort. Completely relaxed in tension.

Become completely self-absorbed, not self-aware. There's a crucial difference. Self-awareness creates the split consciousness that kills truthful performance — one part performing, another part monitoring. Self-absorption means disappearing into the character's reality so completely that your consciousness becomes theirs.

Focus all your energy on intention and internal stakes. What does your character want? Why does it matter so desperately? Let these questions consume you until the words become inevitable — not recited but expelled as the natural consequence of internal pressure.

Observe how stillness can be more powerful than excessive movement. How a subtle shift in focus draws the eye more effectively than broad gesture. How the thought that precedes the line creates more tension than the line itself.

In film and television especially, these micro-moments become macro on screen. The camera catches everything — the fleeting doubt, the momentary decision, the thought half-formed before words give it shape. What feels like nothing to you reads as everything to the audience.

The exercises of the Method aren't just about emotional memory or sensory work. They're about creating the conditions for authentic being. For dropping into a reality so completely that words emerge naturally from the character's consciousness, not the actor's memory.

This requires a paradoxical kind of discipline — structured improvisation, controlled spontaneity. You must know your lines so thoroughly that you can forget them. Must prepare so extensively that you can abandon preparation. Must analyze so deeply that analysis dissolves into instinct.

Most actors rush to fill silence. They treat pauses as empty space rather than pregnant possibility. They speak to fill the void rather than allowing tension to build until words become necessary.

Try this variation: Take a monologue you know intimately. Perform it at half speed, doubling the length of every pause. Notice how this changes the subtext. How it forces you to live in the spaces between words. How it creates room for thought to become visible.

Now try it again, but this time, find a specific memory or image that belongs to your character during each pause. Something that justifies the silence. That makes the pause not empty but full. Not an absence but a presence.

This is where the most compelling work happens — in these moments of apparent nothing that contain everything. In the breath before the confession. In the hesitation before the lie. In the silence that follows the revelation.

The Russian director Konstantin Stanislavski once said, "Silence is the loudest noise in the theater." He understood that what happens in stillness often carries more weight than what happens in action. That the spaces between words often reveal more truth than the words themselves.

This approach connects directly to the character work we've been exploring. All that preparation — the autobiography, the relationship mapping, the objective analysis — it creates the rich internal landscape that fills these moments of stillness. Without that foundation, pauses become merely technical. With it, they become revelatory.

Building the Character's Universe

Try speaking the autobiography aloud once it's written.

Notice how the character's natural speech patterns emerge — their rhythms, their vocabulary, their particular way of organizing thoughts. These patterns contain the seeds of the character's inner monologue — that constant stream of consciousness that runs beneath their spoken words. The greater the gap between this internal world and their external expression, the more complex and compelling the performance becomes.

The spoken autobiography reveals physical dimension of character's self-expression — tension patterns that manifest during specific topics, breath changes that accompany emotional content, gestural vocabulary that emerges naturally from character's psychology rather than imposed physical choices. These embodied discoveries provide foundation for physical characterization that emerges organically from specific psychology rather than applied mannerisms.

As this foundation takes shape, you begin asking deeper questions — the ones that define your character's place in the universe.

Who Surrounds Them?

Not just character names from the script — living souls with histories, with agendas that help or hinder, with relationships that have shaped your character's perceptions long before the story begins. The nervous laugh your character uses around authority figures? That came from somewhere. The slight physical distance they maintain in intimate conversations? That too has history.

Understanding character within relational context rather than isolation transforms abstract psychological profile into specific human being shaped by particular interpersonal dynamics. Individual doesn't exist in vacuum but develops identity through interaction with others — family systems that create behavioral patterns, friendships that shape values, romantic relationships that influence emotional responses, professional connections that determine status perception. These relationships create specific behavioral patterns that persist long after original relationship that formed them.

Map these relationships with archaeological precision — they've left their marks on everything your character does. A mother who withheld approval has shaped how your character receives compliments. A betrayal by a former friend colors how they approach new relationships. A mentor who believed in them when no one else did gives them resilience during moments of doubt. These relationship dynamics aren't abstract concepts but living forces that influence every choice, every reaction, every unspoken thought.

What Events Are Unfolding?

Not just plot points, but experiential realities. Is your character witnessing something unprecedented or tediously familiar? Are they participant or observer? Instigator or responder? The quality of their attention, the nature of their involvement — these aren't abstract considerations but physical realities that transform how you occupy space within the scene.

Character who's seen this before? Different energy. Veteran carries weight differently than rookie. Initiator moves differently than reactor. Body knows. Organizes itself accordingly. Attention narrows or widens. Emotions register in spine, in fingertips, in breath pattern. These aren't abstractions —

they're physical realities. The texture separating magnificent from merely competent. The lived quality you can't fake.

Where Are They?

Not a set description — a lived environment with atmospheric pressure. Does this space belong to your character or someone else? Is it public territory or intimate ground? The body carries this knowledge immediately — shoulders relaxing in safe spaces, spine stiffening in threatening ones. The air itself carries information — heavy with humidity or crisp with autumn.

Environmental awareness transforms performance from isolated behavior to contextual response. Actor creates not generic character but specific person responding to particular environment with its unique sensory qualities, emotional associations, and contextual implications. Hospital corridor, childhood bedroom, unfamiliar hotel room — each space triggers specific psychological and physiological responses based on character's relationship to environment and previous experiences in similar spaces.

The sensory reality of the environment grounds performance in physical truth rather than indicated emotion. The colors, lighting, sounds, even smells shape emotional responses. Is the light harsh and exposing, or soft and forgiving? Are the colors vibrant and energizing, or muted and melancholic? Is there a persistent hum of machinery? Distant voices? The particular quality of silence that exists only in certain spaces? These sensory details trigger emotional responses more effectively than intellectual analysis.

When Does This Moment Exist?

Not just historical period, but time of day, season, moment in your character's life cycle?

A scene played at 2 AM differs fundamentally from the same exchange at noon. Exhaustion colors perception. Darkness shapes vulnerability. Morning light carries different emotional possibilities than sunset. Thirty-five brings different urgencies than seventy. These aren't intellectual frameworks but lived circadian and developmental realities.

The historical context shapes fundamental assumptions about what's possible or acceptable. A character in 1950s America has different expectations about gender roles than one in contemporary society. Someone living through war experiences security differently than someone in peacetime. The character carries these contextual realities in their body, their expectations, their baseline sense of what constitutes normal existence.

And Why Is Your Character Here, Now, In This Moment?

The driving forces — both conscious and unconscious — create the engine of authentic behavior. What needs fulfillment? What fears demand appeasement? What dreams still flicker despite setbacks? These aren't acting choices but character imperatives — the forces your character cannot help but follow, regardless of what your analytical mind might prefer.

What Obstacles Stand In Their Way?

Conflict creates drama. Without meaningful obstacles, scenes lack tension and momentum. What prevents your character from immediately achieving their objective? Is it another character with opposing goals? Internal limitations or flaws? Social or physical constraints? These obstacles create the resistance against which your character must struggle — generating the energy that fuels compelling drama.

What Tactics Do They Employ To Get What They Want?

Every moment in a scene represents a tactic toward achieving the objective. Some characters use charm to disarm resistance. Others rely on intimidation. Some employ logic while others appeal to emotion. The tactics should flow naturally from who the character is — their background, their habits, their ethical boundaries — while remaining responsive to the immediate circumstances.

What's At Stake If They Fail?

If a character doesn't risk something meaningful, the scene lacks urgency and emotional investment. What could they lose? Status? Security? Love? Identity? The higher the stakes, the more energy the character brings to pursuing their objective — and the more compelling the scene becomes for the audience.

These big questions establish the universe your character inhabits. But equally important are the smaller questions that define their specific existence within that world. What quirks, habits, or patterns define their behavior? What physical actions reveal their inner state? What seemingly insignificant details make them distinctively themselves? The way they adjust their glasses. How they always touch doorframes when entering rooms. The slight hesitation before answering certain types of questions.

Consider too the production context surrounding your character. Who's directing the project, and what's their stylistic approach? What's the writer's voice and vision? Who are the other actors, and how might their performances affect yours? Is the studio or production company known for particular types of content? These contextual elements shape how your character exists within the larger artistic framework.

Osmotic Memorization – The Role Before The Words

Let me be clear— what follows isn't about audition prep. This isn't the sprint to get a few pages under your belt for a callback or day player role.

What we're talking about here is the deep dive. Doing the work you do *after* you've booked it. After the confetti settles and you know your name is going to be on the call sheet. When you've landed an important role—a recurring, a strong support, or a lead—and you're now faced with the vast terrain of the character. Multi-page scenes. A living arc. Someone you have to carry with you... for weeks, possibly for months.

That's where this process begins. Though I'll add—this still works beautifully for any role that intimidates you with lines. For some, that's forty pages. For others? Just one.

I once saw an interview Matthew McConaughey gave, back when he had crossed over from the heartthrob to serious actor. What he described struck me as deeply aligned with what I teach — and call *osmotic prep*.

I paraphrase...

"I read it after a run, when my dolphins are flying...
I read it late Saturday night after a buzz...
I read it after church, in a forgiving mood...
I read it when I'm mad, sad, tired, glad..."

He wasn't talking about running lines. He was talking about letting the role get into his blood.

Not with force. Not with analysis. But with time. Exposure. Texture. He reads the script over and over—not for memorization, but for *variation*. He lets it land differently depending on *who he is* in the moment. And that changes everything. Because the truth is—**you're not the same person every time you read a scene.** And that's the gift.

He doesn't start with answers. He starts with resonance. He lets the material hum in different states — through sweat, joy, guilt, fatigue, grace. He's reading not to decode, but to absorb. To soften the edges around what he *thinks* the scene is about, and allow something unexpected to drift in. This is very similar to the process that Anthony Hopkins employs. "I read the script two hundred and fifty times."

That's not a technique. That's a relationship.

And both McConaughey and Hopkins are wise to warn against grabbing on too early.

"You don't want to grab hold of things you want to take literally too early— You want to stay loose."

Because when you clamp down too fast — when you lock in a choice before you've lived with it — you risk choking out something deeper that might've bloomed later.

What he's describing... that's what I want you to try. Not just for leads. Not just for Oscar bait. But any time you have the privilege of living inside a character for more than just a short beat or two.

Exercise:
- Read your script once or twice a day in a different state of being. A different location. A different state of mind.
- Don't prepare — just read it. Soft eyes. Open ears.
- Let the emotion of the day's moment tint the ink on the page.
- Track what changes in you... and what doesn't.

Do this over time — not as a grind, but as *osmosis*. You'll find certain lines become reinterpreted and echo louder. Others fall away. That's not a mistake. That's the character *finding you*.

Later, once you start building the substructure scaffolding — objectives, actions, tactics — you'll be working from a place that's been well-steeped. Not just read, but *felt*.

And then McConaughey mentions something I've always found worked well for me and my students.

"I write a lot. I'll rewrite the scene eight different ways. Not because I'm gonna say it that way... but because every version I write tells me something about what's already on the page."

That's the trick, isn't it?

For me, it's about revealing the subtext of what *might* be going on. And there lies the alchemy again — *might be going on... could be going on... should be going on* — all interesting, beautiful choices on your palette to pick from.

Should you choose.

You're not rewriting to change the scene. You're rewriting to *understand it*. To talk to it in your own words before it speaks through the character.

Try this:
- Pick a single paragraph of dialogue.
- Rewrite it five different ways:
  - As a voicemail
  - As a love letter
  - As an angry text you might fire off at 2am

218

- o   As a confessional journal entry
- o   As a courtroom defense
- Read them aloud. Do they unearth new truths? If not, are you listening close enough?

McConaughey might not call this a method. But it definitely is part of my curriculum, the "mixed martial arts method of acting".

Because he's doing the thing we forget: **He's letting the character live in his skin before he ever steps into the wardrobe.**

He's not memorizing words. He's remembering purpose.
And when you do that... what about the words?
They'll show up — if you trust it. And remember Hopkins — two hundred and fifty times.

What? You thought this acting thing was going to be easy?

Physical and Vocal Transformation

From this deep exploration, physical and vocal transformations emerge naturally.

A character's body and voice should feel as distinct as their thoughts. Where does this person hold tension? In the neck, hands, spine? How does their weight shift — light, heavy, hesitant, bold? What's their default movement — quick and sharp, slow and deliberate? How do they sit, stand, interact with objects?

Physical choices should emerge naturally from your analysis. A character who grew up in constant danger moves differently than one raised in safety. A person who has spent years hiding their true self carries their body differently than someone who has always been accepted. These aren't arbitrary acting choices but logical manifestations of the character's lived experience.

Try walking across a room as yourself. Notice your natural rhythm, your habitual patterns. Now walk across the room as your character. Allow their different history, different relationship to their body, different perception of the world to alter your physicality. The shifts shouldn't feel imposed from outside but discovered from within — logical manifestations of who this person is.

The physical transformation doesn't start with external imitation but with internal understanding.

Shift in posture happens organically. Rhythm changes. Tension redistributes. All emerging from who this person is — history etched in his spine. Fears locked in her jaw. Relationships visible in the shoulders. Vulnerability evident in the placement and movement of his hands.

Watch a cat stalk a bird.

Precision. Economy. Total commitment. No gap between intention and action. Zero separation. This is what we're after in character physicality — not indicated behavior but integrated purpose.

Not showing. Being.

The voice undergoes similar transformation.

What's their natural tone? Soft, gravelly, crisp, monotone? How do they pace their words? Do they use thoughtful pauses or rapid-fire delivery? What's their speech rhythm — hesitant and unsure, or assertive and controlled? How does their background affect pronunciation, emphasis, or vocabulary?

Voice reveals character as clearly as physical behavior. The executive who expects immediate compliance speaks differently than the new employee desperate for approval. The lifelong New Yorker uses different rhythms than someone raised in the rural South. These aren't stereotypes but specific manifestations of lived experience.

Practice speaking as the character at different intensity levels — from intimate whisper to full projection. Speak at 100% intensity (fully embodied, fully engaged). Then dial back to 50% intensity (refining control while maintaining character). Finally, reduce to 10% intensity (barely whispering, finding the essence of their voice). This exercise helps you find the character's voice at different emotional registers, ensuring that their vocal identity remains consistent whether they're whispering or shouting, casual or intense. The core vocal fingerprint should remain recognizable across all circumstances.

Remember Michael Caine's observation: "Stage acting is talking loud and moving large. Film acting is thinking loud and barely moving at all."

This distinction illuminates the intimate relationship between thought and voice — especially in film, where the camera reads your thoughts directly. Your voice must carry the weight of your character's interior life without pushing or performing. It must reveal without announcing.

As physical and vocal patterns establish themselves, the character's emotional landscape takes shape.

What are their deepest fears, desires, and wounds?

What do they hide from the world?

How do they handle conflict, loss, joy, and power?

What emotions feel dangerous or forbidden to them?

These emotional patterns aren't random but logical, shaped by experience and reinforced by habits. The character who learned early that showing anger led to punishment has a different emotional vocabulary than one who was encouraged to express all feelings freely. Their emotional landscape emerges from their history — not as abstract concept but as lived reality.

Identify the core emotions that define your character. Find personal or imagined experiences that connect to those emotions. Practice accessing each one on cue, learning how these emotions manifest physically in this specific character. This isn't about manufacturing emotion but finding pathways to genuine feeling. The emotion shouldn't feel performed but experienced — with all the messy, unpredictable quality of actual human emotion rather than its theatrical approximation.

Remember Laurence Olivier's warning that "Self-consciousness is the poison of acting."

When you become aware of yourself performing rather than simply being the character, the audience immediately senses the falseness. This self-consciousness — that part of your brain watching yourself perform — creates a fatal division: one part of you is in the scene, another part is judging how you're doing. The antidote isn't self-absorption but self-forgetting — losing yourself so completely in the circumstances that you have no attention left for self-evaluation.

A Walk in Their Shoes

To deepen your embodiment of the role, consider stepping into the character's skin outside the framework of the script — but with restraint and clarity of purpose.

This is **not** a call for total immersion or losing yourself in the identity of the role à la traditional "Method" acting. I'm not suggesting you vanish into the character or live their life 24/7. That's a romantic idea, and it can sometimes be very useful — but often it becomes performative off-screen and misleading, overly self-indulgent on-set.

What I'm pointing to is something far more practical — brief, intentional moments of exploration. Spend an hour moving through ordinary tasks — drinking coffee, walking the neighborhood, writing a letter — as the character. Maybe you speak a line or two aloud. Not to impress anyone. Not to slip into fantasy. But to pause. To observe. How do they hold a cup? What's the rhythm of their thinking? What's their posture in silence?

These aren't acts of identity fusion — they're quiet studies in embodied empathy. You're not becoming them. You're recalling them. As if you've seen them do this before — not in a scene, but in life. A **reflection** of someone you know intimately. The memory of a gesture. The way they said a word. You're letting that reflection guide the behavior, not inventing, just recognizing.

You might blend in some sensory work — how would this character respond to the smell of old wood? A certain kind of music? You might engage in some spontaneous improv — responding in-character to something unplanned. You might even do a bit of contextual research — how their environment or historical setting shaped them. All of this is valid.

These aren't "methods" to swear allegiance to. They're tools. What matters isn't how you get there — it's that the result feels instinctive, lived, real. That the character becomes something you can access without straining — not through effort, but familiarity.

This kind of work — subtle, temporary, respectful — helps bridge the gap between intellectual understanding and **embodied behavior**. And that's where the magic lives: in a character who *responds truthfully under imaginary circumstances*, because you've built a quiet, durable foundation for them to live beneath the surface, ready, but never imposed.

The Paradox of Performance

The final challenge is bringing all this preparation into performance without losing spontaneity. Character work means nothing if it doesn't translate into organic, truthful behavior on camera or stage. The paradox of great acting: the more thoroughly you prepare, the more thoroughly you can abandon that preparation in the moment. When the character's reality is fully integrated, you no longer need to consciously construct responses — they emerge naturally from the foundation you've built.

Your final challenge: bringing your extensive preparation to performance without killing spontaneity.

Character work means nothing if it's dead on arrival. If it doesn't breathe on camera. On stage.

The paradox waits for you here — prepare thoroughly only to abandon it completely. Build the house then forget about the architecture. Learn the map only to burn it later. When a character's reality fully integrates, conscious construct falls away. Responses emerge. Not planned. Not forced. Inevitable. Like water finding a path downhill. Like a breath finding lungs. Like truth finding its way out.

This paradox resolves when preparation transforms from intellectual construct to embodied reality. Thorough character development creates not performance blueprint but alternative consciousness that responds authentically to immediate circumstances. Actor doesn't think "my character would respond like this" but experiences situation directly through character's specific perspective, generating authentic behavior without conscious mediation.

Know the character so well that choices happen naturally. Let go of rigid pre-planned reactions; allow yourself to be affected in the moment. Trust that your thorough analysis has created instincts you can rely on. Remain present enough to respond truthfully to whatever actually happens in the scene.

Every line should be infused with subtext, emotional history, and need. The same words can carry radically different meanings depending on the character's perspective. "Thank you for coming" might mean "I'm relieved you're finally here," "I'm surprised you had the nerve to show up," "I wish you'd stayed away but I'm being polite," or "I've been desperate to see you but don't want to appear eager." Each interpretation creates an entirely different scene while using identical words.

Allow the dialogue to emerge from the character's thought process rather than from memorization. Experiment with performing the same speech under different emotional circumstances — notice how the meaning shifts with the emotional context. Lines shouldn't sound like dialogue but like thoughts being formed in the moment. When the character's inner life is fully developed, their words emerge naturally from their perspective rather than sounding like authored text.

Great acting is never about simply reading lines. It's about creating full, complex human beings — with flaws, contradictions, desires, and vulnerabilities. Your work as an actor is to step into another soul, inhabit another reality, and make that existence feel undeniable to the audience.

As I preach endlessly, "Every great actor has great range... work to broaden yours and it will enrich any role you play... even the role you play in life."

This pursuit of range — the holy grail of acting — requires systematic exploration of characters far removed from your natural tendencies. Each role stretches your instrument, adds colors to your palette, expands your capacity for transformation. The actor who can move effortlessly between comedy and tragedy, between period drama and contemporary realism, between leading roles and character parts — this actor builds a career that can weather the industry's inevitable changes.

This analytical framework isn't academic exercise. It's the bridge. The connector between intellectual understanding and embodied performance.

Each question, when thoroughly explored, creates specific realities. Emotional landscapes. Physical patterns. Psychological textures. Your body recognizes these. Responds to them authentically.

When you've done this work completely — when you've mapped the full territory — something shifts. The intellectual questions dissolve into lived experience.

...you no longer think about these answers. You inhabit them.

Analysis becomes invisible. Yet its fruits remain — specificity, authenticity, the unmistakable quality of a performance that feels not constructed but discovered. Not manufactured but excavated. The hewn marble block reveals the artist's statue unearthed from somewhere deep and true.

This detailed work — crafting a character from internal psychology to physical embodiment — lays your foundation for the next crucial element. The dynamic interplay between characters. The electricity that happens in the space between two fully realized human beings.

It's here — in the contact between those internal worlds — that everything either ignites or evaporates.

Chemistry isn't choreography. It's contact. Collision. Sometimes combustion. What lives between actors — the tension, the tether, the flare of something unscripted — can't be planned. But it can be provoked.

But even craft alone isn't enough. It has to hold up when the opportunity finally arrives.

After all my years in this business — both as an actor, a teacher, writer and a coach — here's what I've come to understand:

You only need one moment. One good scene. One tight, authentic minute opposite an A-list actor. One compelling turn in a hit film or series. That can be enough to launch your career. And that can happen at any age. That one performance becomes the anchor — the proof that you belong.

But here's the truth nobody tells you early on: if that moment comes and you're not ready... it doesn't matter.

If your craft isn't there — if your range is limited, your instincts underdeveloped, your life a mess — you'll be exposed as someone who caught a lucky break, not someone who can carry the weight.

And in this industry, people remember both.

That's why range matters. That's why craft matters. Because the moment will come — if you stick around long enough. You don't have to chase it. You just have to be ready.

I still remember something a casting director said in a workshop early in my career. It stuck with me:

"You will get your shot. If you stay in the game long enough, you will get your shot. The question is — will you be ready to take advantage of it when it comes?"

That's the whole thing, really. Be ready. And stay ready.

Case Study: Willem Dafoe and the Method of Intentional Disruption

"If we go a few takes, I'll deliberately fuck it up — just to see what comes out of it," Willem Dafoe once confessed. This isn't mere improvisation; it's a conscious embrace of chaos to ignite spontaneous discovery. Dafoe understands that within the structured realm of filmmaking, predictability can deaden authenticity. By intentionally disrupting the flow, he creates moments charged with unexpected truth.

In Robert Eggers' *The Lighthouse*, Dafoe and co-star Robert Pattinson dove headfirst into this technique. Their performances brimmed with volatility, precisely because they allowed for intentional missteps and unrehearsed provocations. Eggers noted how their willingness to let scenes spiral unpredictably brought a visceral immediacy to the film. Dafoe's disruptions were never arbitrary — they were calculated risks meant to strip away artifice and unveil deeper emotional currents.

This tradition of intentional disruption isn't Dafoe's alone. Marlon Brando famously rattled scenes to shake out genuine reactions, refusing to let his co-stars settle comfortably into practiced rhythms. Heath Ledger's Joker emerged so disturbingly authentic because Ledger constantly kept the cast and crew off balance, never repeating the same action exactly, pushing the performance into realms of unpredictability. Daniel Day-Lewis, while known more for immersion than intentional sabotage, similarly found authenticity through profound spontaneity, often throwing subtle yet impactful curveballs to keep a scene alive and evolving.

Actors using this method understand something essential: genuine reactions can't be faked. By deliberately throwing off the script, they force their scene partners — and themselves — to respond authentically. This dance with chaos demands absolute trust and vulnerability, but when done well, the results are electrifying.

In your own exploration of character, consider Dafoe's wisdom: embrace the mess, provoke the unpredictable, and trust the chaos to guide you toward deeper truths. Sometimes, the richest performances aren't crafted meticulously — they erupt spontaneously from the intentional disruptions actors dare to invite.

Case Study: Brando's Cue Cards — Spontaneity or Shortcut?

Marlon Brando — iconic, unruly, revolutionary — became famous in the end of his career for refusing to memorize his lines. He'd have them taped them to cue cards, lamp shades, even other actors' foreheads. Duvall once wore a sandwich board cue card for Brando on *The Godfather*. Robert Duvall remembered watching him work that way and thought about trying it himself.

"I tried that once. It didn't work for me. You can do that for spontaneity — to keep it fresh, to be always searching. But I think you can learn the lines perfectly and still have spontaneity."
— Robert Duvall

For Duvall, the searching came *after* the memorization. For Brando, it came *instead of* it. But here's the hard cold facts of that process: *You* can't do what Brando did — not unless you are Brando.

229

He earned that freedom.

He had already paid his dues — first as a disciplined stage actor with a photographic memory, performing night after night in productions like *A Streetcar Named Desire*. He *could* memorize anything. He *had* memorized everything. But eventually came to believe that his famous "naturalism" that once electrified the stage was beginning to look performative under the camera's cold eye.

So, he changed. Or maybe, more accurately — he saw change coming before anyone else. The craft was shifting. Audiences were shifting. And Brando knew what once felt real was becoming gratuitous. He sensed it first — then adapted.

And yes — it worked. He won two Academy Awards, along with multiple nominations, using this technique. The spontaneity wasn't laziness. It was yet another evolution of the *method*, in disguise.

Still, let's be clear: *You* will not be able to show up on set today and ask for cue cards. Not unless your name's already above the title. If anything, it would mark you as unprepared, unprofessional. Brando could get away with it — because he'd already proved, for decades, that he could do the work. Accommodating and trusting him might deliver gold as a director.

The real lesson here isn't the cue card. It's what Duvall called the *"always searching"* process that is part of the internal dialog of the character. That's the heartbeat of great acting — not recitation, but discovery. Not the performance, but the possibility. That's what Brando was chasing. And in the best moments of his career, the beginning, middle or end — that's what he caught.

Case Study: Barry Keoghan in "Saltburn"

Barry Keoghan's performance as Oliver in "Saltburn" demonstrates how modern character creation emerges not through external indicators but through microscopic authenticity that feels slightly off-center. Keoghan builds Oliver from internal truth so convincing that we accept his reality even as it diverges from normal behavior.

Study the dinner scenes where Oliver gradually infiltrates the family. Keoghan's power comes from his listening — the way his eyes absorb information, calculate responses, recalibrate approach. He doesn't play "scheming"; he plays a person absolutely committed to achieving his objectives by whatever means necessary.

The film's most disturbing moments work precisely because Keoghan's performance lacks traditional performance markers. There's no mustache-twirling villain, no "tells" that signal dishonesty. Instead, there's just a consciousness we gradually realize operates by different rules than our own.

What makes this work so compelling is Keoghan's complete inhabitation of Oliver's perspective — morally disturbing but psychologically coherent. We're not watching an actor portray a manipulator; we're watching a character who doesn't recognize his own manipulation as anything but survival. This is character creation at its most sophisticated — building a person whose internal logic feels authentic even when their actions provoke horror.

Case Study: Jeremy Strong in "Succession"

Watch Jeremy Strong as Kendall Roy in HBO's "Succession." Notice what he's *not* doing — there are no broad indicators of emotion, no traditional "acting moments" designed to signal his character's state of mind. Instead,

Strong disappears so completely into Kendall's fractured psyche that we're watching thought itself unfold.

In the Season 3 episode "Too Much Birthday," observe the sequence where Kendall's birthday party collapses around him. The camera catches his minute shifts in awareness — hope curdling into disappointment, confidence crumbling into humiliation. Not once does Strong "show" us these emotions. They simply exist, emanating from him in micro expressions so authentic you forget you're watching fiction.

This is today's gold standard — performance so internalized that the mechanism disappears entirely. Strong builds Kendall from the inside out, creating a consciousness so complete that every gesture, every hesitation, every half-formed word feels inevitable rather than constructed. The technique is invisible yet the preparation must be exhaustive. This is what we mean by "thinking loud and barely moving at all."

What makes Strong's work particularly instructive is his comfort with stillness — with allowing Kendall's thoughts to play across his face without commentary or emphasis. In moments where lesser actors might reach for obvious emotional indicators, Strong simply exists in Kendall's reality. The pauses between his words often carry more meaning than the dialogue itself. This is the power of internal life made visible — not demonstrated but simply existing.

A character created in isolation is only half-alive. Like a heart without blood to pump. A lung without air to breathe. No matter how detailed your creation — how thoroughly you've built the psychology, physicality, voice, and history — a character doesn't fully exist until they collide with another consciousness.

That collision? That's where the alchemy ignites.

You've spent hours in the laboratory. Mapping the timeline. Tracing the wounds. Building the body. Finding the voice. But now comes the real test — what happens when your carefully constructed human being meets another? When your choices crash against choices you didn't make? When your rhythm is interrupted, your expectations shattered, your perfect plan... derailed?

Characters, like people, don't reveal themselves in solitude. They show their truth under pressure. In conflict. In connection. In the electric space between two souls with competing needs.

So now we step into that space — the unpredictable territory where your preparation meets someone else's. Where listening matters more than intention. Where your work stops being a plan... and starts becoming a person.

Welcome to the art of relationship — where characters become people, and technique dissolves into truth.

CHAPTER 7

THE WORKING ACTOR'S SURVIVAL GUIDE

Navigating the Marathon, Not the Sprint

The entertainment industry is an unpredictable mess. Some rare actors book their first major role quickly, then fade away, never to be seen again. Others spend years perfecting their craft before landing any steady work, then claw out a successful character role career that lasts a lifetime. Success is never linear. Never predictable. Never guaranteed.

This reality exists beneath every actor's journey — managing expectations, handling rejection, creating sustainable success in an ever-changing industry. The actors who last understand something crucial: you're building a career, not just booking a job.

Acting is a marathon, not a sprint — the goal is longevity, not just a single project. The industry is built on timing, preparation, and persistence. Many great actors were rejected for years before breaking through. The names you know, the faces you recognize — almost all weathered countless rejections before that "overnight success" the public remembers.

Consider Bryan Cranston. Years of sitcoms, guest spots, commercials — even voiced a few Power Rangers villains — all before he ever stepped into Walter White's shoes on Breaking Bad. What made him unforgettable wasn't just the transformation, but the truth he carried into every phase of it. He didn't break through by reinventing himself. He broke through by *refining* himself and being ready when the role finally matched the man.

Or take Jonathan Banks, for example. Another alum from the Vince Gilligan family of great character actors who elevate great writing. You know him from *Better Call Saul* and *Breaking Bad* — that gravel-voiced, coiled-spring presence in the room. What most people don't know is that he'd been a working actor for decades before those roles found him. Bit parts mostly, character work, lots of television. *Beverly Hills Cop* back in the '80s.

He didn't land Mike Ehrmantraut because he was flashy or new. He got it because he was *consistent*. Professional. Always in the moment. Vince Gilligan said that Banks brings this *under-the-surface threat* — a quiet control — and it was obvious the moment he read for the role. He wasn't performing toughness. He was just *still*. Honest. Minimal. You couldn't look away.

And the kicker: Banks wasn't supposed to have a big arc. His role was meant to be small. The occasional recur. But his work was so layered, so grounded, they wrote more for him. A lot more. Because he gave them something they didn't even know they needed — a man who didn't need to prove he was dangerous, because he *understood what restraint feels like on camera.*

That's what singles you out, not noise. Not desperation. Truth in the moment. Presence. Quietly dangerous in his case. And always professional.

Patience. Resilience. Determination. These aren't just motivational poster words. They're survival gear. The bare essentials.

Try this — grab a piece of paper. Write down exactly where you want to be in five years. Be specific. Be brutal. What kind of work? What kind of roles? What kind of life? Then write down three things you need to do to move the needle, even if they're painful, difficult, and you can't do them today. Training, for sure, should be on your list. That is not saying, "You must take acting classes." No, it means you must begin earnestly your study. Reading this book was already a great first step. Read more. Watch more films, from every era. But watch as a student of the craft, not as an audience absorbed in the story. Break down the performances, the edits, the camera angles, and move... the "mise-en-scène." Look that up if you don't know what that means. Build relationships. Make your plan actionable. But most of all, make it yours.

Your plan becomes your compass. When the auditions are slow, work dries up, when nothing's moving, when doubt creeps in — you'll have something to steer by.

The actors who last — they don't just count bookings. They count *progress*. Maybe you finally got in front of that casting director who never saw you before. Maybe you wrote your own scene and shot it. Maybe you learned something that scared you, or you didn't quite understand before, and now does. These are mile markers. Quiet wins. Proof that you're moving forward — even when the industry isn't calling your name... just yet.

That's how you stay in it and build something that lasts. What's the quote?

> *"The race is not to the swift, nor the battle to the strong...*
> *but time and chance happen to them all."*
> — Ecclesiastes 9:11, The Hebrew Bible

The Reality of Rejection

Rejection is an unavoidable part of an actor's journey. Casting decisions are rarely personal; they are based on an ever-changing mix of talent, look, chemistry, and timing. The actor who takes rejection personally becomes fragile. Brittle. Unsustainable.

The math is simple but brutal: even exceptionally successful actors, considered "working actors," book perhaps 5-10% of what they audition for. Think about that. Actors working steadily at the highest levels still hear "no" 90-95% of the time. This isn't failure — it's the baseline reality of the profession.

This percentage reveals a crucial truth: rejection is the normal state of an actor's professional life. Booking is the exception. This perspective shift removes the emotional sting from individual rejections. They're not personal failures — they're simply part of the statistical reality of a very competitive industry.

How do you handle rejection without losing confidence? You detach from outcome — you are auditioning for a career, not a single role. Evaluate and learn — "What can each audition teach me about my craft, my preparation process, my presentation?" Stay in motion — keep training, networking, and creating even when you're between roles.

I once coached an actress who kept a "rejection wall" in her apartment — she put up *Variety* clips and photos of all the important roles she hadn't gotten in the past. What began as a joke to defuse rejection and laugh with her friends eventually became something powerful — a badge of honor. When she didn't book a role she knew she'd given a strong audition for, she would pin up the mementos beneath the title she'd written above the wall: **"Their Loss."**

This ritual transformed any sense of rejection into evidence of her persistence, her courage to keep showing up despite inevitable disappointment, and — more importantly — a belief in herself: *"No one can do it better... only different."*

It's a quote I share with my students when they've squeezed out every nuance of *"What's available to play?"* A question I repeatedly ask my students to find *within* the script.

Financial Sustainability for Artists

Let's talk about money. No one wants to, but you have to.

Acting work is inconsistent — so if you plan to stick around, you'd better learn how to manage the gaps. Longevity doesn't come from talent alone. It comes from not going broke between gigs.

The smart ones build in survival plans. Side hustles. Passive income. Whatever keeps the lights on while you wait for the phone to ring. And when the big check *does* come in? Don't spend it like it's the new normal. Save 30–40% of anything decent. That's not just for taxes — that's your runway.

Live under your means. Way under. Don't get used to the taste of money just because it showed up once. Build a cushion. Three to six months of expenses. Enough to breathe if it all dries up tomorrow.

And be intentional with your side gigs. Not all hustles are created equal. You want flexible hours — yes. But also something that keeps you in the creative orbit. Teaching, coaching, voiceover, content creation — things that use the same muscle without draining the core. Bartending, catering, waiting tables — sure, they work. But they take a toll. Body and brain.

Some of the best actors I know make half their income teaching. Or coaching tapes. Or doing voiceover for ads no one even knows they recorded. That work keeps them afloat — and often leads to something unexpected. A connection. A referral. A new lane they didn't see coming.

So write it down. All of it. Your monthly expenses. Your income sources. Be precise. Be ruthless. Where's the fat? Where's the dead weight?

Because here's the truth: if you can't survive, you can't create. Financial stability isn't selling out. It's staying in the game long enough to matter.

> *"Your art will ask everything of you — including your rent."*
> — Unknown

Networking: Building Essential Relationships

Success in acting is not just about talent — it's also about who knows you and trusts you. Directors, casting agents, and fellow actors remember professionalism, attitude, and reliability. The industry is small — and the burning of a bridge, intended or not, can have a ripple effect that costs you opportunities years down the line. Your reputation will follow you, precede you, and define you in rooms you haven't even entered yet.

Effective networking in the entertainment industry isn't about collecting contacts or building an email list. It's about building *genuine* relationships. Actors who approach networking as a transaction rarely develop the meaningful connections that sustain a career. But those who focus on authentic engagement — who find shared interests, offer support without expectation, and consistently show up with professionalism — they build advocates. Or as I like to call them, *Champions*.

Champions are the people who promote your work when you're not in the room. Every actor needs these. People in the industry who genuinely admire your work — and wish the world could see the same thing in you they do.

Make a list. Seriously. Write down the professionals you admire in your geography, and consider appropriate, respectful ways to connect with them — through class, through a thoughtful email, through genuine interaction on social media. Attend industry events, film festivals, and acting workshops. Not to "network" in the surface sense — but to be present. Visible. Real.

And be clear: connect without being transactional. Follow up without being intrusive. Stay polite, respectful, and consistent. Let relationships grow over time, not over text. And never underestimate anyone. That PA you barely noticed on set? They may be the producer calling the shots next season.

Remember: your peers today will be running productions tomorrow. The assistant taking your audition details now might be casting major projects a few years down the road. That PA getting coffee, guiding you to your trailer? Could be directing the next indie breakout. So treat everyone with the same level of respect and professionalism — not just the decision-makers. It's not just the right thing to do; it's also a smart career strategy.

So, yes — allow for everyone in your orbit to become your Champion. Do this without being obsequious or pushy. Genuine connection is not about flattery or performance. It's about showing up with humility, consistency, and an openness to being of service to the work — and the people creating it.

I have so many stories I'd love to tell here — actors who made it or broke their careers based on how they presented themselves, on set. But I'm pretty sure that would wind up being another book. So for now, we'll stay focused on the task at hand.

That said, we can't ignore how the game has changed. Social media has transformed how actors build and maintain professional relationships. When used strategically, platforms like Instagram, Facebook, Twitter/X, and LinkedIn can help keep you visible to industry contacts between in-person interactions. The key is consistency and authenticity. Share your creative journey. And be sure to celebrate the work of others. Engage thoughtfully. And above all — I beg you — resist the urge to make it all about you.

On the other hand, I know several decades-working character actors who refuse to post anything about themselves. They find it overly self-serving, even desperate. They believe it cheapens the years of work they've put in — and frankly, I deeply admire that humility. But the truth is, the days of letting the audience come to the artist are long gone. There's just too much noise now. Agents, casting directors, networks, and studios all consider your online presence — they look at your numbers, engagement, and visibility when casting key roles.

So like it or not, you've got to stay visible. The trick is doing it with grace — without sounding like you're shouting for attention. It's a balance. A tightrope. But it's one every working actor has to walk.

Understanding Representation: Agents, Managers, and Your Career

Understanding representation starts with one thing: clarity. You have to know what you need — and when you need it. Agents, for the most part, are focused on the business: securing auditions, negotiating contracts, and managing expectations. *Yes*, I said it. Managing expectations — and I'm sure

I'll ruffle a few feathers for saying that part out loud. But it's true. If you've worked with one long enough, you've felt it.

Now, "managers" — in theory — are supposed to be there for the long game. Big-picture thinkers. Guides. Advocates. Career architects. They help shape long-term strategy, offer feedback, sometimes play therapist, sometimes play traffic cop. Not every actor needs both. In fact, not every actor should have both — at least not right away. But if and when you do assemble the full team, know this: **you have to manage them.** Because if you don't? They'll manage you. And not always in ways aligned with your best interests.

The right representation? It amplifies your efforts. Opens doors. Magnifies your visibility. Strengthens your positioning.

The wrong one? It muddies the water. Creates friction. Slows you down — and sometimes does real damage before you even see it coming.

There's also a big misconception about how the agent-actor relationship works. Your agent isn't your employee. And they're not your personal concierge. They are your **business partner** — and they have other partners besides you. Lots of them. Some of whom may look, sound, and act an awful lot like you. Truth is, you're probably not the only one on their roster going out for that role. And guess what? They don't get paid unless someone books it — so they're hedging bets across a spread. It's not personal. It's math.

Success comes when you understand this. When you shift from expecting to be "taken care of" to becoming an active, strategic collaborator. You want to stand out? Be the actor they *don't* have to chase down. Be prepared. Be easy to submit. Be the one who nails tape on the first pass. Be low-maintenance, but high-output. That's how you earn their advocacy — and their attention.

And remember: your agent can't sell what they don't understand. You have to help them help you — by knowing your type, sharpening your materials, tracking your submissions, and staying visible without being a nuisance. When you build that kind of rapport — and trust — your agent becomes something more than a name on the contract. They become your **first real Champion** in the industry.

Agents have a tough job. It's high-volume, high-pressure, and when done well, it's an invisible art form. When done poorly, it can tank your momentum before it's even begun.

So choose wisely. Show up professionally. And never forget: no one will ever care about your career more than you do. That's not cynicism. That's the job.

To find and secure the right agent, start by researching agencies that align with your current career level, type, and trajectory. Look for those whose rosters suggest room for someone like you — or better yet, someone like you who brings something they're currently missing. Then submit a strong, professional package: updated headshots, a focused résumé, an IMDB link if you have one, and a solid demo reel that showcases your range and presence on camera.

If you're invited to a meeting — whether in-person, over Zoom, or otherwise — treat it like the audition it is. Agents are evaluating not just your talent, but your professionalism, marketability, and whether you fill a casting "type" they're currently lacking in their talent pool. They're not looking to duplicate what they already have — they're looking to complete a puzzle.

Make a list of ideal agents and managers you'd like to work with in *every market* where you're willing to work as a local hire. That's a key phrase now — **local hire** — and if you don't understand what it means, you'll be left behind. Many emerging regional markets offer state tax incentives to producers, and nearly all of them include some form of stipulation that requires local casting. Which means unless you're already a well-established name with a résumé full of studio credits, you'll be expected to cover your own housing, transportation, and airfare — even if you're the best actor for the role.

I won't go deep into the weeds on all the games played with pay rates across different markets, SAG/AFTRA, Non-Union but here's what you need to know: being booked *out of* your L.A. agent into a regional market will usually land you a significantly higher payday — if that option's available. Otherwise, as a local hire, you're working at scale at best if you're in the union. That's a huge difference from what could be negotiated as a "Top of Show" guest star rate for a series. We're talking thousands of dollars in difference. But as I mentioned, this goes deep and wide and is best discussed with your agent manager "after" you've booked a job.

And while more producers are working in regional markets to cut production costs, the industry bias still lingers — the assumption that "out-of-market" talent isn't quite on par with L.A. or New York actors. That outdated perception is often used to justify these lower rates, regardless of actual skill.

The "Local Hire Only" label is a bit of a wink-and-nod game. Everyone knows you don't actually live there. But if you can provide a local address — and be available for callbacks or fittings without a fuss — you may qualify as a "local hire" and book an important role that boosts your résumé and gets you in the room for future work.

These regional markets often struggle to find seasoned talent. Their actor pools are smaller, their training pipelines less developed. Which means:

opportunity. For those who are willing to navigate these challenging and costly logistics — and play the game — there's real ground to be gained outside the traditional hubs.

First and foremost, find the right agent. Not just *an* agent — the *right* one. Do your homework. Research their website. Look at who they represent and what they're actively looking for. Then build an action plan to get on their radar — with intention, not desperation.

The right agent doesn't just book you jobs. They believe in your potential. They see your unique qualities. And more importantly — they *fight* for you. They pitch you for roles that actually align with your strengths, not just whatever's floating through the breakdowns that day.

Now, let's talk red flags. Warning signs of poor representation include: long silences, weak communication, scattershot submissions that don't fit your type, pressure to take inappropriate roles, or consistent failure to negotiate effectively on your behalf. Don't let your hunger for representation keep you stuck in a counterproductive arrangement. No agent at all is better than one who quietly derails your career.

And if it's going sideways — don't be afraid to walk away. Fire them if you have to. They'll fire you without blinking. Just do it with professionalism, candor, and as much grace as you can muster.

But be warned: agents don't like to be fired. It's a one-way street from their perspective — *they* end things, not you. And if you're the one who calls it? You're going the wrong way down that one-way street. They'll remember. And more often than not, they won't forgive.

So don't sign lightly. Do your due diligence. And if you commit — *really* commit. Show up, deliver, and make them look good at every opportunity. That's how you become the talent they brag about.

And remember: as your career evolves, so will your needs. The agent who helped you break in might not be the one to take you to the next level. Transitions are inevitable. But they require tact, timing, and professional courtesy. Don't ghost. Don't burn bridges. This industry is too small — and too interconnected — for scorched-earth exits.

Balancing Artistry and Commerce

The business side of acting doesn't have to kill creativity. Great actors find ways to stay passionate while remaining professional. Set clear boundaries around the roles you're willing to take — but stay open to new challenges. The most successful actors balance commerce with artistry, understanding that both matter, and both must be managed.

The tension between artistic fulfillment and commercial success is a central challenge for every actor. Some roles feed your soul but not your bank account. Others provide financial stability but leave your creative spirit running on fumes. The key is finding an equilibrium — not swinging wildly between extremes, but learning how to navigate both with intention. That's what builds a sustainable, satisfying career.

Keep training. Keep building. Take classes. Work on accents. Develop physical skills. Make your own projects — whether that's short films, theater, or writing. Surround yourself with artists who challenge and inspire you. Because once you stop growing, you start becoming predictable. And in this business? Predictable equals replaceable.

Self-produced content has become an increasingly viable way to showcase range, claim creative control, and attract the right kind of attention. Web series, podcasts, short films — the technology is here, the gatekeepers are fewer, and the industry is watching. These projects don't just pass the time between gigs — they can launch careers, revitalize stalled ones, or bridge the gap between where you are and where you want to be.

I've known actors who completely transformed their trajectory through smart, self-driven content. One actor I coached, constantly cast as "the best friend," wrote and produced a dark psychological thriller that showcased her dramatic intensity. Within months, she started getting auditions for lead antagonist roles. Another, tired of playing the tough-guy bodyguard, created a comedy web series that revealed his timing and vulnerability — suddenly, comedy casting rooms started opening up to him.

Staying Inspired Between Jobs

The working actor understands the long game — that success is about consistency, adaptability, and passion. It's about showing up day after day, regardless of yesterday's triumph or disappointment. It's about treating yourself as both artist and business. As both creator and product.

This paradox sits at the heart of a sustainable acting career — you must care deeply about your craft while maintaining perspective about the business. You must invest emotionally in each role while detaching from outcomes beyond your control. You must be vulnerable in your work while developing resilience in your career.

Staying inspired between jobs becomes an essential skill. Read voraciously. Watch films that move you. Study performances that challenge you. Keep your instrument — your body, your voice, your emotional life — finely tuned and ready. The actor who depends on external validation for inspiration will experience long creative droughts.

Create daily rituals that connect you to your craft regardless of employment status. Perhaps it's voice work every morning. Character exploration through journaling. Scene study with peers. Physical training to maintain flexibility and expressiveness. These practices maintain technical readiness while nurturing the creative spirit that brought you to acting initially.

I recommend all actors develop an "artistic emergency kit" — collection of books, films, music, or exercises that reliably rekindle your passion when motivation flags — and it will. Return to these touchstones during difficult periods — the monologue that first made you fall in love with acting, the film performance that showed you what's possible, the theater experience that changed how you understand human connection through art.

Remember why you started this journey. What moved you. What compelled you forward despite obstacles. That core passion becomes your anchor when the industry's chaos threatens to pull you under.

The Art of Career Longevity

The most successful actors think in decades, not seasons. They understand that a career has its own natural rhythm — cycles of visibility and invisibility, commercial highs and creative pivots, momentum and necessary rebuilding. Holding the long view helps quiet the desperation that often derails developing careers.

Study the paths of actors whose careers have spanned decades. Watch how they adapt to industry shifts, how they reinvent themselves when the work demands it — because it *will*. No one stays young forever. Time brings change — to our faces, our bodies, our energy. And with those changes come new roles — if you've prepared, if you've evolved.

Personal Sidebar: The Call That Pulled Me Back

"Sometimes that's all it takes — one champion, one role, one brief moment of clarity — to remember who you still are."

There was a time I walked away. Completely. Not just from the process, but from the whole identity. I didn't just step back from the business, from the hustle, the classes, the castings, and the callbacks. I let go of it all. The friends. The allies. The champions who believed in me when I doubted myself. People who spent their own political capital — their own time and reputation in trying to keep me in the game.

But I left. Quietly... and they felt betrayed — though I couldn't fathom why. It didn't register until years later, when I found myself on the other side of the conversation. Teaching. Coaching. Talking to producers, directors, agents — vouching for a student, advocating for someone I believed in — as their champion. Recommending them the way others had once recommended me. That's when it hit. The weight of it, the betrayal they felt because of what they'd risked. And what I'd walked away from, despite their personal investment.

Walked away from the mirror. From the discipline. From whatever small ember still burned under the ash of all that came before.

I was out. Gone. For maybe five, six years.

Some personal blows — real ones — ripped me away. Not a choice, not a tantrum, not some moody declaration of reinvention. Life hit hard. And acting, the thing that once tethered me to something meaningful, suddenly felt like a wound I kept tearing open.

So I shut it down. Cold.

I didn't just stop working. I refused to.
Wouldn't think about acting. Wouldn't talk about it. Wouldn't even let myself miss it.

I had to pretend it never mattered.

Had to convince myself it had all been some foolish detour.
Acting was a con. A waste. A romantic mistake.
An embarrassing ex I'd finally grown out of.

That old lover — she was ugly now.
What did I ever see in her?

I stopped watching films. Changed the channel anytime someone mentioned the business.
Rolled my eyes at artists, as if I'd never once longed to be one.
As if I hadn't given everything to the work.

And with that story in my pocket, I tried to rejoin the "real" world.

I put on the shoes. Wore the suit. Talked the talk. Did the business casual. Meetings, perfectly polished corporate speak, strategy decks. Every time I looked in the mirror, I rehearsed a new kind of performance — one that passed for worthwhile, functional. Corporate. Hirable. I told myself I'd finally grown up. I thought I had crushed that old ember. Smothered it completely.

But the thing about identity — the real kind — is that it doesn't just dissolve because you decide it's inconvenient.

So, when my house of cards started to fall — it all fell hard. One domino after another. Jobs, business ventures, marriage, health, finances. Everything I'd propped myself up with, my false identity, collapsed under the weight of that pretending. I was sliding down life.

Eventually, I was sleeping in my car.

No epiphany. No script-worthy moment. Just exhaustion. Cold, fake leather upholstery and the sound of my pathetic breath in the dark.

No work, no job interviews, no safely net, no family to fall back on.

… and that's when the call came.

There was this one agent — an old champion. The kind who still believed in people, not just names.

He knew I'd quit. Knew I wanted no part of the business. But every few months, like clockwork, he'd call.

"Jim, I've got something for you. If you want. Ready to come back?" Every time I'd say the same thing:

"No, but thanks, Mike. I'm done. I've got to make a life."

Truth was, I didn't have one. Sleeping in my car. No prospects. No momentum. I won't go into the details — but enough to say, rock bottom, emotionally, physically, financially.

Then one day, he calls again.
"How you doing?" he asked.

"I'm not," I said.

Instead of pushing a cliché or playing cheerleader, he said:

"Look, I've got an industrial shoot. One day. Fifteen hundred bucks. He'll write you a check at the end of the day. I know the producer." He paused and waited for my response. And when it didn't.

Look, Jim, I can give this to anyone. But I want you to have it. You need it."

I told him I couldn't do it. My self-loathing and lack of self-confidence wouldn't let me believe I could do it.

He said, "Just go do it anyway. For the money, yes — but more than that. You need this. Come by the house and I'll give you some gas money. Pay me later."

So I did... But the thought festered in me, "Could I even go through the motions? As if I were an actor again? What if I'd make him look bad if they had to fire me halfway through the shoot?" But that money, at that moment, was a lot. It could be a lifeline.

So I went. Reluctantly. No confidence, no spark. Just basic primal need.

And then — it happened.

The work was simple. But even without the confidence. I got back on the bicycle.

Shockingly, lo and behold, at "Action!" I could still ride.

They liked what I did. At the day's end, I didn't want to quit. I wanted to keep going. I felt, "I love this. I'm relative again. I have something to offer."

I got paid on the spot then treated myself to a clean and comfortable room for the evening.

But more than that — I felt like a whole person.

It wasn't some big breakthrough role that course-corrected my life. It wasn't validation from the industry.

It was just one job, from an old champion who still believed in me. Giving me one respite. A moment where I could be relevant again.

So cultivate Champions in your life. In the craft or otherwise.

Sometimes that's all it takes. One scene to remember who you are.

Case Study: John Travolta

By the early 1990s, many in the industry considered his career finished. The charm and flash of *Saturday Night Fever* and *Grease* had long since faded, and his recent projects had floundered. But in 1994, Quentin Tarantino cast him — against type — in *Pulp Fiction*. That single role revived his career, reshaped his image, and launched a second act that no one saw coming. But he was ready. That's the key. Reinvention only works if you've done the work.

The smartest actors balance the commercial needs against the artistic, nurturing their creative vitality through every stage of life. These long arcs hold patterns — and lessons — that you can shape to fit your journey.

Case Study: Frances McDormand

McDormand's path offers another valuable lesson. She built sustainable success through character work rather than leading lady roles, creating a career immune to Hollywood's age biases. She alternates between independent projects that feed her artistically and larger films that expand her commercial viability. She disappears from public view between projects, preserving her private life and creative energy. This balanced approach has yielded a four-decade career of consistent growth rather than dramatic peaks and valleys.

The industry will test your commitment repeatedly. It will question your choices, challenge your confidence, and present obstacles that seem designed specifically to break you. The actors who endure aren't necessarily the most talented or the most connected — they're the ones who refuse to be broken. Who learn from rejection rather than being defined by it. Who maintain their creative fire through the industry's indifference.

This is not a profession for the faint-hearted. Not for those seeking external validation or overnight success. It's for the stubborn dreamers. The patient builders. The resilient storytellers who understand that the privilege of bringing characters to life is worth the struggle required to do so.

Your career will have its own distinctive rhythm, its own unique challenges, its own unexpected gifts. The framework offered here isn't a prescription but a perspective — a way of thinking about the road ahead that emphasizes sustainability, authenticity, and the long view. The work is difficult, yes, but for those called or *claimed* to it, nothing else satisfies.

As Konstantin Stanislavski reminds us: "Love the art in yourself, not yourself in the art." This distinction — between ego-driven performance and genuine artistic service — often determines who finds lasting fulfillment in this profession. The actors who endure are those who fall in love not with the spotlight but with the work itself. The discovery. The connection. The transformation. The truth.

Case Study: Octavia Spencer

Octavia Spencer's career trajectory offers a masterclass in persistence and preparation meeting opportunity. For nearly twenty years, Spencer worked steadily in small roles — one-line parts, minor characters, brief appearances. She maintained consistent professionalism, building relationships and refining her craft while supporting herself through consistent if unspectacular work.

When her breakthrough role in "The Help" arrived in 2011 — after two decades in the industry — Spencer was fully prepared. Her technical skills were sharp. Her understanding of character was sophisticated. Her professional network was extensive. The "overnight success" that brought her an Academy Award at age 39 was built on thousands of days of preparation when nobody was watching.

What makes Spencer's journey instructive is how she leveraged her breakthrough rather than expecting it to automatically transform her career. She continued working consistently rather than waiting for only leading roles. She diversified into producing, creating opportunities rather than just responding to them. She balanced mainstream projects with independent films that stretched her artistically.

Spencer represents the working actor's ideal approach — professional persistence, continuous artistic growth, strategic career management, and authentic relationship building. Her success wasn't accidental but methodical, built on the foundation of specific choices made consistently over time. This is how sustainable careers are built — not through magical thinking or desperate grabs for fame, but through the patient application of craft and business acumen in equal measure.

CHAPTER 8

SCENE WORK AND RELATIONSHIP DYNAMICS

The Evolution of Connection

The chemistry between actors has always been essential to creating compelling performances. But in today's landscape, that chemistry manifests differently than it once did.

Where actors once built dynamic exchanges through heightened emotional interplay, today's most effective scene work happens in the spaces between dialogue — in the quality of listening, in the microscopic reactions that reveal thought before it finds words.

Consider *Normal People*. Paul Mescal and Daisy Edgar-Jones demonstrate a rare ability to let silence carry the full weight of emotional complexity. Their most powerful scenes are marked by minimal dialogue; the drama unfolds in their eyes, in barely perceptible shifts of breath, in the tension and release of

256

facial muscles. They aren't performing connection — they're experiencing it, moment by moment, thought by thought.

Or look at Cillian Murphy and Robert Downey Jr. in *Oppenheimer*. Their relationship dynamic is conveyed not through dialogue but in the quality of the silence between them — charged, dangerous, and thick with history. Every glance is loaded with calculation. Every pause reveals a story untold. The space between them speaks volumes.

This microscopic approach extends beyond prestige drama. Even in action-driven projects, the standard has shifted. Watch Pedro Pascal in *The Mandalorian*. For much of the series, his face is hidden behind a helmet. And yet, his connection with other characters is palpable — revealed through subtle head tilts, the tempo of his movements, and the deliberate precision of his physical stillness. Dynamics don't need exposition. They're written in the body.

This demands a profound shift in preparation. Scene work today requires not just knowing your lines but authentic listening — genuine reactions born from real-time impact, not predetermined beats. Thought must be made visible. Subtext must carry more weight than text.

Relationship dynamics now reveal themselves through the quality of attention — the way one character receives another's words, the slight adjustments in proximity or gaze. The camera captures all of it — the tiny tells, the unguarded moments that reveal history, power, longing, and betrayal.

It's all visible.
It's all exposed.

The Fundamental Connection

No performance exists in isolation. Even a monologue is a dialogue — not with another character, but with the audience or with the silence itself.

The actor may stand alone, but the work is never solitary. A monologue is a living exchange — the actor listening not with their ears but with their body, their breath, their whole being. Feeling the weight of the audience's attention, even when they remain silent. Shaping the performance moment by moment in response to that unseen other.

Acting isn't simply about delivering lines; it's about listening — and responding. Whether with a partner or with the audience, the principle remains unchanged: acting is reaction. It's the art of surrendering to what is alive in the space between.

Great actors aren't just masters of their own craft; they are masters of connection. Scene work is where voice, body, emotion, and character cease being isolated disciplines and come alive in an interactive, spontaneous exchange. Acting doesn't begin when you speak. It begins when you listen.

And sometimes, that listening must be directed inward — to yourself.

This isn't the same as self-awareness.
Self-awareness — the monitoring mind that asks, *How am I doing?* — is the death of craft. It freezes impulse and fractures presence.

Self-absorption, on the other hand, is the beginning of true craft. It is private listening — the willingness to turn inward, to hear the voice beneath the voice, to live in the shifting currents of thought and feeling before anything is spoken.

In this space, you are not performing for others. You are simply living the character's life — sometimes so quietly, so deeply, that the outside world vanishes. Yet paradoxically, this is the moment when the world — the camera, the scene partner, the audience — feels your presence most acutely.

The difference is not subtle. It is everything.

Even alone, the actor is never truly alone.

Remember the actor's golden rule: *Acting is reacting.*

It's not just a catchy phrase. It's the foundational truth many actors — even experienced ones — forget under the pressure of performance. Lines aren't announcements; they're responses. Each word emerges from what was just received, not from a predetermined plan.

A scene is a shared moment. No actor drives it alone. True acting happens when you're fully present, responding to your partner's energy in real time. Every action must be driven by a need arising from the other person, not just from internalized emotion.

I once worked with an actor who was technically brilliant — sharp instincts, well-honed craft, clear emotional arcs. On paper, she had everything. Yet, her scenes still felt mechanical. Something essential was missing.

The problem was simple but fatal: she wasn't truly listening. She performed *at* her partners, not *with* them. She knew her lines. She understood her character's emotional journey. But she wasn't present for her scene partners. She inhabited her own bubble — crafting isolated, thoughtful choices — failing to let those choices be shaped by the living moments around her.

While her instincts were strong in isolation, her work came across as disjointed and untruthful. If the performance had existed in a vacuum, we might have admired it for its precision. But acting is not solitary. What we saw instead was a performer disconnected from the intent of the scene's arc, blind to the ensemble's gifts and the shared rhythm that brings a scene to life. She was focused on her dialogue, her emotional beats — not on the story unfolding between the characters or on the dynamic breath of the scene as a whole.

Performance, especially in ensemble work, is never just about your line, your emotion, your moment. It's about what happens *between* — the invisible thread spun from true presence, shared energy, and mutual responsiveness. Without that, even the most polished technique rings hollow.

Try this: run a scene with a scene partner without you speaking. Respond only with breath, facial expressions, and body language. This silent listening exercise forces you to stay present. It sharpens your reactive instincts and stops you from retreating into your head, planning your next move while your partner is still speaking.

What you'll find is this:
Your body knows how to respond before your mind does. Trust it.

This exercise often proves revelatory. Actors discover just how much attention they've been giving to anticipating (false intending) their next line rather than absorbing the now. Forced into silence, they find themselves reacting, not performing reactions. The difference is immediate and unmistakable — the difference between constructed acting and acting that feels alive.

The Architecture of Relationship

Every scene has structure beneath its surface. To create dynamic, compelling performances, you must identify three essential elements:

your objective (what you want),

your tactics (how you get it),

and your stakes (why it matters).

Your objective — what do you want?

Every moment must have a clear intention. The stronger the objective, the sharper the scene. Vague desires produce vague performances. Be specific. Make it primal. Make it urgent.

I once worked with an actor preparing for a critical audition. When asked about his character's objective, he said, *"To get information."* Too general. We dug deeper. *"To get information about his missing sister."* Better. Finally, *"To force this person to reveal what they know about her last movements because he believes she's still alive — and he's running out of time."* Now we had something he could pursue with urgency and truth.

Specificity transforms performance. Your character doesn't want "to be loved" — they want "to make this person look at them the way they did before the betrayal." They don't want "to succeed" — they want "to prove to their dying father that his sacrifice wasn't wasted." Specific objectives create truth.

Your tactics — how do you get what you want?

Characters rarely state what they want outright. They pursue it. They employ tactics. Instead of begging for love, they charm. Seduce. Accuse. Retreat.

Watch Bryan Cranston in *Breaking Bad*. His Walter White cycles through tactics like a master strategist — intimidation, rationalization, pleading,

261

manipulation — each rising organically as the last one fails. This tactical flexibility keeps scenes unpredictable and alive.

Dynamic performances pivot — shifting tactics the moment one fails. This is where real chemistry ignites: in the space between failure and new strategy.

Your stakes — why does it matter?

If the stakes aren't life-and-death — personally, emotionally — why should the audience care?

Stakes must be personal. *Saving the world* is abstract until we understand what that world means to the character. In The Hunger Games, Jennifer Lawrence's character Katniss Everdeen isn't fighting for abstract freedom — she's fighting to return to her sister. It's specific, making the political personal and the stakes visceral.

Stakes power the scene. They determine how hard you fight, how deeply you listen, how much you care and how much you'll risk.

Take a short scene. Break it down: what's the objective, what are the tactics, what are the stakes? Rehearse it, adjusting these variables. Watch the scene transform.

Chemistry and Conflict: The Twin Engines

Relationships on stage or screen are built on chemistry and conflict. They are the twin engines that drive emotional impact — whether the story is one of love, rivalry, betrayal, or alliance.

Chemistry isn't just about romance. It's about energy exchange — the invisible current between fully realized characters. Authentic chemistry emerges from mutual impact: the sense that these two beings shape each other.

Look at Jesse Plemons and Kirsten Dunst in *The Power of the Dog*. Their chemistry is forged in small moments of recognition — the sense that each sees something in the other that the world overlooks. It isn't manufactured. It arises from deep character work and genuine connection.

Techniques to build chemistry are simple but powerful:
Eye contact.
Mirroring.
Vulnerability.

But chemistry alone isn't enough.

Conflict — not noise or shouting, but real, rooted opposition — forms the backbone of drama. Conflict arises when two agendas collide.

Think of the dinner scenes in *Succession*. The conflict isn't in the yelling — it's in the strategic maneuvering. The glances. The false pleasantries masking veiled threats. The most compelling conflict lives not in the spoken but in the unspoken — the power dynamics, the history, the wounds.

Try this: rehearse a scene without words. Use only body language, distance, proximity, and shifts in energy. Notice how much is communicated without dialogue. Observe how much richer the scene becomes when you trust the silence.

The Power of Silence

Some of the most powerful moments in acting happen when nothing is said.

Watch the final scene of *Lost in Translation*. Bill Murray whispers something inaudible to Scarlett Johansson. The words don't matter. What matters is what passes between them in the silence afterward — a moment heavy with all that cannot be said.

Great actors play not just the text but the tension between text and feeling. They allow contradictions to coexist within a moment. And the camera, especially today's intimate close-up, reads it all — the smile that doesn't reach the eyes, the firm words undermined by hesitation.

Take a scene. Run it once fast, with full delivery. Then again, allowing pauses. Notice how silence invites the audience in. Observe how it fills the scene with life.

The pause is not an empty thing. Learn to love the pause. It's filled with thought, struggle, and with the unsaid.

Directors like Denis Villeneuve understand this. In *Arrival*, the most profound moments come not from dialogue but from Amy Adams processing, choosing, and silently revealing.

Living Spontaneity

Great scene work demands spontaneity — the ability to stay present, to react, and to adapt.

The technical demands of film and television work against this... Multiple takes, shooting out of order, long days on set.

To counter this, many productions borrow from independent filmmakers — use multiple cameras, longer takes, and allow for improvisation within the framework. Improvisation keeps performances alive. It trains actors to respond, not plan.

I once worked with an actor who rehearsed everything — every pause, every glance, every breath. His work was polished, precise — but lifeless. He was classically trained and had spent years immersed in Shakespeare, where even the breaths are measured and intentional. On stage, he was brilliant. His technique, his command of language, his physicality — all of it came together to create performances that were rich, powerful, and undeniable in a theater.

But for the camera, it didn't translate. And by *didn't translate*, I mean it read. We could see the process. The work was visible — the choices, the timing, the calculated breaths. What felt alive on stage felt deliberate and constructed on screen.

As a result, his talent, which had been so celebrated in theater, wasn't as fully appreciated in film and television. The camera demanded something different — a looseness, a spontaneity, an interior life that didn't announce itself.

When we introduced structured improvisation into his preparation, everything changed. We didn't abandon his craft — we freed it. New life poured into the work. His technique didn't vanish — it became invisible, serving something deeper and more truthful. What once felt mechanical began to breathe.

Try this: perform a scene as written. Then again, improvise only the subtext while maintaining the objective. Return to the script afterward. Notice the difference. Notice what stayed alive.

The Rehearsal Process

Some actors — and even some directors — resist rehearsal. They have their reasons, and they aren't wrong. It's their process, and if it didn't work for them, they wouldn't rely on it. But for me, rehearsal is where the scene is *found*. It's where the work stops being theoretical and becomes lived. Where the raw material of instinct and preparation is shaped into something truthful.

I approach rehearsal in three distinct phases:

First, Discovery.
This stage is without pressure. Read the scene. Question it. Explore the relationships and histories buried between the lines — not just your character's, but those of the others as well. Look for what's not said. Look for what might be living beneath the text.

Second, Experimentation.
Try different emotional states and physicality. Test extremes. Play the anger as humor. Play the grief as detachment. There are no wrong choices here — only discoveries. This is where you expand the possibilities rather than narrow them too soon.

Third, Refinement.
Now, lock in the strongest, most dynamic, most truthful choices. Polish. Clarify. But be careful not to over-smooth. The goal is to keep the vitality, the layered complexity you uncovered in the earlier phases — not to lose it to mechanical repetition. Refinement is about clarity without flattening.

The Alchemy of Truth
Scene work is the alchemy where craft meets unpredictability.
A great scene isn't a recitation of lines.
It's two living beings, thinking, breathing, reacting — together.

When it works, it transcends technique.
The text falls away.
What remains is life.

This is the goal. Not perfection.

Not performance.

Truth.

My Three-Phase Approach: Safe – Top - Bottom

You've done the groundwork. You've walked the timeline, dissected the scene, mapped the character's wants, needs, wounds. You've traced the moment before — so your character doesn't just appear out of thin air like some ghost with amnesia. All those big and small questions... answered.

Now what?

Now we play.

This is where it gets interesting — where instinct meets structure, and truth begins to emerge. I take actors through three deliberate phases. It's a process. A system. My personal shorthand for discovering something honest, unexpected — alive. We don't chase "the right take." We explore the full terrain.

Phase One: Play it Safe

We begin where most actors stay. Do it safe. Do it clean. Straight down the middle — exactly as written on the page. No special flair. No clever invention. Just the scene on the page, played as it might be read in a first table read.

We run it until the rhythm settles in the body. Until the lines and tone and pace become comfortable, second nature. Until you stop thinking about blocking or beats or breath. This is calibration. It's the warm-up lap. The rehearsal before the rehearsal.

But that's all it is — a starting point. Foundations aren't the house.

Phase Two: Finding the Top

Now, we blow it open.

"Find the Top" means you stretch — explode — everything available in the scene. You push past realism. You go theatrical. Surreal. Musical if need be. Laugh on the word that should make you cry. Flirt when you're supposed to threaten. Break rhythm. Overstep. Interrupt. Stutter. Step on the other actor's lines. Break the fourth wall.

You try the version no one else would dare to submit.

Think Dafoe. Think Cage. Think Walken with nothing left to prove. This isn't about showing range. It's more about freedom — discovering the edges of what's possible. We push this until even *my* notes start getting weird. When you feel a little lost — now you're close.

But we don't stay here. We only visit, because this phase shakes loose the predictable. It breaks the polite actor in you — the one who wants to be good, wants to get it right. I don't want *right*. I want real. Authentic. Awkwardly. Drunkenly. Truthful.

Phase Three: Find the Bottom
Now we go the other way. What's the least I can play?

Strip it all down. Find "the bottom" — the place where you're barely playing anything, and yet everything is there. The murmured version. The silence. The look that doesn't land, but lingers. Talk to the floor. Talk to yourself. Play it like no one's watching — because sometimes, they aren't.

Think *Mumblecore* meets Robert Bresson. Think 2AM — no one left awake but you and the ache of the moment. The thought buried deep inside the character.

Think Greta Garbo in *Flesh and the Devil*, her eyes alone doing what most actors can't in a monologue. Of Lillian Gish in *Broken Blossoms*, trembling hands and terrified stillness speaking louder than any scream. Of Lon Chaney in *The Phantom of the Opera*, every gesture carved with pain and precision — a face behind a mask, and a thousand more behind that. Or Harold Lloyd in *Safety Last!*, dangling from the clock face not just for laughs but to show us how vulnerability *moves*.

These performers didn't have the crutch of dialogue. They had to transmit story, emotion, inner life — entirely through body, face, timing, stillness. They were masters of control. Minimalism. Precision. Every blink mattered. Every pause carried weight.

And that's the key here — you keep it *small ball*. You don't go big. You don't perform grief, or loss, or fear. You embody it. Contain it. Let it flicker just beneath the surface of the skin. Physicality becomes the language. Your breath, your posture, your glance — that's more the dialogue now. But yes, we keep the dialogue, if it serves us. Or use your own.

Because in this phase — in the bottom — it's not about reaching the back row. It's about pulling the camera *in*. About trusting the lens to catch the *internal*, what you almost didn't let escape.

This is the version you whisper. Where subtext does the heavy lifting. Where thought is louder than voice. The performance you almost don't notice... until it wrecks you.

Only after exploring all three — Safe, Top, Bottom — do we find the real terrain of the *opportunity* of the scene. But sometimes, even after you've mapped Safe, Top, and Bottom, there's value in stepping off the map entirely.

The truth lives somewhere in that tension. And now you've mapped it. You've seen where it stretches and where it breaks. You know where your performance breathes.

This isn't a technique for tricks. It's a map for discovery. A method for letting go. A way in.

This three-phase process works beautifully in rehearsal — but when we reach Chapter 9, *The Art of the Audition*, we'll see why it pays to adjust the approach.

Beyond the Top

And that's where we go beyond the Top. and into the place where craft meets chaos, and chaos makes craft. There's a kind of alchemy in going too far — in leaning into a take you know is beyond the boundaries of the scene as written. Call it a *Mirror Universe* pass. Flip the given circumstances on their head. Push tone, energy, or intention to an extreme — not to live there, but to see what unexpected gems shake loose.

Sometimes you'll hit the very "top" of a scene — the biggest emotional or physical moment that feels authentic and available to play — and then, on a whim, with a little courage, you risk it. Exceed it. You step beyond the map. Jump out of the plane without a parachute. That excess risk will always leave a mark. A residue of what once was. Then, the next time you run the scene, even if you pull it back within the confines of the script, a ghost of that excess remains. The air is charged. The muscles remember. The eyes carry it. The camera sees it.

Think of Willem Dafoe's gleeful provocation: *"Let's fuck it up. And see what comes out of it."* That's not chaos for chaos's sake — it's *chaos to craft*. In fact, for a time, I nearly made *Chaos to Craft* the subtitle of this book. That's how central this alchemy is to the work. But as much as it captures the spirit, it didn't speak to the full thesis of the book — the larger arc of history, evolution, and craft I wanted to cover. Still, the idea remains at the core.

This is permission to crack the safe open and see what's inside. Most of what you find won't make the final cut — but an echo might. And that echo can be the difference between a scene that works, and a scene that lives and breathes beyond the moment — the kind that lingers in the mind of a casting director, a director, and, finally, an audience.

Pushing the scene past its edge does two things: it shows you the full range of possibility, and it frees you from the safety of doing only what's on the page. And the more you do it in rehearsal, the more available that spirit will be when the director calls *Action*.

Case Study: Ayo Edebiri in The Bear

Following the *Three-Phase Approach*, Ayo Edebiri's performance in *The Bear* — particularly in Season 2's episode "Fishes" — this case study offers a vivid, modern embodiment of the *Find the Bottom* phase. Here, we see an actor working at the peak of internal control. Not pushing. Not showing. Just *being* — in the middle of a storm.

Her portrayal of Sydney is a masterclass in restrained authenticity. In the chaos of the kitchen — tensions exploding, egos colliding — Sydney maintains a surface calm. But behind her eyes, something remarkable is happening. We're watching her think. Not just feel — *think*. We see mental calculations, shifting strategies, and unspoken realizations unfold in real-time, all without a single line announcing them.

This is "small ball" acting at its best. No grand gestures. No overwritten emotional displays. Just micro-shifts in posture, voice, and gaze that reveal a character trying to stay afloat without letting anyone know she's drowning.

It's a lineage that goes back to the silent film masters. Greta Garbo in *Flesh and the Devil*, Lillian Gish in *Broken Blossoms*, Lon Chaney in *The Unknown*. Performers who transmitted emotion with no dialogue, using only the body, the face, the flicker of an eye. Edebiri channels that same economy of expression — updated for a world of high-definition lenses and hyper-attuned audiences.

In one particularly charged sequence, her interaction with Carmy contrasts sharply with her response to Marcus or Tina. Each relationship has its own temperature, its own undercurrent — and she calibrates accordingly. That calibration is the work. That's the scene.

This case study reinforces the heart of our thesis: in today's performance landscape, the most compelling work happens not in the declaration of emotion, but in the *containment* of it. Not in the result, but in the process. Not in telling us what the character feels — but in letting us discover it by watching them struggle *not* to show it.

Next, we'll explore the art of auditioning — how to deliver your strongest, most truthful work through a lens. In an era where nearly every casting begins with a self-tape, the camera is your first audience. We'll cover how to craft performances that feel alive, spontaneous, and authentic — even in your living room at 2AM. From taped submissions to live Zoom sessions, to finally walking "into the room" for callbacks or interviews, the challenge is always the same: make it feel real. Make them forget they're watching a recording. Make them believe.

CHAPTER 9

THE ART OF THE
AUDITION

The Evolving Audition Landscape

The audition landscape has transformed as dramatically as the performance itself. Self-tapes have replaced most in-person auditions, creating new challenges and new opportunities. Where actors once performed in rooms with immediate feedback, they now must create intimate, camera-ready performances in isolation. This shift, accelerated by the pandemic of 2020 but driven by industry efficiency, has permanently altered how actors secure work.

This evolution demands a complete rethinking of the audition technique. The sometimes broad, energetic approach that might have commanded attention in a casting office can often read as overplayed on camera. Instead, successful self-tapes capture the same qualities we've identified as essential to contemporary performance — internal life made visible, thought process as compelling as emotion, and authenticity rather than demonstration.

Yet this new format brings unexpected advantages. Gone is the nerve-rattling purgatory of the waiting room — that clinical silence, the clipboard shuffle, the dreaded "You're next," like a summons to execution. Instead, actors now have the opportunity to create intimate, focused conditions on their own terms. No distractions. No audience of strangers. Just you, the camera, and the work. You can control the frame, the lighting, the pacing — crafting a space where thought-based, detailed performance can breathe. Where the camera doesn't just observe you — it *witnesses* you. Up close. Personal. Undiluted.

Whether in-person, virtual, or self-taped, auditions remain the gateway to opportunity — those high-stakes moments where your preparation, presence, and skill must converge under pressure. Unlike scene work, which is collaborative and exploratory, the audition is a performance test. Casting directors, directors, producers aren't just looking for talent — they're scanning for adaptability, confidence, and marketability.

Make Your Own Movie

In the age of self-tapes, you have an unprecedented gift: the chance to make your own movie, first and foremost. To shape the frame. Pace the rhythm. Set the tone. This isn't just a reading — it's a performance with direction, cinematography, and intention. A world you've built around the truth you bring. So don't waste the opportunity trying to guess what they want. Show them what *you* see — what's possible when the work is yours.

And remember: you're not just auditioning for *this* role. You're auditioning for every role that comes next. You may feel you're not quite right for the part — too young, too old, too something — but the casting director might remember you for another project. The showrunner might see a fit you hadn't imagined. A director might send your tape to the lead actor for feedback — and that actor might see the spark they want to play opposite... in this or in the future.

This isn't just an audition. It's a calling card. A signature. A small film with your name on it. Make it count.

Self-Tapes: The New First Impression

In today's industry, the self-tape is the front door. No more warm handshake. No room full of nervous energy and eye contact. Just your file in a queue — your performance compressed through pixels and bandwidth. And yet... it's never been more personal.

A self-tape isn't just a technical step. It's a creative act. A moment of authorship. You're not only the actor — you're also the director, the DP, the sound designer, the editor. The tape you submit doesn't just show what kind of performer you are — it shows what kind of *storyteller* you are.

So don't treat it like a chore. Treat it like your short film. Because for once in this unpredictable process, you *do* have control.

Yes — get the basics right. Clean background. Natural or soft lighting. Good audio (buy whatever gear you need to do this right). No clutter. No chaos. Frame it properly: medium close-up for most scenes, slightly wider for physicality. Show them you're ready for a professional set — because in this moment, you already are one.

But remember, technical polish is just the entry fee. What matters is what *comes through* the lens.

The good news? You don't need a scene partner on camera to create a dynamic relationship. You just need someone offscreen — ideally in the room — or, if not, on the phone, recorded, or preloaded into your editing software. Even if that someone is you, reading with yourself, as long as the energy is right. The presence matters.

Unless otherwise directed, keep your eyeline close to the lens. Let the camera feel like another person — not a device, not a test, but a *witness*.

The best self-tapes feel like stolen moments. Like we stumbled into something we weren't meant to see.

Use a bit of "business" — something small to open the scene, so it doesn't look like you suddenly blinked into existence on "action."

Open with something small — a breath, a glance, a physical beat — so the moment doesn't begin with the line.

And when allowed, submit two takes for each scene. If it's a short one — a "They went thataway" kind of line for a day player — consider submitting three. But make sure each take is *truly different*. If you can't find three distinct versions, you haven't done the work.

Remember the Three-Phase Approach: Safe, Top, Bottom. That process isn't just for exploration — it can guide your final tapes. Just be sure your final choice is the one that breathes.

Because in the end, the golden rule of auditioning still holds:

Don't be boring.

That's the difference between acting... and being seen.

press play... the clock is ticking.

What They're Really Looking For

So what are they really looking for?

276

It's not just talent. Not just training. Not even the perfect "look." They're looking for the actor who solves their problem. Who fits the world they're building? Who shows up — not just prepared, but alive in the moment.

Yes, preparation matters. Yes, presence matters. But what makes someone book consistently? I once asked a top casting director that exact question. She said simply:

"I'm looking for actors who solve my problem, not create new ones."

Read that again. Because that mindset can change everything.

It's not a judgment of your worth — it's a search for the piece that makes the whole thing click. Your audition is your proposal: *"Here's how I can help bring this story to life."* When you stop chasing approval and start embodying **value**, everything shifts. Your energy in the room changes. Your focus sharpens. Anxiety drops away.

The casting process isn't built to reward desperation. It responds to clarity. Generosity. Specificity. And yes — a sense of ease. The actors who book aren't the ones performing for approval. They're the ones inviting collaboration.

So before you hit record on that self-tape — ask yourself: *"Am I offering a solution? Or just hoping to be chosen?"*

Which Take Comes First - Risk Toward Refinement

I get asked a lot, "If I'm submitting multiple takes, which one should I lead with?"

It's a fair question, but the answer is nuanced, tricky, and not quite straightforward.

Casting directors sift through hundreds, even thousands of submissions. They're not hunting to discover you — they're scanning for easy reasons to eliminate actors who don't fit.

So, do you open boldly? With your most vivid, risk-taking interpretation in order to get their attention?

The answer... Maybe.

Common wisdom says, "Put the safe one first. Get it out of the way, then experiment with something more daring afterward." But here's the nuance: if the casting director already knows you — if you've been in their room before or booked through them — then yes, lead with your safe take. They'll likely watch all the takes you submit. You've earned that privilege. They're looking to be reminded, not convinced.

So that's your submission strategy. Safe take submitted first, exactly what's on the page.

But what's your shooting strategy?

Here's a tip — more like a secret weapon — you probably haven't heard it elsewhere: your self-tape audition process shouldn't start safely. Begin with the *top*, the throwaway take, the one that terrifies you just a bit. Go all out. Explore the subtext, your invented backstory. Let the lines blur into something deeper. Don't think about hitting the implied marks that might be in the action lines.

Find the essence of your character, the core truth of the scene, and wring the life out of it. Make your little movie. Claim your Academy Award in the confines of *what's available to play* on the page. Even if you never submit this take, it's crucial you shoot it. Because it's where the gold lives. Where the risk lies, and where authenticity breathes. Get that take down first, work it

278

to death until you're thrilled with it. Then — and only then — do your safe take.

Yes, you heard right — this approach runs counter to conventional wisdom and all typical set practices. On set, directors secure the safe take first. Only after securing a good take are they sometimes willing to experiment with a different version, if time allows. Budgets, schedules dictate those practicalities.

But your audition tape doesn't have those constraints. So go *top* first, unshackle yourself from all caution.

Why?

Because once you've captured the audacity of that initial, fearless performance, your *safe* take, however small or controlled, will carry an echo, a residue of the depth you've already mined. That resonance isn't artificial, laid on top — it's deeply embedded in the character's DNA now. It's the secret, subtle advantage of working from risk toward refinement.

If you've made it this far in the book and still haven't found enough practical value, take this last piece of advice to heart. The time and money you've invested will return more dividends than you can imagine at this moment.

When the Camera Turns Into a Room

Most auditions today begin and end with tape. You submit. They watch. No handshake, no banter, no room. Just your work out there in the void, doing the talking for you.

But sometimes — when you're being seriously considered for a more significant role — the process shifts. You may be invited to a callback via Zoom, or, on rare occasions, asked to come into the room, wherever that may be. These are mostly for things like guest star, recurring role on a series, lead or co-lead in a film. This is often just a vibe check with the director, producers, or even the current attached star.

It's still an audition — but now it's *live*. Real time. No second take. No editing. No lighting tweaks or reader swaps. Just you.

That's when the work shifts again. And that's when this truth matters most.

Your Mind Walks In First

Before they hear your voice, they feel your presence.

If you enter the room (or the Zoom) needing approval, it shows. It leaks through your voice, your posture, your pace. But if you arrive believing you have something to offer — a take, a truth, a point of view — everything changes. That's not arrogance. That's alignment. Humble confidence is usually your best positioning.

Casting directors, producers, filmmakers — they read energy. Long before they evaluate your choices, they register your clarity. Your confidence. Stillness. Steadiness. Your self-trust.

Early in my acting career, I was told something that didn't resonate at the time, but it stuck with me until I eventually understood the value and learned to make the most of it.

While in a workshop, a well-established LA casting director said:

"I can usually tell in the first five steps the actor takes entering the room, whether an actor's going to be worth watching. Ninety-nine percent of the time, I already know before they begin."

At the time, I thought it was a self-important generalization. But he took it further — made it part of the workshop exercises. There were about twenty of us. He sent us outside, and one by one, we knocked on the door, walked in, and introduced ourselves. Over and over. Just the walk, the entrance.

Back then, like most of the others in class, I dismissed its value — as just a noteworthy anecdote. Now?

Now, I understand exactly what he meant, the deeper value, well beyond that first introduction and entrance into the room.

It wasn't about posture. It was about presence. Ownership. Whether we walked in as if we already belonged there, or as if we were asking for permission to be there. That's the physical truth of it... It speaks before anything else can.

Recently, I saw an interview with Gil Junger discussing the casting of Heath Ledger in *10 Things I Hate About You.*

Junger: "I had read 253 Guys for 10 Things. Marcia Ross, who was the head of casting, said, look, I don't know this last kid, it's a favor for an agent that I respect. So the door opens, and Heath walks in. I didn't know him. And he took about four steps towards me. And this is exactly what I thought, 'If this guy can read English, I'm going to cast him.' Why? Because there was just a presence about him. There was a confidence. He just walked in as if to say, 'This is who I am.' He was 100% Heath Ledger. He clearly didn't pay any attention to the stage directions. And that won me over like a wave. When he left, I told Marci, 'Hire him immediately.' And he was hired before he got to his car."

So yes, we're back to the body, physicality, *business* again, back to how you carry yourself — not as a performance, but as evidence of who's showing up to do the work.

So take the time to prepare. But let go of perfection. Presence isn't born of polish — it's born of an internal stillness. A breath and practice.

So before the session, settle yourself. Not with tricks — with breath. Drop your shoulders. Loosen your jaw. Take three full, intentional, deep breaths before entering the frame or entering the room. Let everything tighten, then release. It's not about faking confidence. It's about remembering that you've done the work — then letting that truth settle into your body.

That's the version of you they need to see. The one who already belongs there.

Breaking Down Sides Quickly and Effectively

When you receive your sides, how you analyze them will make or break your audition. Many actors dive immediately into memorization without understanding the scene's purpose, the character's function, or the overall narrative context. This is a backward approach that, at best, yields technically accurate but emotionally empty performances.

Before you make choices — before objectives, tactics, or intentions — ask yourself: *Where the hell am I?*

Ask: Where does this moment actually take place?

Is it an alleyway or crowded diner with the echo of silverware and overlapping conversations in the background? A dark hallway where overhead fluorescents flicker like they're on their last leg? A memory-soaked childhood bedroom and something from an older era?

What time is it—morning, night? Summer? Fall? Before or after the thing that changed everything?

Is the air cold, stiff, humid, dry? What's the light like? Are you standing or sitting? Alone or exposed? What do your clothes feel like on your skin? Too tight? Too thin? Too familiar?

Then go even deeper: What does it smell like? Taste like? What *just* happened the moment before — five minutes ago, five years ago, that still clings to this moment?

The actor's first and most sacred job is to *be somewhere.* Fully. Not vaguely. Not generically. You can't want something until you know where you are. You can't live in the truth of a moment if you're floating above it like a puppet, hoping it will land somewhere convincing.

So, before you figure out what your character wants, figure out where they're standing — what surrounds them, what weight the space holds, what texture is under their fingertips. The details of those granular, invisible facts are the foundation of everything else.

Once you're there — *really there* — then, and only then, ask: What does this character want?

Not what they say they want, not what the line suggests on its surface, but what they *need* underneath it all. Why they ache for it. Fear they won't get it. Fear they *will*.

Sometimes, in a break-up scene, the character might insist they want freedom, but the real drive — and more interestingly — might be more twisted: to hurt the other person first, to force a reaction, or to avoid the shame of being left behind.

Desire, like people, is never simple.

Then comes the next inevitable layer: *Why now?*

Why does it matter here, in this scene? In this moment? What happens if they don't get what they need? What breaks? What truth gets buried? What opportunity gets lost? What pain gets repeated?

The complete stakes are rarely found in the dialogue itself. They live in the unsaid — in the history that isn't on the page but bleeds through, despite the lines. They live in the context — the fight from last night, the anniversary forgotten, the voicemail unanswered. This is the engine that moves the scene. Without it, you're just reciting words with an attached emotion.

And then — only then — can you begin to feel the shape of the scene.

Every well-written moment has an architecture. It shifts, it turns. There are moments of hesitation, escalation, reversal. You feel the temperature drop. The clumsy eye shift. The smile that isn't a smile anymore. The *notes* to play within the possibility of a scene.

So, where does it turn? When does the power shift? When does the air go still?

Mark those places — make note — not rigidly, not as *checkpoints to hit* — but as emotional terrain to allow to explore. Without them, the scene flattens into a single one-note performance. With them, it pulses. Becomes authentic.

And now that you've metaphorically walked the scene's space, sat in the silence, and traced the edges of the character's need — now you can ask the most dangerous question: What is *your* specific way in? What might *you* understand about this character that others will miss?

What do you carry — quietly, privately, personally — that allows you to touch this role in a way no one else sees?

This isn't about being strange or clever. It's not about making a choice that "pops." It's about *owning the soul of the moment*. Boldness doesn't mean noise, loud, or anger. It means *clarity*. It means specificity. It means you've chosen something real — and *real* always reads.

So when you're handed new material — those five pages, that monologue, that audition side — don't start with *performance*.

Give yourself ten minutes to ask and answer the only questions that matter:

Who am I?

What do I want?

What's in my way?

How do I get it?

Why does it matter?

Then—trust yourself. Trust the space you've built in your mind. Trust the instinct that lives under your preparation.

Don't plan it to death.

Perform it as if you were only now discovering it.

Because that's what the audience wants to see — *not you showing them something, but you finding something right along with them.*

In real time.

That's the difference between acting that might impress... and acting that *transforms*.

The Technical Craft of Audition Mastery

Memorization? Absolutely — it's non-negotiable. You've got to know your lines cold. But here's the catch: rehearse it too clean, too tight, and you strangle the life out of it. I see this all the time with actors who've done a lot of commercial or corporate work. That over-polished delivery becomes a trap. Every move, every beat, prepackaged, exactly. Executed, not discovered. And the thing is — today's audience can *feel* that. They may not know exactly what's off, but they sense the machinery underneath. The intention behind the intending. The "Here comes my next line. Here is where I move to my next mark. My hand goes here." energy. It's false. Polite. Empty. And even if the audience can't name it... they can see it. And they *smell* it.

Techniques for natural memorization start with understanding the *subtext* and logical flow of the scene rather than rote repetition. I often write the lines out by hand as another mental perspective to reinforce retention. I also audio record the scene in a neutral tone and listen back while rehearsing.

Physical action helps. Always. Run the scene while making your bed. Unloading the dishwasher. Try eating an apple — eating and saying your lines is a very good exercise, by the way, in general. Take a long walk. While doing these, your body begins to associate the words with motion. Muscle memory kicks in. The subtext becomes clearer, and the lines stop feeling like "lines." They just *are*. Like living, breathing thought. They don't sit on top of the page or the moment — they come from *inside* your character.

For those rare in-person auditions, the initial moments (walking into the room), as previously mentioned, can often determine your success. So enter with confidence and focus — casting directors notice energy before words. Never complain about traffic and what it took to get there. Have the attitude that "Everything's just fallen perfectly into place for you to be here at this moment." It couldn't be any easier or more ideal. Make eye contact and acknowledge the room with a genuine, relaxed greeting. Carry yourself like a professional who belongs there, not someone hoping to be chosen.

Be warm and upbeat in handling small talk and introductions — casting directors have tight schedules. If asked, say something brief but memorable about yourself. Something you've practiced a hundred times, but can make it look like you've just thought about it for the first time. Never force humor or over-explain. Don't apologize or overthink — you belong in that room. So act like it.

The slate — your introduction before performing — merits special attention. Many actors treat it as a throwaway moment, but smart performers recognize it as their first acting choice. Your slate should demonstrate the energy and presence you'll bring to the role — not necessarily in character, but aligned with a hint of the project's tone. A procedural crime drama audition might warrant a focused, direct slate, while a comedy could allow for warmer, more upbeat, charming, personable energy.

For self-tapes, your slate should follow precisely the requested directions, usually detailed in the audition request, while still conveying your unique presence. State your name clearly, the role you're reading for, and any other requested information. Keep it brief but not rushed. This might seem minor, but casting directors often report that an actor's slate immediately signals their experience, professionalism, and camera awareness. In this new era of self-tapes, the elimination of an actor can happen at the slate. The *slate* should look completely comfortable, like you're not trying but were born to play this part. That does not mean that if you are auditioning for the role of an astronaut, you should be wearing a pressure suit, but rather, as an astronaut, comfortable in his street clothes, at home.

Taking Direction: The True Test

Plenty of actors crush the first take — only to crumble the moment an adjustment is thrown at them. It's not about talent. It's about adaptability. That moment — when the casting director leans in and says, "Let's try it a little different"—that's where the job is often won or lost.

Taking direction isn't just following orders. It's reading between the lines. Interpreting the *intent* of the note, not just the words. And doing it without losing the integrity of the character that got you in the room in the first place.

When you're given a note, repeat it back. Not robotically — just to confirm. "So, a little more conversational, less intensity?" That tiny moment shows you're present, collaborative, and not guessing. It also gives them a window to clarify. Because "less intense" can mean a dozen things—softer, slower, more internal, less heat but not less focus.

Then make a bold shift. Clean. Deliberate. Don't half-split the difference between your first read and the adjustment. Don't play it safe. The note is a gift — it's a second shot. Show them you can pivot without unraveling. That you can adjust while still owning the scene. That you're directable. That you're *hirable*. And that you have *range*. The secret sauce of craft.

Some common notes and re-directions might include comments like: "Pull it back" (reduce intensity without losing investment); "Let's see it underneath" (keep the emotion but express it more subtly); "Make it more conversational" (find natural rhythm rather than performed speech patterns); "Speed it up" (increase energy and pace); "Take the air out of it." (don't pause as much between sentences or ideas) or "Take your time with it" (find the important moments rather than rushing through).

As an exercise, you might have an actor friend give you unexpected adjustments mid-scene. Try responding without breaking character or losing flow. This builds the muscle, range, and adaptability — perhaps the most valuable quality an actor can possess in the audition room.

The callbacks process presents unique challenges. You've passed the first hurdle, but now face higher expectations. Callbacks both in the room and on Zoom often include more decision-makers — the director, producers, studio executives, each with different priorities. Stay consistent with what got you the callback while remaining open to any new direction.

For a callback from a self-tape, resist the urge to completely reinvent your performance. The initial submission earned you the opportunity, so build on that foundation rather than starting from scratch. Make refinements based on feedback provided, but maintain the core choices that originally distinguished you from other actors.

The Live Virtual Auditions: Another New Reality

Though most auditions these days are self-taped submissions, the pandemic accelerated the industry's shift — first toward virtual, live online auditions. Zoom, Teams, and whatever else they decide to throw at us. Each with its own quirks. It's not a self-tape. It's not in-person. It's something in between... and it requires a different kind of calibration altogether.

While these are becoming rarer, let's cover them — just to make sure the nuance isn't lost. There are things here that matter more than you might think.

These auditions are scheduled at a specific time, which means a tech run-through is essential. You'll most likely be standing, so position your camera or webcam at eye level. Not above. Not below. Looking down shrinks your presence. Looking up? Unflattering—and a little desperate. Frame yourself from mid-chest up. Give yourself room to move with any business or action the script calls for, so you're not sliding out of frame mid-beat.

Lighting matters. Place your key light in front of you, just behind the camera, slightly elevated. Fill light on either side helps eliminate shadow. And never — *ever* — sit with a window behind you. Unless you want to look like a silhouette in a docuseries about poor decisions.

Connection speed matters too. Use wired internet if you can. Shut down background apps. Do a test run with an actor friend. And have a backup — hotspot, audio dial-in, something. Because if the tech fails — and it *does* — and you've got no Plan B? That's on you. And it's all for nothing.

Case in point: a few years ago, I had a *Live* callback through a casting director's proprietary platform. I tested everything days before and again and hour before my audition time. So I sat in the virtual "waiting room" with confidence. Watched the countdown as I moved up the queue. Then — right as the CD came online — the system crashed. Theirs, I think, as it didn't seem to like my connection or operating system. We tried again 3 more times in quick succession. Then rescheduled for later that day. Same result. Never got back in. And here's the truth: it's been at least four or five years, and I haven't been invited back by that casting office since. Not blaming them one bit. That's on *me*. Other actors made it work. I didn't. And casting directors don't have time for tech excuses — even the honest ones. So just a word of caution.

That said, I know plenty of CDs who *prefer* live virtual auditions. It allows them to offer real-time direction. If you get one, take it as a compliment — you've already been vetted. They're interested. It's a chance to make a live connection through the screen and, often, for the CD to cut together your session and send it along to the film or series director with their stamp of approval.

These particular auditions are a little different. You're usually asked to read to camera — directly into the lens. Not at the face on your monitor. It feels strange, but on their end, it reads as eye contact. Let the reactions live on your face. Stay in it.

And energy? This is where actors most often miss the mark. Self-tapes can be low flame. In-person? You'll need a lift. Virtual live? Right in between. About 10 to 15% more energy than you'd use for a self-tape — just enough to push through the flatness of the screen. Not manic. Not dead. Think *vibrant stillness*, not caffeinated chaos. Of course, this is in general terms and scene-dependent.

Every detail counts in this format. The frame. The lighting. The timing before you speak (or don't — "take the air out"). The way your energy lives inside the space.

Casting directors don't have time to fill in the blanks. Your job is to make the frame work for you, not against you.

That's how you turn a digital square into a doorway.

The Aftermath: Learning from Every Audition

After an audition, let it go. Immediately. Overthinking won't change the result. Give yourself a day — that's it. Reflect, make a note, learn what you can, then move on. The actor who obsesses over yesterday's audition misses today's opportunity. The one who celebrates too long? Misses tomorrow's preparation.

You'll never know how close you were — or how far off. That part isn't yours. What *is* yours is the next shot. The next moment. The next tape.

And if you're lucky enough to get feedback — take it. Apply it. But don't drag it backward into the last performance. Use it to sharpen the next one.

You're not auditioning for a role. You're auditioning for a career. Never forget that.

The smartest actors I know keep track of their auditions. Not a diary. Not a confessional. Just clean, useful notes. What you wore. Who was in the room — casting director, producer, assistant, intern with a clipboard. What project it was, who directed it, what network or studio was behind it. What scene you did. What the vibe was. And any feedback, even the offhand kind.

Over time, these notes start to show you something. Patterns. Maybe a certain casting director responds better when you lead with stillness, not business. Maybe you prep better when you rehearse late at night instead of first thing in the morning. Maybe your shoes mattered, how you felt in them. Or they didn't.

You start to see the audition process not as a crapshoot, but as something you can actually *shape*. And that's where the real shift can happen — from chaos to craft. From guessing... to working.

The audition is your moment of power — a chance to prove you are prepared, present, and confident. Mastery of auditions means mastery of the industry. The actor who books isn't always the most talented. They're most often the most prepared. The most present. The most adaptable.

They're the actor who walks into the room as if they already have the job. Who performs not from desperation but from confidence. Who knows their worth and demonstrates it without apology.

This isn't just about securing a role. It's about building a career one audition at a time. About transforming each opportunity — whether it ends in booking or rejection — into a stepping stone toward mastery of your life-long craft.

Case Study: Adam Driver and the Power of Stillness

Adam Driver is known for intense presence and emotional precision, but what often surprises casting directors is how *quiet* his auditions are. In a conversation with *Backstage*, a casting director remarked that Driver "doesn't perform the scene, he *lives it* — even in the smallest frame."

When auditioning for *Girls*, Driver didn't try to project charm or likability — he leaned into awkward silences, odd pacing, and moments that *should have felt wrong*, but didn't. They felt lived. Because he wasn't acting like a guy trying to land a role. He was a guy simply responding to a given moment — on camera, under constraints, but fully in the room.

What stands out in his audition approach is how unpolished it is — deliberately so. Driver focuses less on delivering "moments" and more on listening and reacting. He allows the frame to do the work. His gestures are minimal. Eye lines specific. He doesn't fill the space unnecessarily. It creates a kind of gravitational pull — the camera leans in, rather than pulls away.

The Shift: From Survival to Evolution

His work reminds us that success in on-camera auditions isn't about high energy or strong choices for the sake of visibility. It's about clarity. About holding tension in the body. About making silence feel dangerous — or safe — or full of unspoken stakes.

Driver didn't get the role because he showed the casting team what he could do. He got it because he made them believe that in that space, in that moment, they were watching someone authentic — an original moment.

Survival isn't the same as thriving.

You've learned to navigate the business. To build champions. To manage rejection. To create financial sustainability in a world that offers only uncertainty. These are the tools that keep you in the game — standing, breathing, fighting for the next opportunity.

But the actor who merely survives eventually withers. They become stagnant. They start repeating themselves, recycling what worked yesterday instead of discovering what might work tomorrow.

The difference between the actor with a job and the actor with a lifetime of meaningful work isn't luck. It isn't connections. It isn't even raw talent. It's evolution.

It's the willingness to keep growing when no one's watching. To polish the instrument when no one's listening. To expand your range when no one's demanding it. It's the commitment to train not just for the role you have, but for the artist you're becoming.

In this industry, the moment you stop growing, you start dying. The techniques that book you work today might be obsolete tomorrow. The performances that moved audiences a decade ago might feel mannered or false to the next generation. The casting category that carried you through your twenties won't sustain you through your forties.

So how do you not just endure — but evolve? How do you transform survival into mastery? How do you build a practice that keeps you vital across decades, not just seasons?

That's where we turn next. From the actor who survives... to the artist who transforms.

PART IV

THE
ARTIST'S PATH

The Long Becoming — The Actor Who Endures

Acting isn't just something you do. It's something that seeps into the way you listen. The way you watch people. How you hold tension in your body during an argument, or catch yourself slipping into a different voice at the dinner table — hoping nobody notices. It becomes how you move through the world, consciously or not.

This final section shifts focus. Less about craft in isolation, more about the long arc. About what it means to live this work over time — years, decades, a lifetime — with all the highs, lulls, pivots, and unexpected recalibrations, reinventions along the way.

We'll look at sustainability. Not in a buzzword sense, but practically: how do you keep showing up when it's been a while since anything landed? How do you stay sharp and ready when the request for auditions slows or stops altogether? How do you keep your fire lit when the industry trends seem to favor something else entirely?

Because that moment will come. It does for us all. Always.

When the roles stop resonating.
When the work dries up — or worse, becomes mechanical. It will.
When the people around you start quitting. They will.
When you catch yourself wondering if you missed your window. You didn't.
Or if maybe it was never there to begin with?

This is where endurance becomes less about resilience and more about philosophy. Not talent. Not technique. Not who you know. But something internal — quieter — that still believes in the work, the love of craft, even when there's no audience for it.

There's a paradox at the center of acting that becomes more visible the longer you stay around: You work for years to master your process — voice, body, impulse, range — only to realize the real goal is to let it all drop. To trust it's there without holding onto it.

That's the leap.

I remember asking an early acting coach — someone I deeply respected — how you're supposed to do it all at once. "How do you hold all of this in your head," I said, "and still do the scene… and remember the words… and not fall apart?"

He smiled. Told me it's like walking into an empty room you've slowly filled with furniture. A chair here, a lamp, a table, a couch. Over time, the space becomes yours — cluttered maybe, but familiar. At first you have to be careful, navigate it with awareness. But eventually, he said, you can walk into that room blindfolded and know exactly where to sit, where to put your feet up. It's all still there. You just don't have to think about it anymore.

That metaphor never left me. Because that's the work. You build it up, piece by piece, and then... you stop trying to hold it all. You just live in it.

True mastery means not needing to perform the mastery. It means you're free to respond — to the moment, the other actor, to the space — with nothing in the way. You're not acting anymore. You're available.

It's not perfectionism. It's the highest tier of craft. And it's rare — but not unreachable.

Most actors catch glimpses. A few can get there more often. What matters is that you know it's possible — and you learn how to return to it, not by chasing the feeling, but by building a foundation strong enough to support it when it comes.

These final chapters won't hand you that. But they'll point you toward it. With language. With questions. With a bit of perspective. Enough to help you find your own way back when things get quiet... and the work asks more of you than it used to.

CHAPTER 10

THE ACTOR'S LIFELONG TRAINING ROUTINE

Evolution, Not Stagnation

An actor's training cannot remain static in an evolving industry. Methods that once perfectly prepared performers for 1990s cinema or early 2000s television often fall short in developing the skills demanded by today's productions. If the medium changes — and it always does — your training must change with it.

This doesn't mean discarding classical foundations. It means adapting them. It means supplementing traditional training with work designed specifically for the nuanced, thought-driven performances that today's cameras demand. The intimacy of contemporary film and television doesn't reward size or projection — it rewards interiority, precision, and authenticity.

Modern training should emphasize *thought visibility* — the ability to think truthfully on camera, not just act. *Micro expression control* — understanding how the smallest facial movements communicate volumes. *Internal monologue development* — cultivating a rich, unspoken inner life that subtly animates the performance. *Technological adaptation* — learning how different camera setups, frame sizes, and digital formats alter performance requirements.

Much of the most relevant training today comes not from the classroom but from studying today's best performers with analytical eyes.

Watch Florence Pugh's minute shifts in awareness.

Observe Steven Yeun's compelling stillness.

Track Jodie Comer's ability to make her thought patterns visible without a word.

Break down their work frame by frame — not for what they *do*, but for *how they think* on camera.

The actor who evolves alongside the industry doesn't just survive — they thrive.

Range today isn't only about playing different characters.

It's about adapting to different mediums, evolving technologies, and shifting stylistic approaches as the art form itself continues to change.

The ones who endure are the ones who evolve.

The Never-Ending Apprenticeship

The most successful actors in the world never stop training.

Just as athletes continually refine their mechanics, actors must keep sharpening their craft — not for accolades, but for survival. The industry evolves. The work demands new techniques. And growth — both personal and artistic — constantly changes the way an actor approaches the craft.

Why does the training never end?

Because acting is a muscle.

Without consistent use, it weakens.
It dulls. It loses responsiveness.

Every new role presents new challenges.
Every new medium — film, television, streaming, digital — demands fresh adaptation.
Mastery isn't about knowing everything. It's about staying open — alert to what you don't know yet.
Repetition isn't stagnation. It's refinement. It sharpens instincts, making them faster, clearer, more reliable.

Look at the ones who endure:
Meryl Streep still works with voice coaches decades into her career.
Anthony Hopkins, well into his eighties, continues to refine his technique.
Viola Davis regularly returns to theater between film projects to maintain her technical foundation.

These are not beginners clinging to the basics. They are masters who understand that real mastery is never finished.

Try this:
Identify three areas of your craft where you feel weakest.
Voice work? Movement? Emotional range?
Create a six-month training plan to address those weaknesses.
Be specific. Be consistent. Be honest about where you need work.

Many actors avoid precisely the areas that need the most attention.
The naturally charismatic performer avoids technical precision.
The technically gifted actor sidesteps emotional vulnerability.
The dramatic actor shies away from comedy.
But true growth requires the courage to confront weakness, not sitting in your comfort zone relying on your strengths.

The work never ends. And that — more than anything — is why it stays alive.

Best Practices: Monologue & Scene Work

Always have at least three polished monologues ready to go in your back pocket. You should be working on these with your coach or actor partner on a weekly basis. To develop your best monologues, you need to have several that you are working on and rotating as your top three. This is an ongoing process that will keep you sharp and ready to go at a moment's notice when the opportunity arises. Work these until you are sick of them, then rework them some more. Find new ones that will challenge you and make you fail miserably. Then work harder to uncover what weakness is holding you back. You will need a second pair of eyes to assist with this process, so be sure and find a good coach or trusted actor who is able to give you notes objectively.

I've watched actors shift their entire trajectory — not through big breaks or some magical revelation, but through quiet, consistent daily practice. No drama. No rituals. Just commitment.

One actress used to warm up her voice every morning in the shower. Ten minutes. Nothing fancy. Over time — and I mean, over years — her range, control, and vocal presence expanded so naturally, even *she* didn't realize what had changed at first. But everyone else could hear it.

Another actor — he used his morning commute like a rehearsal lab. He'd borrow someone's walk, their posture, even their accent. For a few blocks, he'd become someone else entirely. Then let it go. No performance. No feedback. Just the habit itself — that *was* the training.

These weren't grand gestures. They weren't dramatic. But they *stacked*. Quietly. Layer by layer. And over time, they built something solid — a flexible, responsive instrument that could be played on cue.

Most of the actors I've worked with? They've been doing some version of this since they were kids. Long before they called it "acting." They were already studying people. Mimicking. Testing things. Trying on other ways of being. That's how you know the impulse is real — it shows up early, without permission.

The best daily practice does two things: it maintains what you've earned... and it pushes you somewhere new.

Maintenance keeps the edges sharp — voice, body, focus. Growth stretches your range. Without both, you stall. If you only maintain, you start repeating yourself. If you only chase the new without grounding it, your work gets wobbly. Unreliable.

So balance both. And once a week — make it count.

Pick one thing. Go deep. Work a monologue, top to bottom. Beat it out. Rehearse it. Film it. Do a cold read. Grab a partner, hit a scene. Do some improv. Watch it back. Sharpen the blade.

That weekly reset? It keeps you honest. Keeps the rust off. Keeps the fire lit.

Because when the call comes? That's not when you start warming up. That's when you're already ready.

Beyond the Comfort Zone

Growth doesn't happen where it's comfortable. And it doesn't happen where things are already working — not really.

That's the trap.

You find something that clicks. Gets a laugh. Earns praise. So you stay there. You lean on it. Sharpen that one edge again and again until it shines — but the rest of your instrument starts to dull. Over time, you stop discovering. You start repeating.

We've all done it. It's survival, in a way. A rhythm you can trust. But artistry lives on the *edge* of that rhythm — just past it, in the unknown. Where you stammer. Miss. Second-guess. That's the space where your instincts either expand... or harden. And only one of those keeps you moving forward.

So stretch — on purpose.

Take the role that doesn't feel like it belongs to you. Say yes to the audition that scares you. Play softness if you usually lead with edge. Try chaos if you're always composed. Accept the part that feels a size too big — and grow into it.

Make space for the awkward phase. That moment where nothing's landing yet. Where it all feels uncertain. That's not failure. That's *risk*. And risk is the birthplace of anything honest.

Let your technique bend a little. Or bend a lot. Try classical structure. Absurdism. Butoh. Meisner drills. Do a monologue without punctuation. Perform a scene in a language you don't speak — not to show off, but to disturb the habits you didn't know you had.

Push the instrument.

Take up dance. Dialect work. Fencing. Improv. Let your voice crack. Let your body lose its balance. Forget your breath — and don't rush to fix it. Stay inside the disruption. Because what you do *next*... that's where the acting lives.

And when in doubt — flip the script.

Take a scene you know cold, and invert it. If you led it with logic, try leading it with fear. If you performed it from the chest, whisper it from the gut. Not to be "different," but to shake something loose. To knock a few layers off. To surprise yourself.

Because you have habits — right now — that you don't even know are habits. We all do.

And sometimes failure — real, present-tense, sweaty-palmed failure — is the only thing loud enough to show them to you.

The actor who always explodes might discover the truth inside restraint. The one who charms through every beat might find something rawer in stillness. These aren't just new choices — they're new *options.* And that's what range really is: the freedom to choose.

Some of the biggest shifts I've seen in actors? They didn't come from scenes at all.

They came from cross-training.

Study a visual art. Learn an instrument. Take up martial arts. Or sculpture. The painter learns patience and shape. The fighter learns timing and rhythm. The sculptor teaches you how to stop just before you ruin it.

None of these take you away from acting. They take you deeper into it. They widen your expressive range. They add new tools — new energies — new *languages* to move in.

306

Cross-training doesn't scatter your focus. It refines it. Teaches you how to listen differently. Move differently. Respond with nuance you didn't have before.

And when the time comes — when the scene turns, when the silence holds, when the director doesn't cut — those layers will be there.

Not because you rehearsed a clever choice.

But because something in you got wider.

And that's the quiet power of stepping beyond your comfort zone. You don't just expand what you can *do* — you expand what you're made of. You create new terrain inside yourself. So when the moment comes?

You'll have somewhere real to go.

Not because you planned it.
Because you earned it.

The Collaborative Nature of Training

You can rehearse a monologue alone. You can drill lines, stretch your range, run breath work, record a dozen takes until the lighting feels right. But acting — *actual acting* — doesn't fully come alive until it meets another human being.

Because the moment another actor enters the frame, everything shifts. Your rhythm bends. Your certainty wobbles. The scene becomes a conversation, not a solo. It's no longer about what *you* feel, but what *you* provoke — and what you absorb. The space between you becomes the actual performance.

That's where the growth lives.
In the between.

Scene partners don't let you stay asleep. They push back. They surprise you. They miss a beat and force you to find another one. They make you listen, really listen. And the moment you stop listening, they let you know it. Directly or indirectly — but unmistakably.

Workshops wake you up. Peer rehearsals catch you slipping into habit. They throw you into friction, into heat, into awareness. And the best collaborators hold up the kind of mirror you can't avoid — the kind that says, *This. Right here. Look again.*

You can practice technique in isolation. You can refine breath, gesture, vocal strength. And you should. But the relational magic — the live pulse that carries truth across a scene — only happens when another soul is standing across from yours. Acting isn't constructed in a vacuum. It's discovered in exchange.

Seek that out. Not occasionally. Consistently.

Join a scene study group. Trade sides with a friend. Cold read with strangers. Find the actors who throw you off balance — who challenge your rhythm, not reinforce it. And don't stop there. Train with dancers. With writers. With musicians who breathe in different time signatures. With poets who hear silence as music.

Every creative language you learn? It echoes back through your work.

The actor who trains only with familiar actors runs the risk of repeating themselves. They get slick. They get competent. But they start echoing the room instead of stretching beyond it. Those who step outside — who cross-train across disciplines — return different. Sharper. Stranger. More alive.

And then there's feedback.

Not flattery. Not applause. But clear, unsentimental, trusted feedback. The kind that sees you and says the thing you've missed. That gesture you always fall back on. That breath you skip when the stakes rise. That unspoken habit you've stopped noticing.

One note can shift everything.

I've watched it happen. A single observation — one honest, precise mirror — and suddenly an actor's whole presence can shift. Their work opens up. The scene breathes. And they're not *performing* anymore. They're *being*.

That kind of breakthrough? It never happens alone.

It happens in the room.
With pressure.
With risk.
With another set of eyes that support seeing you grow.

That's the work. That's the gift.

And that —
That's the alchemy of acting.

The Long View: Sustainable Growth

Longevity in this craft isn't built on raw talent alone. That might open the door, sure — but it won't keep you in the room. What sustains a career over time is something quieter, something far less celebrated. It's the ability to stay close to the work, even when no one's watching. Even when the world forgets your name for a while.

A lasting career grows from consistency, curiosity, and a deeper kind of love — the kind that doesn't need applause to keep showing up. You have to find ways to keep the craft alive during the slow seasons. To nourish it. To keep it flickering. Even when nothing is being asked of you, you have to keep asking something of yourself.

There will be plateaus. Long ones. Periods where everything feels flat. Where your voice dulls, where your instincts start to feel mechanical or uninspired. You'll think, *maybe I've lost it.* But that's not failure — that's digestion. It's the invisible part of growth. The part that doesn't get applause, but quietly prepares the next breakthrough. Push through too fast, and you interrupt it. Pull away completely, and you risk losing the thread. But if you stay near — just close enough — something builds. Quietly. Steadily. Out of sight.

Take a break when you need to. But don't vanish. Don't let too much dust settle between you and the work. Watch something that challenges your perspective. Read something dense, with difficult syntax or sharp insight. Spend time with a painting that doesn't let you look away. Let art reshape your angle of approach. Let life do the same. Explore without agenda. Create without a finish line. Because everything you experience becomes part of your instrument — whether you meant it to or not.

Start keeping a log. Just once a week. One moment of resonance. A line that moved you. A performance that struck a nerve. Don't make it formal. Don't write an essay. Just jot down what it stirred — and maybe why. It might feel trivial at first, but over time, that journal becomes a mirror. A map. It shows you the quiet shifts in your taste, your range, your questions. It gives you a way to track the becoming.

Because this isn't a business of straight lines or smooth arcs. Growth happens in fits. In spirals. In circles that somehow widen with time. You'll think nothing's happening — and then something will. You'll say a line differently. Not because you rehearsed it that way, but because you've changed. The line stayed the same. You didn't.

The more you train, the less you have to think. Not because it gets easier, but because the work has moved into you. It's living there now. The body remembers. The breath responds. You stop trying to be present — and simply are.

Every hour you've invested — every class, every cold read, every awkward self-tape you deleted and started again — it's all building something. And you won't always know what that is until later. But it's there.

Then one day the camera rolls. The room goes quiet. And something drops in — clean, honest, alive.

That's the payoff. That's the reason.
Not just to be better.
But to stay *connected*.

Training isn't what you do before the work. It *is* the work. Not an obligation. Not a box to check. A conversation. One that continues — through auditions, through setbacks, through long seasons of silence and the rare, electric moments when something clicks and you remember why you started all this in the first place.

And if you stay close — if you keep the tools warm, the mind open, the body responsive — the line between practice and performance starts to fade. Because what you'll have built isn't just skill, or readiness, or range.

You'll have built a way of being.

And that — more than credits, more than roles, more than applause — is what makes this a life.

Case Study: Daniel Kaluuya's Evolving Approach

Daniel Kaluuya's evolution between *Get Out* and *Judas and the Black Messiah* is more than just a study in range. It's a map — a guide showing how serious actors reshape their process to meet the unique demands of the work.

Kaluuya has emphasized in interviews that his preparation isn't fixed. Instead, it *shifts* depending entirely on the character in front of him. That flexibility — his willingness to let the work change him — is what makes his process so instructive.

For *Get Out*, his work was internal. He immersed himself in the psychology of hypnosis and the mechanics of fear, training his breath and body to reflect the paralysis of the "sunken place" — not as a performance, but as a lived experience. It was breath held at the edge of panic, subtlety over spectacle, precision instead of affect. He made the invisible visible.

With *Judas and the Black Messiah*, his approach deepened. He didn't just study Fred Hampton's speech or stance — though he did that meticulously. He absorbed the texts Hampton consumed, internalized the philosophy that drove his choices, and let those ideas live *underneath* the character's every gesture and breath. Nothing was loud; it all was quiet but foundational.

What makes Kaluuya's approach so compelling is not just his range — it's his adaptability. He doesn't show up to each role with a preset method. He begins with a simple question:

"I ask the script, 'What do you want me to do?'"

Then, he listens. His training becomes a dialogue — between actor and character, instinct and investigation. Alive. Specific. Unpredictable.

This reveals something deeper about craft itself.

Training is not an inventory of static skills. It's a living relationship. One you have to renegotiate each time you step into a new life. Some roles demand physical transformation. Others feel like intellectual excavation or emotional exposure so intense it toes the edge of danger. And no two characters ever ask for the same preparation or the same tools.

The actor who endures is the one who learns to listen — to the material, to the moment, to the mystery. They evolve, not through rigidity, but through humility. They're always ready to begin again.

Daniel Kaluuya's work reminds us:

Craft evolves because we do.
The best actors meet that evolution with curiosity, with openness, and with integrity. They're willing to be changed by the work — not simply serve it.

CHAPTER 11

THE INTEGRATED ARTIST - LIVING A LIFE OF ART AND MASTERY

Integration Over Specialization

This is where everything comes together — range, readiness, response. The actor's ability to hold nuance, timing, instinct, and stillness simultaneously, sometimes within the space of a single breath. You don't need to be fluent in every method, but you do need to borrow wisely. The future doesn't belong to purists. It belongs to the hybrids.

The great actors today resemble mixed martial artists more than traditional craftsmen. They train across disciplines, absorb what works, discard what doesn't, and integrate the rest. It's not about flash or performance for its own sake — it's about readiness. That's the real art. That's the edge.

An actor's journey now is more than the pursuit of roles. To truly live as a modern artist, you must balance the craft, the business, and the deeper soul of the work. Too often, actors burn out because they cling to only one part of the equation — refining their technique while neglecting the realities of the industry, chasing auditions while letting their creative fire die, or curating a public image without deepening the private instrument. True mastery comes from integration, the alignment of artistic fulfillment with professional sustainability.

Acting is not simply a job. It is a way of engaging with the world — a lens through which humanity comes into sharper, sometimes more uncomfortable focus. The best actors sustain both professional ambition and personal artistic growth. Without balance, the risks are real: the soulless careerist measuring success by visibility alone, or the purist clinging to rigid ideals while the industry evolves past them. Both paths lead to the same destination — disillusionment.

I have watched countless actors sacrifice artistic integrity for commercial success, only to find themselves trapped in roles that pay but leave them creatively starved. I have seen others refuse commercial opportunities to preserve artistic purity, only to grow bitter and isolated as financial pressures mount and opportunities dwindle. Neither extreme leads to a sustainable or fulfilling life in this craft.

Try this: Write down your greatest artistic joys — the aspects of acting that excite and sustain you. Then write down your career goals — financial, professional, personal. Compare them honestly. Are your daily actions supporting both sides of that equation or pulling them further apart? The distance between those lists is the real work ahead — the integration required.

Creating Your Own Opportunities

In today's industry, waiting to be cast is no longer a strategy. The most successful actors create their own momentum. They write, direct, produce, and collaborate. They generate work when the industry sits silent.

The tools have never been more accessible. A smartphone with a decent lens, basic editing software, and a clear creative vision can produce work that reveals facets of your talent casting directors may never see. Self-generated projects sharpen your instrument, broaden your capabilities, and provide tangible evidence of your artistic voice.

Independent film, theater, web series, and digital platforms offer a measure of control over your artistic path that previous generations could only dream of. Actors who wait become passive participants in their own careers. Actors who create become architects of their futures.

Consider Issa Rae, who launched *Awkward Black Girl* when traditional channels didn't offer her a seat at the table. Or Phoebe Waller-Bridge, whose one-woman stage play became the foundation for *Fleabag*. These were not side projects; they were strategic acts of creation that opened doors traditional routes never would have.

Try this: Write a one-page monologue or scene built around a character you are eager to play. Film it. Refine it. Use it — as a self-tape, as an audition piece, or as the beginning of a larger project. This is not just a creative exercise; it is professional development and a reclamation of artistic agency.

The greatest shift happens internally. When you begin to create your own work, you move from being a passive recipient of opportunities to an active maker of them. Desperation gives way to purpose. Anxiety transforms into direction. Helplessness becomes agency.

The Artist's Mind: Constant Curiosity

Acting does not happen in isolation. The richest performances come from actors who feed their work with a steady diet of curiosity. Read widely — novels, poetry, philosophy, history. Study psychology. Watch international cinema. Expand your lens beyond the conventions of your immediate environment.

Every experience becomes material. Every conversation reveals something about human nature. Every observation adds color to the palette you will eventually draw from.

Curiosity must be embodied, not merely intellectual. What does it feel like to stand at the edge of a cliff? To knead bread by hand? To dance until exhaustion? To sit for an hour in silence? These experiences become more than memories; they become reference points for future roles, expanding your emotional and physical vocabulary.

Try this: once a week, engage in an artistic practice outside of acting. Visit a museum. Watch a dance performance. Listen to a new genre of music. Observe how different forms translate truth through rhythm, movement, light, and shadow.

The painter understands composition and negative space. The musician internalizes rhythm and tempo. The dancer knows how to tell stories without words. The actor who absorbs these lessons creates work with greater texture, dimension, and nuance.

I once worked with an actor who had very solid technique. Nothing wrong at all with what he was doing — he hit the beats, took direction well. But something in his performances never quite landed in a way that made you take notice. It was hard to convey to him without causing confusion — or worse, setting him back. His takes weren't bad... they just lacked soul. Not a word I'd ever say to an actor directly, but that's what it was. And it wasn't something that could be fixed with another round of scene study.

So instead of assigning more material, I asked him to spend some time in a museum before our next session. No task. No scene to prepare. Just go. Walk around. Look. Notice things.

How painters *suggested* emotion through the framing of a moment. How sculptors worked with tension and stillness — sometimes both in the same piece. How a photograph could say everything without saying anything. It wasn't about translating any of it into performance. Not directly. It was about perspective. And how you start to understand something without needing to analyze it.

He came back with a renewed perspective that opened him up more than I could've reached in a dozen more sessions. Because up to that point, he was trying to fix it — whatever "it" was — through hard labor. Through effort. He was convinced the answer had to be in working harder, pushing further, tightening the screws. But sometimes the work isn't about effort. It's about seeing it differently. Feeling it differently.

That shift — that release — was joyous to witness. Because I knew how hard he would've worked had I let him believe something was off. That he wasn't measuring up. That his work was behind his peers. He would've turned it into a problem to solve — when what he needed was a door to open.

And the museum visits did that. They opened something in him I would've struggled to teach. They gave him access. Not to a new technique — but to a new way of receiving the world.

He returned to the work more grounded. His scenes didn't suddenly get louder or more "expressive," but there was more presence in them. More patience. Stillness. A quiet kind of gravity when it was called for. He wasn't just delivering the scene anymore — he had started to live inside it.

His technique hadn't changed. He already had the tools. But something in how he saw the work — how it registered in him — started to shift. It reached a deeper, more lived level. And it stayed with him.

Emotional Sustainability

Sustaining a long-term acting career requires emotional resilience. The highs and lows are inevitable in this profession, and learning to protect your mental wellbeing while remaining creatively open is not optional — it is essential. Develop daily rituals that center and stabilize you. Practice mindfulness, meditation, or any grounding technique that allows you to reconnect with yourself. Surround yourself with supportive artistic communities that uplift rather than drain you.

The actor's instrument is uniquely personal: body, voice, emotional life — there is no separation between the artist and the tools. This intimacy brings vulnerability. When your work is criticized, it feels personal in ways few other professions experience. When the roles dry up, it can trigger not just frustration but existential doubt. These challenges require deliberate emotional management, not just resilience.

Each night, make a simple practice of reflection. Write down one thing you learned, one thing you struggled with, and one thing for which you are grateful. Over time, this builds self-awareness and mental clarity, keeping your artistic life in perspective. The actor who maintains perspective survives the inevitable rejections, disappointments, and long gaps between opportunities. The actor who loses perspective becomes brittle — vulnerable to every industry wind.

The integrated artist understands that emotional health is not separate from artistic development — it is fundamental to it. Burnout, bitterness, and cynicism damage more than your personal wellbeing; they corrode your creative capacity. An actor depleted emotionally cannot summon the openness, the vulnerability, or the presence that great performance demands.

I have seen too many talented actors undone not by lack of opportunity but by the inability to manage the emotional demands of the profession. The erratic scheduling, constant scrutiny, financial uncertainty, and the invisible but pervasive sense of being evaluated — these pressures accumulate over time, undermining even the most gifted. Sustainable careers require more than talent and strategy; they require emotional infrastructure built to withstand pressure.

Over time, I learned this lesson myself. In the early years, I approached my craft with a painful, frenetic urgency, chasing the imagined steady working life of a character actor hoping for major films or a long-running television series. I clung to those ambitions ferociously, believing that fulfillment would only arrive once I achieved a certain level of visible success. However, somewhere along the way, without even realizing it, I let go of that chase. I stopped striving for a singular definition of what my career *had* to look like. When I did, something remarkable happened.

I found myself fulfilled in ways I hadn't anticipated. I still work in front of the camera from time to time, but my life has expanded beyond those early goals. Screenwriting, directing, producing, mentoring up-and-coming filmmakers, teaching acting and film studies, and coaching talented professional actors — these became not side projects but central, sustaining parts of my life. Over the decades, I found the perfect fit for the talents I had developed. And with it came a quieter pride — not just in my own work, but in the successes of those I've had the privilege to teach and mentor along the way. Watching their growth, encouraging their journeys, celebrating their breakthroughs — that, too, has become its own kind of fulfillment.

It's not the life I once pictured.

It's better.

Redefining Success on Your Own Terms

Actors often struggle with inherited definitions of success — fame, wealth, awards. While external validation can be gratifying, true success lies elsewhere: in living a life that aligns with your creative values and personal integrity.

What does success look like to you — beyond accolades and recognition? Are your career decisions grounded in your artistic values, or are they simply reactions to industry trends? How do you define fulfillment beyond financial gain?

The integrated artist cultivates clear internal measures of success, remaining stable even in the absence of external recognition. The satisfaction of fully embodying a complex character. The quiet joy of discovering new insights to the craft of technical skills. The connection felt when a performance resonates with an audience member. The personal growth that comes from stepping beyond familiar territory. These intrinsic rewards sustain you when the industry offers little in return.

Try this: Write a letter to yourself ten years from now. It doesn't have to be elaborate, just a brief description of the artist and person you hope to become. Focus not on awards or contracts, but on growth — the type of work you want to be doing and the kind of life you aspire to live creatively.

Let this letter become both your compass and mirror — showing you the direction you hope to move toward, while also allowing you to reflect on the distance you've already traveled.

You may find that your definition of success evolves.

The new actor, driven by dreams of recognition and acknowledgment by his peers, often matures into an artist more concerned with meaningful work, creative collaboration, and continued personal growth in their craft as well as within the industry. This evolution isn't a compromise — it's development. Growth. It reflects the deepening of values as craft matures and experience accumulates.

I've seen this shift firsthand in many actors I've mentored across decades. One of them, a veteran of television and film, once told me: "In my twenties, I wanted fame. In my thirties, it was respect. In my forties, I cared about security. But now? I just want to keep working in this craft I've come to love from so many different angles. I want to be part of projects where I can contribute, maybe even help lift the work a little higher. I still love the feeling of being in front of the camera — but I take just as much pride in helping bring a project to life however I can."

This progression isn't a diminishment of ambition — it's ambition refined.

The Integrated Artist

The integrated artist lives at the intersection of craft, career, and calling. They move easily between the practical demands of the profession and the deeper, sustaining work of artistic exploration. They understand that technique without heart is hollow, and passion without skill is incomplete. They recognize that the business side of acting isn't separate from the art — it's the structure that allows the work to reach an audience.

This kind of integration isn't just a strategy — it's a necessity for the long game. It's what sustains a career through seasons of change. It's the difference between a brief, bright flame and a steady fire that evolves and deepens over decades.

You've come this far. You've studied the craft. You've learned to navigate the business. You've sharpened your instrument. Now comes the real work — not dividing these pieces, but bringing them together. Not keeping your artistic life separate from your professional one. Not isolating the classroom from the audition room or the rehearsal from the performance. But weaving them into a single, fully integrated approach to a demanding, unpredictable, and deeply rewarding profession.

This is the point where it all converges — where preparation meets opportunity, where discipline allows for freedom, where technique dissolves into presence. Where an actor becomes an artist. Where the job becomes a life.

This is your path now — your journey. The integration of everything you've learned, everything you've endured, and everything you are still becoming. The work won't end. The growth won't stop. And the art will never fully give up its secrets.

But that's the beauty of it. That's the challenge.
That's the joy.

Welcome to the life of the integrated artist.

Integration in Practice: Olivia Colman

Background

Olivia Colman didn't segment her career. She didn't wait for permission to pivot. Those early years — British sketch comedy, sitcoms, slapstick, and satire — were no detour. They were boot camp. Timing. Specificity. Emotional truth tucked inside absurdity. She didn't see a boundary between "funny" and "serious." Only an opportunity to sharpen tools that would serve both.

Every set, every laugh-track, every over-lit soundstage — she approached it the same: character first. Real stakes, even in farce. The audience laughs harder when the actor doesn't reach for it.

Approach

Colman's method isn't about reinvention. It's about expansion. Deliberate. Steady. She carries the discipline of comedy into drama — micro-calibrated timing, restraint where another actor might signal. And she smuggles vulnerability back into comedy, grounding the joke in something breakable. Human.

Her craft isn't split between genres. It's fused. She accepts the projects — the heavy, the light, the layered — not to escape type but to refuse confinement. She doesn't compartmentalize; she cross-pollinates.

Integration Example

Watch *Tyrannosaur*. Harrowing. Intimate. Bleak. And at the same time — quietly alive with the subtle comic timing she honed in those years on the BBC. The lift of an eyebrow. The hesitation before an answer. Not comedy in the traditional sense — but the recognition that humor and heartbreak drink from the same well.

She filmed *Tyrannosaur* while still appearing in lighthearted projects. She didn't toggle between modes. She blended. Letting the authenticity demanded by each infect the other. She found the same humanity beneath both. Genre became irrelevant. Only truth mattered.

Sustainability Factors

Colman resists classification. She lets the work reshape her, not the other way around. She never positioned herself as a "serious" actress after comedy — she simply kept moving, kept choosing, kept growing.

Long before awards chased her, she built slow credibility — project by project, director by director. Not flashy. Not strategic. Just steady, authentic expansion. She understood: it's not status that sustains you. It's the work. And the refusal to calcify.

Lessons Learned

Colman teaches what most resist: integration isn't about shedding old skins — it's about weaving them together. The body of work isn't an escape route. It's an ecosystem.

Her career proves that technical precision and intuitive freedom aren't rivals. They're dance partners. Presence isn't a rejection of craft. It's the full flowering of it.

The sustainable life of the artist — the one that endures the seasons, the droughts, the reckonings — doesn't come from specializing. It comes from integrating. Expanding. Allowing contradictions to coexist. Making a home there.

Integration in Practice: Cate Blanchett

Background

Cate Blanchett's foundation isn't one tradition; it's a collision. Laban movement analysis. Yat Malmgren's psychological gestures. Two disciplines — one structural, one intuitive — braided together in her bones long before the world took notice.

She didn't choose between intellect and instinct; she fused them. Built a method that thinks with the body and feels with the mind. Embodied intelligence — not just learned, but lived.

Approach

Blanchett assembles characters the way an archaeologist excavates ruins — piece by piece, object by object. She starts with research, sure — the desk work, the biographies, the facts — but that's only the frame. The real work happens in the objects.

She gathers a talisman, a worn sweater, a chipped cup — little altars to the character's unseen life. Each object a portal. Each arrangement a map. She builds not from words, but from touch, from weight, from texture.

It's ritualistic, physical, nonverbal. The character breathes in the arrangement long before a line is ever spoken.

Integration Example

Blue Jasmine — her masterclass in contradiction. Blanchett didn't just play Jasmine's collapse; she constructed it, physically and spatially. Trinkets from a life she can't quite let go of — pearls, prescription bottles, the heavy hang of expensive fabric worn like armor.

She moved among these artifacts, letting their gravitational pull alter her gait, her gestures, her voice. Technique — the research, the psychological structure — was never abandoned, but also never alone. The physical world infused the interior. Thought and instinct were braided so tightly they became indistinguishable.

Sustainability Factors

Blanchett's process never ossifies. It renews because it requires reinvention — new objects, new rituals, new maps for every role. Intellectual rigor keeps the process sharp, while physical ritual keeps it alive.

She doesn't approach the work as a destination to reach but as a territory to wander — uncertain, shifting, alive. It protects her from repetition, from stagnation, from herself.

Lessons Learned

Blanchett teaches what few dare admit: the mystical and the mechanical are not opposites. They are two halves of the same key. The actor is not a puppet of impulse nor a slave to intellect, but a vessel where the two converse, argue, and seduce each other.

True integration is not balance; it's fusion. Technique dissolving into instinct. Instinct sharpened by technique. Each feeding the other until the craft disappears — and only the living thing remains.

CHAPTER 12

TRUTH BEYOND TECHNIQUE

From Structure to Surrender

T he greatest lie we tell ourselves as actors is that we can prepare for everything. We can't. We shouldn't. The map is never the territory; the script is never the full weight of human experience it tries to capture. What separates mechanical actors from transformative ones isn't technical precision — it's presence. It's being fully alive within contradiction. It's standing at the narrow intersection between discipline and abandon, structure and chaos, control and surrender.

I didn't come to this philosophy through theory or tradition. It arose from necessity — from watching truly talented actors sabotage themselves. Locked in their heads, they overthought their performances into sterile perfection, hitting every mark while leaving audiences unmoved. They had all the technique but none of the life.

Audiences don't crave perfection. They crave humanity. They don't want cleverness. They want you — the real you — messy, contradictory, and surprising even to yourself. Not as you wish to be seen, but as you are.

This isn't about rejecting technique. Technique is essential — like the strong back of a dancer or the breath control of a singer. It's the subtextual analysis that honors the writer's intent. It's the unseen architecture that holds the work together. But technique alone is empty. Impressive, perhaps. Nourishing? Never. What feeds both actor and audience is truth. And not some grand, fixed truth, but the fleeting, shifting truths that slip through our fingers the moment we try to capture them — the kaleidoscope of impulses, contradictions, and fears that make a single moment real and unrepeatable.

I teach actors to chase those moments. To prepare rigorously, then surrender completely. Some days those moments never arrive. That's part of the work, too.

The greatest performances weren't constructed — they were discovered in real time. The actor isn't an architect; they are an explorer. They find, rather than build. And that requires a courage no technique can teach — the courage to not know what's coming next, the courage to be changed by a scene partner's glance, the courage to let a character alter your own cellular structure.

Our industry resists this at every turn. It prefers consistency, predictability, and safe excellence. It wants your performance contained within repeatable boundaries. Resist that. What moves an audience isn't watching someone execute a plan — it's watching someone navigate uncertainty with their full humanity. Think about the performances that haunt you years later — they weren't technically flawless, necessarily. They linger because, in some fleeting moment, something unrepeatable broke through.

I've worked with actors who could hit every emotional beat with precision yet leave the room untouched. And I've worked with others who struggled with technique but who brought a reckless vulnerability to the work — and those were the ones who moved everyone to tears.

Technique can be taught. Presence must be cultivated.

Yes, this approach makes acting harder. More unpredictable. Less controllable. But also — more alive. And in a world increasingly flattened by screens and algorithms, the simple act of being fully present is revolutionary. What we practice in rehearsal becomes the way we move through the world.

Presence is not something we can force. It can only be invited — by stripping away certainty, by surrendering to curiosity, by listening with your entire nervous system. Your job isn't to decide how a scene should go. Your job is to prepare so thoroughly that you can let it all go when the moment demands it.

This is the paradox at the heart of great acting: complete preparation, complete surrender. You must know the lines so deeply they disappear. You must understand the character so completely that you can abandon your cleverness when the moment calls for something rawer, truer.

The sacred moment — the living moment between actors — can't be manufactured or replicated. It happens when we stop performing and start responding. When we stop showing and start seeing. When we become fully available to be changed.

This is the philosophy behind everything I invite actors to explore. Not because it wins awards, although it often does. Not because it guarantees commercial success, although it often leads there. Because it keeps our art form necessary — vital — human.

In the end, it's not your technique the world needs. It's your humanity — channeled through story, character, and language. That's the gift only you can offer. That's the work that matters.

So go. Be braver than you think you can be. Trust more than feels safe. Listen harder than seems possible. React — to your partner, your surroundings, your own heartbeat. Risk it. Don't ask for permission.

And remember: the performance isn't in your preparation. It's in your presence.

Living as an Integrated Artist

Great acting has never been about simply reading lines. It's about creating full, complex human beings — contradictions, flaws, desires, vulnerabilities, and all. Your work is to step inside another soul, inhabit a different reality, and make that existence feel undeniable to the audience.

What has changed isn't the purpose but the level of authenticity demanded. Today's audience can spot falseness in an instant. They've been educated by decades of subtle screen performances and sharpened by artists who keep pushing the edges of naturalism. They live in stories told with an intimacy no previous generation of storytellers ever achieved.

The analytical framework we've explored isn't theory for theory's sake — it's the bridge between intellectual preparation and embodied performance. Character creation must become so complete that the mechanics disappear entirely. No matter how detailed your analysis, no matter how thorough your transformation, the viewer should see only the living character — never the scaffolding that built it.

You Are Never Going to Be in Control

I once had a role on a very popular television series. The director, who hadn't met any of the new cast members, invited us to dinner the night before a complicated shoot. After introductions, she turned to me and said, "Jim, I just want you to know — your audition tape was the easiest casting we've ever had. We all looked at each other after your first take and said, 'That's our guy.' We didn't even watch anyone else."

It was flattering, especially sitting at a table full of established, respected character actors, many of whom I had admired for years. Just days earlier, I had watched one of them in a favorite series of mine, never imagining I'd soon be sitting across from her, having dinner, preparing to share a scene the next day.

That compliment gave me real confidence. I slept well that night, thinking my job would be simple: deliver what the director liked so much in the audition. Easy enough, right? I knew the material inside out and backward. I was comfortable. I even had a pat on the back from the director before stepping on set.

But then came the day of the shoot — and everything was behind schedule. After wardrobe, makeup, and hair, the other six actors and I waited for hours in holding area, long past our call times. When we were finally brought to set, the tension was thick. As we arrived, the director was already strongly dressing down the second AD. An unease hung over the entire crew. You could feel it in the air.

She addressed us sharply: "We're way behind. We're losing our lead actress in one hour due to a personal emergency. We're going to knock this out in a couple of takes. I expect everyone to be one hundred percent on their game. No mistakes."

The usual first-day nerves spiked into something sharper. Still, I held onto my confidence, comfortable in remembering her praise the night before.

We blocked quickly. No rehearsal. Just marks. "We're rolling. Speed. Action!"

My scene partner, a young actor, barely got two words out before freezing — completely blank.

"Cut! Damn it. You don't know your lines? Feed him the damn line! Let's go, let's go. Back to one!"

The tension only thickened. The room shifted from creative to survival mode. Fear of failure replaced the search for truth.

After some scrambling and broken starts, it was my turn. The director called out, "Let's go, Jim! I expect perfection. Action!"

I began — giving exactly the same performance I had in the audition, the one she had praised not 12 hours before.

I barely got three words out before — "Cut! Come on, Jim! Too slow. Faster. Back to one. Rolling!"

I adjusted. I tried to rush the words without losing the work. I stepped on my partner's lines, threw away beats, and forced pace over feeling.

"Keep rolling. Jim, way too slow. Faster. All of it — faster! Action."

By the next take, I abandoned any semblance of the audition performance. It wasn't about craft anymore — it was about getting the words out fast enough so the lead actress could make her exit.

"Cut! Jim! Faster! One thousand times faster!"

At that point, I gave up trying to control anything. I surrendered to what the day demanded. It was not my best work, but it was what the day called for. And after all, this is a business. The pages got done, the actors wrapped, and the show must go on.

And that — that is the paradox of this work. You show up prepared, rehearsed, ready to deliver your best. You think you're steering the ship, hands firmly on the wheel. Then the ground shifts. The tide turns. And you realize control was only ever an illusion.

That's the real lesson. Let go. Embrace the uncertainty, the limitation, the unpredictability. Ride the wave. Because control? It was never really yours to begin with.

The Quiet Revolution: Mumblecore to Streaming

Cinema evolves. The spiral turns.

In 2005, at the South by Southwest Film Festival, sound editor Eric Masunaga coined a term — *mumblecore* — while discussing films like *Mutual Appreciation*, *The Puffy Chair*, and *Kissing on the Mouth*. The name stuck. Not because it was flattering, but because it was true.

These films mumbled. They wandered. They lingered in rooms where nothing seemed to happen — and yet, everything did.

Low-budget. Loosely scripted. Emotionally raw. Mumblecore wasn't rebellion — it was refusal. A refusal to inflate, to polish, to force meaning into scenes that were already full of it.

Where Dogme 95 stripped away technical artifice, Mumblecore dissolved narrative scaffolding. The characters didn't arc. They meandered. They didn't project. They reacted. Dialogue stumbled, overlapped, stalled. Emotions hesitated. Truth leaked sideways.

It wasn't small. It was specific.

In *Funny Ha Ha*, Kate Dollenmayer's Marnie doesn't telegraph her emotions. She absorbs them. A flinch. A laugh that doesn't land. A drink sipped too fast. Performance, not as display — but as accumulation. She isn't acting. She's responding.

Mumblecore didn't last as a movement — but its DNA spread everywhere. *The Big Sick. Lady Bird. Medicine for Melancholy.* And behind them, the deeper, stranger waves: *Mumblegore* merging naturalism with horror. Sean Baker's *Tangerine* and *The Florida Project* dragging us even closer — into lives not dramatized but lived.

Mumblecore didn't invent authenticity. It just made room for it. It said: You don't need spectacle to matter. You just need people. Imperfect, restless, listening.

And from that silence — something new was waiting.

Streaming as Movement

Now, here we are.

Past Mumblecore's handheld intimacy, into something sharper. Hungrier. The camera hasn't stopped trembling — it's just learned to choreograph the tremble.

Streaming didn't just change how stories are watched. It changed how they're told. It changed what we ask of actors. And it changed what audiences are trained to see.

Episodes aren't episodes anymore — they're essays, they're chapters, they're poems. Time stretches, contracts. A single breath might last five minutes. Or flash by in silence.

The lens? Closer. Tighter. Less forgiving.

Shows like *The Bear*, *The Studio* — they aren't just well-made. They're rituals. Especially the one'er — the single, unbroken shot — a gauntlet thrown at the actor's feet. Five, ten, fifteen minutes without a break. No rescue. No cutaway. Presence, demanded without apology.

And yet — is it really new?

Or is it a return? A throwback to the Silent Era. When the actor's body was the only line. When a glance, a gesture, had to carry the whole world.

Today, it's the same — only closer. Inches from your skin. High-definition, 4K, unblinking.

Station Eleven. Beef. Reservation Dogs. Euphoria. The Rehearsal. Works pushing performance past the edge of what craft can plan. Past technique — into something lived.

The actor's task isn't just to hit marks anymore. It's to stay alive inside the unbearable proximity of the moment.

Streaming didn't invent this. It revealed it.

Presence — not performance.

The Truth Inbetween

The craft, like the breath before the line, waits patiently — for the actor ready to listen.

You know the feeling — the same instincts, the same preparation, the same energy you've brought to a dozen scenes before. And yet... it doesn't land. Not this time. Something's off. But it's not you — not entirely.

The ground has shifted under your feet.

The old rhythms, once so reliable, now feel just a beat too long. A thought too late. The camera, the style, the audience — they're all whispering something different. Something quieter.

They're not asking you to perform. They're asking you to live. Microscopically.

Feel the thought hit before the word does. Trust that the lens — that the audience — will catch it.

I've worked with actors who've felt this shift. The sense that the room changed, but no one told them the new rules. That what once read as raw now feels loud. That what once worked — now works against them.

They're not wrong.

Audiences have changed. Their sensitivity to truth — real truth — is unnervingly sharp. If you're still acting like it's 2002, you're already behind.

But this isn't cause for panic.

It's a call to adapt. Because while the medium changes, the work — the real work — doesn't. It just demands a different touch. A different kind of silence. A different kind of bravery.

High-definition cameras bring the audience closer. Six inches away, phone in hand. Seventy-five inches wide, 8K resolution. They don't want to be impressed. They want to be invited.

And if you fake it — even a little — they feel it. And you lose them.

The performance space has collapsed. No longer a proscenium. No longer a medium shot, safely framed. Now, it's the trembling of an eyelid. The hesitation behind a blink. The breath caught before the word.

The work happens not in dialogue — but between it. Not in action — but in the moment before action. The decision. Or the refusal.

Moonlight — the diner scene between Chiron and Kevin. The silence, thick with unspoken history. Fear, longing, wrapped tight beneath a glance.

Elisabeth Moss in *The Handmaid's Tale*. The camera holds her hostage. She can't safely speak — but her skin betrays her. Rage. Resistance. Grief.

Phoebe Waller-Bridge in *Fleabag*. Her glances to camera aren't winks. They're ruptures. Three layers of consciousness folding into a single look: what she shows others, what she shows us, what she hides from both.

Across the best work today, performance isn't shown. It's lived. We're not watching characters act. We're watching them think.

And that's what makes it real.

Not emotional display. Cognitive presence.

Just One More Thing

"Don't think. Thinking is the enemy of creativity.
It's self-conscious, and anything self-conscious is lousy."
— Ray Bradbury

Now that you've done the work — the lessons, the analysis, the training. Now that you've won the audition, memorized the lines, gotten to set, made your call time, passed through wardrobe, makeup, and hair.

Now that you're standing on your mark, lights set, sound checked, the director says, *"Let's run it once."*

Now — it's time to let it all go.

Trust what you've built. It's already in you.

The audience doesn't want to see the architecture. They want to feel the life moving inside it.

You've got this. Throw it away — and just be.

Elia Kazan once said to his actors, *"They can fire you, but they can't eat you."* It's worth remembering. This work will test you. It will humble you. It may break your heart. But it won't break you — not if you trust what you've built. Not if you let go and meet the unknown without fear.

That's the paradox: only by releasing everything you've learned can you fully embody what you know.

Pretend. Play.
Like a child, fearless of being wrong.
Jump — and trust you'll figure out the parachute on the way down.

The work you've done is there — etched into your instincts, your body, your breath.

The preparation, the study, the choices, the exploration — none of it is lost. It's deeper now. Beyond memory. Living inside you.

When the moment comes, the actor who clutches technique will drown. The martial artist doesn't think about foot placement mid-fight. The musician doesn't count frets mid-performance. The dancer doesn't calculate steps mid-flight. And neither should you.

I've seen it happen — brilliant actors who've polished every surface until no life can slip through. Safe choices. Predictable moves. The ghost of a performance.

Real artistry doesn't live there.

It lives in what you dare to release. In the breath between intention and action. In the surrender to what's alive right now.

You've built the house. Now live in it. Not as architect. Not as builder. As a soul with nowhere else to be.

Trust it. It's there. It always was.

You've got this. Throw it away — and just be.

— Jim Blumetti

THE ECHO
THAT LINGERS

Not everyone will understand what we do — or why we do it. And that's alright. Because this work — when done honestly — isn't about being understood. It's about revealing. About standing, fully present, in the small and sacred act of *becoming*... even if only for a moment.

You don't walk away from this book "ready." You walk away *in motion* — more curious than certain. That's the point. Mastery in this craft isn't a finish line — it's a rhythm. You move forward, then sideways, then sometimes back, and eventually... inward. What once felt like technique begins to feel like truth. What once felt like performance begins to feel like presence.

You'll forget most of what you've read. That's fine. Let it go. Let it sink, however slowly into your bones, somewhere behind the eyes and underneath the breath. The work you've done thus far — the hours, the questions, the stubborn courage to keep showing up — it lives in you now. Not in words, but in preparedness. In your silence before the line. In the space between action and cut. In the look that wasn't planned, but was authentic, organic, honest.

And maybe that's all we get. That one honest look.

But if it's real — *truly* real — it's enough to light up the dark.

So go on.

Be brave.

Be strange.

Be willing.

Let the craft shape you, and the chaos sharpen you.

And when you no longer know what to do next...
do less.
Then listen.

That sound you hear?
That's the role becoming you.

APPENDICES

APPENDIX A

A FIELD GUIDE TO FILM MOVEMENTS

(For the actor who wants to understand the frame they're walking into)

These aren't just historical footnotes. They're weather systems. Each one reshaped what cinema could be — how performance was captured, how truth was revealed. Understanding them doesn't just make you a smarter actor. It roots you in the evolution of the craft itself.

You don't need to memorize the timelines. Just feel the shift in temperature of the times, the rhythm of rebellion, the tone of the truth trying to break through.

- **Silent Film Era – 1890s–1920s**
  Before dialogue, there was only the face and the frame. Gesture had to carry it all.

- **Soviet Montage – 1920s (USSR)**
  Cutting as thought. Conflict in the edit. Performance as part of a greater dialectic.

- **German Expressionism – 1920s–1930s (Germany)**
  Shadows and silhouettes. Emotion turned architectural. The internal made visual.

- **French Impressionism – 1920s (France)**
  Cinema as poetry. Subjective experience on screen. Mood over logic.

- **Surrealism – 1920s–1930s (France, Spain)**
  Dream logic. The unconscious unshackled. Acting from the underworld.

- **Poetic Realism – 1930s (France)**
  Everyday beauty. Tragic characters. A soft glow of fatalism before the fall.

- **Italian Neorealism – 1940s–1950s (Italy)**
  Real people, real places, real struggle. Truth without makeup.

- **Film Noir – 1940s–1950s (USA)**
  Hard light. Harder choices. Morality twisted in shadow and smoke.

- **Japanese Golden Age – 1950s (Japan)**
  Stillness meets spirit. Formality and fury in quiet balance.

- **French New Wave – 1950s–1960s (France)**
  Jump cuts and personal truth. Actors discovered the frame could break rules.

- **Free Cinema / British New Wave – 1950s–1960s (UK)**
  Working-class grit. Regional accents. Kitchen-sink defiance.

- **Cinema Novo – 1960s (Brazil)**
  Political urgency with poetic soul. Hunger, heat, and resistance on screen.

- **Direct Cinema & Cinéma Vérité – 1960s (USA, France)**
  Documenting life unfiltered. The actor becomes subject — or disappears entirely.

- **New Hollywood / American New Wave – 1960s–1980s (USA)**
  Antiheroes. Improvisation. Method's rawness hitting mainstream.

- **Parallel Cinema – 1970s–1980s (India)**
  Art over formula. Actors as agents of societal reflection.

- **New German Cinema – 1970s (Germany)**
  Post-war ghosts. Personal rebellion. Performance as provocation.

- **Fifth Generation – 1980s–1990s (China)**
  Tradition torn open. Symbolism and silence. Landscapes of the soul.

- **Korean New Wave – 1990s–present (South Korea)**
  Stylized chaos. Genre-bending. Performance that burns from within.

- **Dogme 95 – 1995–2005 (Denmark)**
  No lights. No sets. No lies. The actor stripped to nerve and impulse.

- **Mumblecore – 2000s–present (USA)**
  Dialogue that rambles. Performances that feel like eavesdropping.

- **New Argentine Cinema – 2000s–present (Argentina)**
  Quiet revolutions. Understated power. Characters barely holding it together.

- **Romanian New Wave – 2000s–present (Romania)**
  Long takes. Awkward silences. Bureaucracy meets human ache.

- **Hyperrealism / Heightened Naturalism – 2010s–present (Global/Streaming)**
  Ultra-close. Ultra-quiet. Acting so real it feels like surveillance.

Let this serve as *a map of moods* — not just movements. Each one opened new space for the actor to explore... or survive inside.

APPENDIX B

SELECTED BIBLIOGRAPHY & INFLUENCES

T his list isn't comprehensive. It's personal.

These are the texts I've returned to over years of craft and contradiction — dog-eared, underlined, sometimes hurled across the room only to be picked up again when the work demanded it. They're not rules. They're reference points — fixed stars in a shifting sky.

Start here. And then let your own list unfold.

Foundational Texts on Acting & Process

- Konstantin Stanislavski – *An Actor Prepares*
  He laid the bones. We're still building the muscle.

- **Sanford Meisner & Dennis Longwell** – *Sanford Meisner on Acting*
  Moment-to-moment truth. React, don't invent. Live it.

- **Uta Hagen** – *Respect for Acting*
  When you want the work to feel honest and precise — she brings the scalpel.

- **Stella Adler** – *The Technique of Acting*
  Imagination is oxygen. She gave permission to breathe deeply.

- **Michael Chekhov** – *To the Actor*
  Everything external becomes internal. Movement as magic.

- **Lee Strasberg** – *A Dream of Passion*
  Controversial, yes — but his deep excavation of self remains foundational.

- **Viola Spolin** – *Improvisation for the Theater*
  The games that crack you open. Where play becomes presence.

Cinema & Film History

- **David Bordwell & Kristin Thompson** – *Film History: An Introduction*
  A structural lens for those who need to see the forest, not just the trees.

- **Robert Bresson** – *Notes on the Cinematographer*
  Minimalist poetry. Acting with breath instead of effort.

- **Alexandre Astruc** – *"The Birth of a New Avant-Garde: La Caméra-Stylo"*
  The camera as pen. The moment I understood film as handwriting.

- **François Truffaut** – *The Films in My Life*
  Filmmaking as autobiography. Watching cinema grow up through him.

- **Andrei Tarkovsky** – *Sculpting in Time*
  Pure metaphysics. Stillness stretched until meaning leaks through.

Contemporary Perspectives & Tools

- **David Mamet** – *True and False*
  Blunt force truth. Take what resonates — ignore the bark.

- **Kristin Linklater** – *Freeing the Natural Voice*
  The voice as instrument, not performance. Breath, vibration, thought.

- **Michael Caine** – *Acting in Film*
  Direct, clear, and British in the best way. An actor's manual for the lens.

- **Elisabeth Moss** – *Inside the Frame* (Interviews & Essays)
  If you want to understand thought-on-camera, study her closely.

- **Gena Rowlands** – *On Gena* (Collected Interviews & Writings)
  Every frame of her work is a lesson in risk. The body unguarded.

Other Voices in the Room

- **James Baldwin** – *The Devil Finds Work*
  Film criticism as soul work. Race, performance, and truth unvarnished.

- **Phillip B. Zarrilli** – *Psychophysical Acting*
  Where breath, body, and spirit intersect — deeply rooted in eastern traditions.

- **Antonin Artaud** – *The Theatre and Its Double*
  Raw. Chaotic. Revolutionary. The actor as spiritual weapon.

- **Eugenio Barba** – *The Paper Canoe*
  How tradition becomes transformation. An anthropologist of gesture.

- **Peter Brook** – *The Empty Space*
  Theatre as a crucible. A space waiting to be filled with human need.

Suggested Reading for the Actor

These books don't just teach acting — they illuminate it.

Foundational & Canonical Works

- Konstantin Stanislavski – *An Actor Prepares*
  The root of the tree. Every technique that followed traces its lines back here.

- **Stella Adler** – *The Art of Acting*
  Adler rejected emotional memory in favor of expansive imagination — and elevated the actor's responsibility to culture.

- **Sanford Meisner** – *Sanford Meisner on Acting*
  Presence. Repetition. Listening. Living truthfully under imaginary circumstances, moment by moment.

- **Lee Strasberg** – *A Dream of Passion*
  The father of Method Acting. A psychological deep dive into memory, truth, and transformation.

- **Michael Chekhov** – *To the Actor*; *On the Technique of Acting*
  Psychological gesture, imaginative play, and energy work — the most poetic of the major systems.

- **Uta Hagen** – *Respect for Acting*; *A Challenge for the Actor*
  Clear, detailed, rigorous. She gave actors tools to live truthfully and with courage.

- **Viola Spolin** – *Improvisation for the Theater*
  Theater games that unlocked generations. The foundation of modern improv and ensemble work.

- **Peter Brook** – *The Empty Space*
  Deadly, Holy, Rough, Immediate. A poetic lens into what performance can be.

- **Patsy Rodenburg** – *The Second Circle*
  An actor's return to presence — onstage, in speech, in life.

- **Cicely Berry** – *The Actor and the Text*
  Voice, breath, and muscularity in language — especially for heightened and classical text.

- **Kristin Linklater** – *Freeing the Natural Voice*
  A revolutionary voice approach. Relaxed, organic, and emotionally connected.

- **Robert Cohen** – *Acting Power*
  Explores behavior, objectives, and human motivation. Less mysticism, more method.

Also Suggested

- **Mike Kimmel** - *50 SECRETS NOBODY TELLS YOU IN HOLLYWOOD*:
  The Working Actor's Guide to Avoiding Pitfalls and Super-Charging Your Career

This one's written by a good friend, but I'd recommend it even if he weren't. Mike's been in the room, on the set, and in front of the classroom for decades. He's written several books of scenes and monologues that actors can actually use — not just academic exercises, but material that plays.

APPENDIX C

BONUS CASE STUDIES

These aren't scenes pulled from performance. They're moments — lived, observed, and remembered — that reveal something useful about the craft. Each of these actors or directors has articulated something aligned with the principles we've explored: internal dialogue, presence before words, subtext, stillness, active listening. Not theory — experience. Not technique — insight.

They didn't say these things to be profound. They said them because they were working through it — solving it — trying to stay honest under pressure. These fragments, these comments, these glimpses behind the work... they matter. And if you look at them closely, they'll echo things you already know but maybe haven't put words to yet.

So read them like field notes. Not to quote — to absorb. Let them reinforce what you've felt in the room. What you've known in the silence. What you've chased in the scene.

Harold Pinter – Silence as Structure

Pinter's plays aren't remembered for soaring monologues — they're remembered for what no one said. His use of the "Pinter Pause" wasn't decorative. It was the beat where a character's truth slipped through —

hesitation, restraint, threat, longing. It forced the actor to listen. To stay in it. To make the audience uncomfortable. And that's the work.

Actors love to fill space. But what if the space *is* the point? Pinter once said his pauses "should be natural." Not actorly, not emphasized — just lived. His scripts demanded it. *The Homecoming* had 224 pauses. *Betrayal*, 140. These weren't stutters. They were land mines. Emotional terrain built into the breath.

As an actor, you don't *do* the pause. You let the pause happen because there's nothing else honest to say. That's the work — the moment before, the impulse to speak, and the choice not to. Learn to love that pause. There's more performance in it than five clever lines.

Ingmar Bergman – Stillness and the Self

Bergman was a master of stillness. He understood that the most powerful moments on screen often came when nothing was said — not because the character had nothing to offer, but because they were *overwhelmed by the truth of it all.*

He once described his own relationship to silence this way: "Sometimes I go for days without speaking to a soul... To be silent... reach behind the silence for clarity." That's the space actors rarely train for — the moment when language isn't available. The actor isn't preparing the next line. They're *inside* the line that hasn't yet arrived.

In *Persona* or *The Silence*, characters live between sounds — tension pulling tighter with each second of held breath. For an actor, this means letting go of control. No signaling. No indicating. Just availability.

Stillness isn't emptiness. It's the pressure of unspoken truth. Let it press against you. Let it wrinkle your breath. Don't break it too early. And don't let the camera find you doing nothing. Let it find you *being*.

Elia Kazan – Subtext is the Director's Language

Elia Kazan didn't teach actors to perform words. He taught them to perform *what's underneath the words*. He directed Brando, Dean, and Wood — all actors defined by their inner life bleeding through the frame.

He once said: "Subtext is one of the film director's most valuable tools. It is what he directs." When Kazan watched actors in rehearsal, he wasn't following dialogue. He was tracking the battle underneath it — want, fear, memory, hunger, resistance. The stuff that doesn't show up on the page.

You don't need permission to bring that into your work. It's the actor's job to supply it. Not to "play the subtext," but to *live it*. If you're preparing a scene, ask yourself — what thought comes between those two lines? What memory interrupts the beat? What do you *almost* say but don't?

That's the space Kazan worked in. The space between the script and the actor's truth. And that's where your work lives too.

Bette Davis – Listening with Your Eyes

Long before anyone called it "micro expression," Bette Davis understood that *stillness could speak louder than speech.* Her close-ups weren't just visual compositions — they were internal storms you could feel building from the inside out. She didn't wait to speak. She *reacted* to what she heard, even when she had no lines to deliver.

A young actor once asked her what her greatest acting tip was. She said, simply:

"Listen. With everything you've got. Because your moment may not come in your line. It might come in theirs."

That's the work. Thinking while listening. Not waiting for your turn. Not preparing to act — but allowing yourself to respond truthfully to what's happening in the room.

If the eyes don't move, if the thought doesn't shift behind them, the camera sees it. And worse — it sees when nothing's going on. Bette Davis never let that happen. She filled the silence. She filled the frame. She *gave space weight*.

Meryl Streep – Thought Behind the Pause

Meryl Streep once described acting as **finding the similarity in what is apparently different**, then discovering herself in there. In other words, she doesn't chase cool impersonations — she burrows, quietly, until subtext blooms from likeness, not mimicry.

A director once noted she begins with **a secret** — an unseen knowing she carries onto the set. That secret, that internal landscape, gives weight to silence, to a look, to the listening breath that doesn't come from dialogue at all. She's fetched into the moment by something only she understands — but the camera and audience feel it.

This is your world, you tell actors: not what's said, but what isn't. The pause, the breath, the micro-expression... those are the seams where truth peeks through. Study her quiet moments. Feel the secret. Let your body speak the lines your mouth didn't.

Anthony Hopkins – Stillness as Power

Anthony Hopkins prepares so deeply that he learns lines until he can deliver them **without thinking** — then deliberately *throws away the text*, letting the moment and the truth take over.

He's called his approach "like a submarine": invisible, submerged, then suddenly present. He's earned silence before words, presence without noise. That stillness — the calm before the storm — is what makes his Lecter scenes unforgettable.

To embody this is to train your inner quiet until the moment before the first line strikes. Let the pre-scene breath gather you. Let the camera find you — not the performance. As Hopkins shows — and Kazan taught — it's what isn't said that hits hardest.

APPENDIX D

IMAGE CREDITS

The following images are reproduced under fair use for the purposes of education, commentary, and critical reference.

The Kid (1921)
Theatrical poster. Written, directed, and produced by Charles Chaplin. Released by First National Pictures. Poster artwork in the public domain.

The Birth of a Nation (1915)
Theatrical poster. Directed by D. W. Griffith, based on The Clansman by Thomas Dixon Jr. Distributed by Epoch Producing Corporation. Poster artwork in the public domain.

The Mummy (1932)
Theatrical poster. Universal Pictures. Artwork featuring Boris Karloff. Original poster design now in the public domain.

On the Waterfront (1954)
Theatrical poster. Columbia Pictures Corporation. Illustration in the public domain due to non-renewal.

All brand names, product names, and trademarks mentioned or depicted remain the property of their respective holders.

ACKNOWLEDGMENTS

To the actors I've worked with over the years — thank you for letting me in. You gave me a front-row seat to your breakthroughs, your stumbles, your moments of pure presence. I didn't take any of it lightly. And like every good teacher or coach will tell you — you've taught me more than I've given you. So thank you, for all these many years of shared excitement — for the wins, and for the support through our collective near misses.

To all those brilliant talents who mentored me, directly or through their work — thank you for leaving the breadcrumbs. They became clearer, and more essential, as I clung to this path. Sometimes straying, but never abandoning. I followed, and I cherish your words of wisdom now longer than I ever realized I would at the time.

And to the quiet voice inside that kept nudging me to keep pushing forward in the craft — and to write these observations down — I'm listening more closely than ever. And I'll keep listening, as long as you keep whispering.

Thank you all. Ghosts, goblins, and heroes alike.

ABOUT THE AUTHOR

Jim Blumetti has spent a lifetime working at the intersection of craft, character, and mentorship — onscreen, in the room, and behind the camera. He's not a theorist. He's an acting coach, a mentor, and a deeply practical observer of what makes performance land. Any performance — whether it's a film scene or a CEO delivering an annual address to shareholders. He's trained and coached many of them for that very reason.

He's also a screenwriter, a speechwriter, and writes both fiction and nonfiction under the pseudonym *William F. Blume.*

He developed this book not to add more noise to the extensive shelf of well-written acting texts, but to cut through it — to offer something useful, durable, and discerning. A practical map for actors facing what he sees as the greatest challenge in today's craft: a changing industry with ever-moving targets.

His method isn't prescriptive. It's evolutionary. Built to adapt. Built to last for the long game.

He works privately with professional film and television actors by referral only.

Further Exploration

Stay connected:
Website: jimblumettibooks.com
Contact: https://jimblumettibooks.com/contact
Join the Mailing List: https://jimblumettibooks.com/mailing-list

www.ingramcontent.com/pod-product-compliance
Lightning Source LLC
Chambersburg PA
CBHW060404130626
46555CB00005B/1987